FATHER OF THE BLUES

FATHER
OF THE BLUES

AN AUTOBIOGRAPHY

BY

W. C. HANDY

Edited by Arna Bontemps

With a Foreword by Abbe Niles

SIDGWICK AND JACKSON
LONDON

First published in this edition 1957

Made and printed by Offset in Great Britain by
William Clowes and Sons, Limited, London and Beccles

Foreword

By Abbe Niles

To me in Connecticut in 1913, came the *Memphis Blues*, an olive among the marshmallows of that year's popular music. I didn't know wherein it was so different: I did not identify what was to become the "blues pattern," and I cannot say that I then and there consciously recognized the fact that here was a mature voice, speaking in its natural accents. But at any rate I kept my copy, which I still have, and I worked out a special piano version to my own taste, which I have ever since played. Thus, it now seems, I was merely exhibiting an automatic human reaction to the music of William Christopher Handy; for it has since become proverbial that there are as many versions of *Memphis'* great successor, the *St. Louis Blues*, as there are musicians.

Though it turns out that I had no choice in the matter, I regarded myself as a discoverer in those days. Accordingly, when twenty-seven years later I found myself sitting by the composer at the Library of Congress, as he signed the copyright renewal application that brought his wandering tune home to his hands, I felt that I, too, had been somewhere and got back.

I should not care to be placed in the position of professing to introduce to the public the most famous and the most affectionately regarded American Negro, and only two functions occur to me which I might now discharge. One is to give his full name, which he has forgotten to mention. This

I have done. As to the other, be it remembered that W. C. Handy is a lyric poet. As such, he is under a certain disadvantage in the larger forms, since he proceeds by association rather than toward organization. The chronological leaps in his manuscript, however justified by inner truth, were confusing from other standpoints, and have now been corrected by his editor. And in order to answer in a measure the questions which any edited work must evoke, I propose to reproduce here a few passages from the author's own dictated letters to myself. They may at any rate give an idea.

Our correspondence, now of some sixteen years' accumulation, has been principally on business, so my quotations must be fragments. Mr. Handy in his music publishing office, Tin Pan Alley, New York, is still primarily the artist. The firm is essentially a private-works project for a large, charming, talented, and temperamental family, nimble at the fiddle and the bow, willing to lay down the shovel and the hoe, apt thus to awake the noble rages, the biting humor, and the high prophetic laments of the patriarch in their midst. Between storms, he reigns serene, solving old and insoluble difficulties by sheer force of character and personality, laying the firm foundations of new and worse ones, doing justice, spending money, borrowing more, paying other people's debts, planning good works, buying songs in magnificent haste, repenting at leisure, arranging the beloved spirituals that well up from his early memories, soliciting advice upon contracts after allowing them to become binding, telling good stories to his innumerable visitors, and arranging for parties and trips, whereby to have yet more fun. He tells of having been worried. I have seen him troubled, but never scared. He is an expansionist at heart, and he would retain the grand manner in jail or in the poorhouse; but he won't have to. As he remarked (at about sixty-six) in the face of a threat: "I don't think anything can stop me now." So much for background.

November 13, 1933. Handy is in Chicago, on tour with the Joe Laurie "Memory Lane" company (see Chapter XVIII). His description of the getting away from New York may be compared with the parallel scene in Chapter XIX. The *dramatis personae* are his office staff:

We did five shows Saturday, five Sunday; our rehearsals for new stands are called for eight or nine o'clock in the morning. Mr. Laurie likes for us to be on hand about an hour ahead of time, so you can readily understand that we have very little time of our own. Then, too, there are interviews, phone calls, personal visits back stage, etc.

I got off to a bad start when I left Tuesday at 12:30 o'clock. The night preceding I didn't get home until two o'clock in the morning. Bill and his wife, Lucile and Kathryn, had been to see me. Kathryn remained and I talked with her and her husband until three o'clock and then retired. I was up at nine next morning, finished my packing, phoned the office, and found Miss Tyler, Bud Allen, Schlesinger, and a new man, Lou Singer, all waiting with nothing to do. Later, I went by Bill's . . .

I asked him to rush to the office because there were many things he could help me to do before time for my departure. I had new glasses fitted, phoned the office for a check, but Miss Tyler couldn't get into the safe; so, I had to wait on Bill, and consequently when Miss Tyler did arrive with the check it was almost train time. Miss Tyler had phoned Bill upon my request— to bring my baggage in a taxi to the train, and after waiting unusually long, I had to show up without him so that Mr. Laurie wouldn't be upset. About fifteen minutes before train time Bill showed up, without my trumpet. Miss Tyler happened to discover it, so she brought it to me. Then, my brother in trying to help out, got another taxi and came down, making four individual taxi fares to do what Bill could have done . . .

I will be sixty years old Thursday Nov. 16. How am I doing? With sincere regards, I am

Yours truly,

W. C. HANDY

March 11, 1935:

Dear Mr. Niles:

Bill just won't quit. Saturday night we added to our family another grandson.

Very truly yours,

W. C. HANDY

November 13, 1935:

I had an appointment with Mr. —— of —— & —— and when he proposed my undertaking to take the part of De Lawd in their filming of "Green Pastures," I expressed myself as being unable to do the work. He said that he had seen me with Joe Laurie and at other times and felt that I could do the work. They had had many tests but he felt that my kindly or benevolent face expressed the type they were looking for. Then I requested time to sleep over the matter.

He was taking a plane for California last night, so I am sending you a copy of the letter sent him.

Very truly yours,

W. C. HANDY

October 11, 1938. Handy is appearing at a night club (two shows nightly):

I had my first aeroplane flight Friday morning to Charleston, S.C. Left here at ten o'clock, arriving in Washington in one hour and twenty-five minutes, with a fifteen minute stop there, arriving at Charleston at 2:15—15 minutes ahead of schedule. The Carolina Air Line will not carry a Negro, so I could only buy a round trip on the Eastern Air Lines. I drove by automobile from Charleston to Columbia, arriving there in a little more than two hours (120 miles), and witnessed a performance of a play "Cavalcade of the Blues," written by a 17-year-old colored girl around my life and work. She had seen the cartoon sent out by the American Society and used her imagination to produce this play. In the last act I was crowned "King of the Blues" and made a speech. My trip was sponsored by the Nina Mae McKinney Literary and Dramatic Club, which is organized to encourage the

youth of our race in creative work. I thought you would like
to know this. . . .

I am dictating from home to Pearl because of the interruptions
I would have in the office. These interruptions leave me fatigued
in the afternoon, and the work at the club would be too much
of a strain. Then too, I have the usual worry of everybody coming late but Pearl and —— and it seems as though they plan to
sleep later and do less after they find I am working at the Cotton
Club. So I'll have to lay down the law. . . .

I am not answering your last letter but just letting you know
about the trip, Cotton Club and other things in a casual way.

November 4, 1938. Handy is reporting a benefit "birthday
party" to be given for him by one of the Spanish Democracy
organizations:

When Miss B. came to me the second time I sent her to F., and
when I saw F. she told me she didn't give her any encouragement
because they were a bunch of communists. I am no communist
but I have taken part in their programs for the Scottsboro Boys
and felt very good in doing so. I have taken part in benefits for
the flood sufferers, Jews, Catholics, Negroes, whites and everybody else and at the time I was sympathetic with the Loyalists
of Spain.

September 10, 1940. Reply to a criticism of this autobiography:

I disagree with you in the matter of deleting the reference to
birds and animals in the second chapter. By all means keep that
in, it establishes a very important fact. The genius doesn't find his
music in books and notes but in nature. He hears the music of the
stream, the brook, the ocean, and makes notes out of them. I
would not consent to take this out.

Fifteen years ago I wrote a text to Handy's anthology of
the blues, which Miguel Covarrubias illustrated. ("*My Lord,*"
a Texan lady is said to have remarked, "*a Mexican, a Yankee
and a nigger!*") My last quotations are from Handy's letters
of January 25 and 26, 1926, commenting on the personal passages of that manuscript:

I would think it hardly necessary, inopportune to use the word "pickaninny" in referring to my school-mates who include such men as Dr. Lewis Moore, former Dean of Howard University, in fact, Southern children of our times and locality never had themselves referred to as "pickaninnies" and the term is used by Northerners inadvisedly. The Negro press has practically won its fight against spelling Negro with a small N and is waging a crusade against referring to our women as Negresses. It is therefore to be hoped that these words will be omitted as indicated, otherwise I will have to stand for a lot of unpleasantness.

On page 23—we say the colored Public Schools furnished better instructions than those for Whites, which is in error. It is unnecessary to invite comparison, but to dwell on the fact that my teacher Prof. Y. A. Wallace from Fisk University conducted classes in vocal music with the results given in your statement.

To this day I have never had a desire for craps nor any pleasant association with crap shooters although I may have associated with persons more objectionable, hence the correction on page 24. . . .

It was the Memphians and Southerners and not Mr. Crump himself who boasted to New York leaders of the superiority of this dance tune *Mr. Crump* later known as the *Memphis Blues.*

Page 31.—The tango rhythm is accentuated in the last strain of the *Memphis Blues* instrumental copy, and I did not obtain the idea from a Florida Negro as stated on page 36, but wrote what I felt. . . .

The achievements of Clarence Williams, writer, recording artist, and pioneer publisher, have been so marked that to leave his name out of this list might be charged to a feeling of which I am incapable. I would therefore thank you to mention him and his wife, Eva Taylor. . . .

Throughout the Southland a Spiritual, *Somebody's Wrong About the Bible* is heard but there is one rendition of it I have failed to hear other than at Beale and Third streets, Memphis, Tenn., sung by a blind woman, usually in the early summer's evening—sung in long drawn-out tones and a strong voice that may be heard for blocks away. As I passed I always stopped to listen to her, and drop in a few pennies. My associates in music would laugh at me taking so much time with this particular person, when there were so many to be heard in this vicinity. They did not hear what I heard, and I doubt whether there is a parallel in Christendom, that is a two-note melody. I noticed this fifteen years ago and harmonized the melody, but had no occasion to make practical use of it until the Scopes trial at Dayton, Tenn., when I got a lyricist to write appropriate lines on this event for phonograph recording. . . .

You will note that I got an inspiration from the various expressions and more incomplete parts of musical phrases;—in other words my inspiration comes from contact with people who say and sing what they feel at the moment. . . .

In Memphis a saloon was operated called "The Monarch." A piano player was hired to play without stopping from an early hour in the evening to four or five in the morning. It would take quite an artist to hold such a job, and this artist, his name unknown to me, was the inspiration of *Beale Street Blues*. If you will notice the first strain of *Beale Street Blues* the melody in the left hand and high notes in the right you will see what set me to work.

I did not appropriate any part of his theme, but standing across the street I did hear on the highest part of the keyboard thrilling chirps on the piano with no bass and then a lead to the bass with no melody or harmony.* I listened to this for sometime which became more interesting, paid the artist a visit, he remarked in his own way that he was resting one hand at a time and when the boss came in he played with both hands.

New York,
April 10, 1941

* An illustration of the style of the man at the Monarch will appear in the author's text.

Author's Acknowledgments

IN 1933 Wendell P. Dabney (editor of the *Union* and author of *Cincinnati's Colored Citizens*) accompanied by the late Arthur A. Schomburg, curator of the 135th Street branch of the New York Public Library, sat up all night at my home trying to convince me of the importance of writing my life's story and offering to collaborate.

It was suggested that I leave the city in order to concentrate on the necessary material at some quiet retreat. Instead, however, in the noise of Broadway and the interruptions of my office routine, I dictated material under the title "Fight It Out," finally completing a first draft with the able assistance of Dr. Laverne Barber. Since the title "Fight It Out" did not express a musical career, I have changed it to "Father of the Blues."

To N. B. Handy of Lynchburg, Virginia, whose family settled on the Eastern Shore of Maryland in 1632, I am indebted for an invitation to visit Princess Anne, Maryland, with him to search the records for confirmation of the information our family Bible contains of my forbears, whose names have inadvertently been deleted from my original manuscript, most important of which are those of my great-grandparents, James Handy and Mary Brown of Baltimore, who, I was told, obtained their freedom before *The Star Spangled Banner* was written. My uncle Hanson Handy who was sold into Arkansas, is one of a long line of Hanson Handys—the name coming from John Hanson of Maryland, President of the Continental Congress.

I make due acknowledgments to Mamie St. Clair, who showed me the historic spots in and around the quaint town of Princess Anne. She advised me to read *The Entailed Hat*, by George Alfred Townsend, which would throw further light on the people and customs of the times, when my grandfather in his effort to escape bondage was evidently kidnaped by the Patty Cannon gangsters and sold into Alabama. This gang even sold white men and free Negroes into bondage.

In the chapter "The Blues Get Glorified," three important names are omitted, that of Gilda Gray who introduced *Beale Street Blues* to Broadway and sang the *St. Louis Blues* around the world; Artie Shaw who made the first record of *Chantez les Bas* ten years after its publication and too late to be included in the original text, also, Roscoe Conkling Simmons, the gifted orator and columnist who was the first to cite the significance of the blues in his addresses. I have learned that Mr. E. H. Crump was and is quite unaware of my employment to play in connection with his 1909 campaign, and I am sure he would have been easily elected without me. Moreover I must now confess for the first time that once in the same campaign I also played the tune that later became known as the *Memphis Blues* for an opposing candidate, Walter W. Talbert, and received a check in payment from his own hands.

W. C. HANDY

Contents

FATHER OF THE BLUES

CHAPTER ONE

Handy's Hill

WHERE the Tennessee River, like a silver snake, winds her way through the red clay hills of Alabama, sits high on these hills my home town, Florence. Here I came into the world, as my parents often told, "squalling for six months straight," from the six-months' colic. They used to place the date of some particular event as "so many years before, or so many years after surrender." This of course referred to Lee's surrender to Grant, which resulted in the emancipation of my race. I began exercising my vocal organs "eight years after surrender"; to be exact, November 16, 1873.

My parents were among the four million slaves who had been freed and left to shift for themselves. I was born in a log cabin which my grandfather had built. The logs were evenly hewn. Our first kitchen had a dirt floor which my father had beat down so that it looked almost like asphalt. There was a three-acre orchard with cherries, pears, damsons, quinces— every native fruit of that soil, where mocking birds and other songsters varied their diets by feeding on insects that infest such places.

Across the road from the cabin were miles of dense woodland and more birds of every variety. Here all sorts of wild flowers, berries and nuts were in abundance. Here squirrels, rabbits and foxes burrowed; buzzards circled overhead daily till carrion was scented in the woods or streams. Whippoorwills, bats and hoot owls, with their outlandish noises, often gave me throughout the night a feeling of depression until I learned to drive the owls away by putting a poker in the fire. Why the hoot owls really left I do not know, but it never failed. Technicians tell me that radio waves are reflected into the atmosphere by a magnetic ceiling. Perhaps somewhere in this idea is hidden the secret of this peculiar phenomenon.

Cypress Creek washed the fringe of the woodland on one side, with high rocky cliffs on the other. In this stream could be found perch, trout, catfish, and the bony sucker, as well as a substantial supply of eels. Turtles sunned themselves on rocks and driftwood until some drizzling rain made them dive into the water, apparently to keep from getting wet. In and near the creek lurked stinging death; water moccasins, in the brush highland moccasins, rattlesnakes, green snakes, black snakes—in fact there were all kinds of reptiles. When I was too small to know what a viper was my mother caught me in the act of picking one up. I had found it on awakening in my bed. But soon I learned to kill every one I came across. I was an expert with a rock, of which there was no scarcity. I knew every haunt of this woodland for whatever adventure my fancy conjured, and I knew the music of every songbird and all the symphonies of their unpremeditated art.

The long walk that led from my grandfather's house to the front gate was beautified on each side by flowers of every description. In our yard were the usual flower beds, and near the chimney corners were fig trees. My cabin home was a temporary one due to the fact that my grandfather's will could not be settled until my youngest uncle, Louis, reached seniority. In dividing the property the plots of land were shared equally amongst each one of seven heirs. The portion that fell to my father probably was on the highest elevation in Florence and was at one time desired by the city as a spot upon which to build a reservoir. Here on this site my father erected a better home.

The west side of Florence still bears the name of Handy's Hill, since William Wise Handy, my grandfather, a Methodist minister after Emancipation, became the first colored man to own property there. He built the first colored church in Florence and several others in Lauderdale County. He and his two brothers had run away from their masters in Princess Anne, Maryland, taking advantage of the "underground railroad." One escaped into Canada, the other to some portion of the East. But my grandfather was overtaken and sold into Alabama where, still urged by the desire for freedom, he started an insurrection for escape, and was shot but not killed. Unknown to his masters he acquired a liberal education and became an honored and respected citizen of Florence. When I was a small boy, Mr. George W. Karsner, one of the oldest white citizens of Florence, stopped me, and after inquiring my name said, "Sonny, if you become like your grandfather, you will be a great man."

Grandfather's son, Hanson, was another fearless man, who would not let his overseers or his masters whip him. They admired this gameness, but they sold him into Arkansas, just as one would get rid of an unruly mule. He was never heard of again. My own father used to cry in church whenever anyone raised the familiar spiritual, *March Along, I'll See You on the Judgment Day*. Once, quite innocently, I asked him the reason for these tears. He answered, "That is what the slaves sang when the white folks sold Brother Hanson away."

Contrast these characters with that of my maternal grandfather, Christopher Brewer. When his master, John Wilson, had given my Grandfather Brewer his freedom, he preferred to stay near Mr. Wilson as his trusted servant. At one time, nearing the close of the Civil War, guerilla warfare was common in this locality. Three robbers were eventually hanged five miles out of Florence. These thieves had undertaken to rob John Wilson. They stripped him and tortured him to death by burning paper and searing his body to make him tell where his money was hidden. He refused. My Grandpa Brewer likewise knew. They shot him to make him tell. He also refused. But when his wounds had sufficiently healed he went to Nashville and brought his young master, Coonie Foster, back home and disclosed to him the hiding place of the money.

It is probably my inheritance from these two characters that enabled me to submit to certain hard conditions long enough to fight my way out and yet be considered sufficiently "submissive" by those who held the whip hand. The word "diplomacy" was not a part of their vocabulary.

My father, Charles B. Handy, had been pastor of a charge at Guntersville, a small Alabama town, where he met a local banker who, on a trip to Nashville, had met and was impressed by many colored people of wealth and culture. The banker inquired why the colored people in this town were so backward, and why they could not acquire a standard of culture similar to the Nashville group. Father explained that such things depend upon local race conditions. "In a community of cultured white folks, there will be found a similar group of colored people," he said, "but in any place where backward whites predominate, there will always be found a group of backward and uncultured colored people."

Florence had some very fine white people of the old aristocracy, and therefore a goodly number of progressive colored people. My father often pointed out to me the excellence of character and carriage of certain aristocrats as a sort of object lesson. As a boy I was acquainted with the first Governor E. A. O'Neal, who often stopped at the old Exchange Hotel and read the prevalent news of the day to friends grouped around him. And it was my daily custom to eavesdrop and hear the political news discussed by these men.

The governor had a forceful, positive, yet sonorous voice, and whatever credit I may have received in school for elocution most certainly came from emulating this fine Alabamian.

Florence was the home of the Rapiers, who gave James T. Rapier (Negro) to Congress in reconstruction days; also, the birthplace of Oscar DePriest, the first Negro elected to Congress from the North. My teacher was trying to fit me for such leadership.

With all their differences, most of my forebears had one thing in common: if they had any musical talent, it remained buried. My mother admitted a fondness for the guitar, but she could not play it because the church put a taboo on such instruments. My Uncle William went so far as to forbid his sons to whistle. There was nothing about music in Grandpa Handy's history. The one exception was Grandpa Brewer, who told me that before he got religion he used to play the fiddle for dances. That had been his way of making extra money back in slavery days. His master, the kindly man that I have mentioned, allowed him to keep what he earned from playing.

In his day, Grandpa Brewer explained, folks knew as well as we do when it was time for the music to get hot. They had their own way of bearing down. A boy would stand behind the fiddler with a pair of knitting needles in his hands. From this position the youngster would reach around the fiddler's left shoulder and beat on the strings in the manner of a snare drummer. Grandpa Brewer could describe vividly this old method of making rhythm, but for his own part he had forsaken such sinful doing, and I had to wait for Uncle Whit Walker, another old-timer, to show me just how it was done.

Uncle Whit, lively and unregenerate at eighty, selected his favorite breakdown, *Little Lady Goin' to the Country*, and would let me help him give the old tune the kind of treatment it needed. Uncle Whit fiddled and sang while I handled the needles.

Sally got a meat skin laid away
Sally got a meat skin laid away
Sally got a meat skin laid away   .
To grease her wooden leg every day.

Uncle Whit stomped his feet while singing. A less expert fiddler, I learned, would have stomped both heels simultaneously, but a fancy performer like Uncle Whit could stomp the left heel and the right forefoot and alternate this with the right heel and the left forefoot, making four beats to the bar. That was real stomping. Country gals and their mirthful suitors got as much enjoyment out of a fiddle at a breakdown or square dance as jitterbugs or rug-cutters get nowadays from a swing band.

Grandpa Handy, who hadn't even sown any musical wild oats, died the year I was born, leaving a widow Thumuthis, and her three children, Lucy, Ellen and Louis. This widow was not my father's mother, but I knew her as grandmother. She was very dark, proudly handsome, and walked like an Ethiopian queen. She was the family physician, who could cure a fever with the juice of peach leaves which she gathered and mashed. Mullein tea and Jimson weeds were her remedies for swellings, sassafras tea for thinning blood, catnip tea for hives, and the marrow from hog jowls for the mumps. Some of her doses were hard ones. I remember that when I had a bad sore throat bordering on croup she made me gargle with my own urine, and when we had the measles she gave us tea made from sheep manure. But we never questioned her remedies, and we all lived.

Grandma Thumuthis was open-hearted and generous, but she was thrifty on principle. Although she often gave me money, she made a point of never allowing me to see the inside of her pocketbook. Always she turned her back, adroitly concealing her money from my inquisitive eyes. This was not merely reticence. Grandma Thumuthis was concerned with fundamentals, and she did her best to convey to me the implications of the gesture.

Grandma Thumuthis was the first one to suggest that my big ears indicated a talent for music. This thrilled me, but I discovered almost immediately that life was not always a song. While the mechanics of living were simple, hard cash was a scarce article in our family. We had to adopt the custom of barter and exchange. I once traded a gallon of milk for a copy of Benjamin Franklin's *Poor Richard's Almanac*. Cattle, hogs and poultry were plentiful, and there was little real anxiety about food. Still there were times when the currency of the realm was essential. For example, a nickel was required for Sunday School and a dime for the church collection. Later— considerably later—there was the important matter of a guitar.

I was compelled to invent methods of earning money for such necessities of my own. During the spring and summer I picked early berries, and sold fruits from the orchard. In the fall I gathered chestnuts, walnuts and hickory nuts. Old iron and rags found a market. I learned to make lye-soap. The woods were usually full of bones, but if these were not enough, a near-by slaughterhouse always produced a ready supply. These bones I would gather in a pot. Over them I'd place an ash hopper filled with ashes from hickory wood. I would then pour rain water over the ashes. The water would seep through, extracting from the ashes chemicals which turned it into lye-water of a very strong solution. This, in turn, would cleanse the bones of their residue of meat and fat. When the bones were thus stripped clean, I would take them out of the solution, heat what was left in the pot and then let it cool. This would congeal into soap which I would cut into cakes and sell.

This sort of enterprise pleased my father. His gospel was that an idle brain is the devil's workshop. With this in mind perhaps, he kept me home from school one day and took me to a neighboring field where a mule and a plow waited in the sunshine. Placing the reins in my hands, he explained that to a mule "gee" means to the right and "haw" to the left. The instructions were as simple and brief as that.

"Hope you won't have to do this for a living," he added, "but the work sure won't hurt you."

Nothing much came of this effort, because I never seemed to have any luck with horses or mules. Even when I fed them, they grew feeble and pined away. As a birthday present he gave me a heifer (Beulah) from which I raised some Jersey cattle. I sold to Will Connor one calf for seventy-five dollars as soon as she was old enough to wean. At the age of twelve a neighbor, Sandy Crawford, got me a job as water boy in a rock quarry near Muscle Shoals, at fifty cents a day; and apprenticeships in plastering, shoemaking and carpentry followed. I pulled fodder, picked cotton, cradled oats, clover, millet and wheat, and even operated a printing press. Sheriff George W. Porter gave me a job at the courthouse, a job that paid two dollars a day during certain sessions. The white Baptists held meetings in another section of the courthouse. They employed me as their janitor. Out of my earnings I bought clothing, books and school supplies, and began saving small sums in the hope of buying a guitar.

Meanwhile the trumpet playing of Mr. Claude Seals fired my imagination. He had come from Birmingham to play with the Baptist choir. Almost immediately I set my heart on owning a trumpet. Since buying one was out of the question, I tried making my own by hollowing a cow horn and cutting the tip into a mouthpiece. The finished product was a useful hunting horn but certainly not a trumpet. I decided to content myself for the time being with the hope of a guitar.

Work meant nothing now. It was a means to an end. But saving was slow and painful. My wages were divided into three equal portions, of which I kept one and gave one each to my father and mother. And since my earnings were usually not more than three dollars a week, the amounts that I could pinch out from week to week were not large.

Setting my mind on a musical instrument was like falling in love. All the world seemed bright and changed. I spent more time in the three-acre grove behind our cabin and took greater delight in the cherries, pears, damsons, quinces and other Alabama fruits that grew there so profusely. I paid more attention to the birds and the riotous carnival they held among the trees. Perhaps they were not more numerous than they had been in the past, but now something sang in me and I felt drawn to them.

With a guitar I would be able to express the things I felt in sounds. I grew impatient as my small savings grew. I selected the instrument I wanted and went often to gaze at it lovingly through the shop window. The days dragged. The fact that I had told no one of my intention created an additional hardship. I had no one to whom I could talk.

My father must have guessed that something was wrong. He noticed me mooning and did little things to please me. He gave me an old Civil War musket, which I learned to use, though I continued to prefer a bow and arrow for hunting. He took me to the river and tried to teach me to swim. This failed, and I only learned later on by diving into the treacherous Blue Hole on Cypress Creek when nobody was around. It was a case of swim or drown then, and I swam, and then completed my self-education by doing the same thing in a swift and deep stretch of the Tennessee River.

The name of my ailment was longing, and it was not cured till I finally went to the department store and counted out the money in small coins before the dismayed clerk. A moment later, the shining instrument under my arm, I went out and hurried up Court Street. My heart was a leaf. I could scarcely wait till I reached home to break the news to my father and mother. I knew how the other youngsters would gather around, bug-eyed with curiosity and admiration, and I had no doubt that soon I would be able to entertain the girls royally.

When I came into the house, I held the instrument before the eyes of the astonished household. I couldn't speak. I was too full, too overjoyed. Even then, however, I thought I saw something that puzzled me. A shadow seemed to pass over the faces of my parents. Both of them suddenly lost their voices.

"Look at it shine," I said finally. "It belongs to me—*me*. I saved up the money."

I waited in vain for the expected congratulations. Instead of being pleased, my father was outraged.

"A box," he gasped, while my mother stood frozen. "A guitar! One of the devil's playthings. Take it away. Take it away, I tell you. Get it out of your hands. Whatever possessed you to bring a sinful thing like that into our Christian home? Take it back where it came from. You hear? Get!"

I was stunned. The words dim and far away like words spoken in a dream. A devil's plaything. I wanted to dispute the charge, but I knew that argument would mean nothing. My father's mind was fixed. Brought up to regard guitars and other stringed instruments as devices of Satan, he could scarcely believe that a son of his could have the audacity to bring one of them into his house. Hints of this prejudice had come to me time and again, but I had never taken them seriously. This storm was a complete surprise.

"I hear what you say, and I understand what you mean," I answered weakly, "but I don't think they'll take it back."

"They'll exchange it. For the price of a thing like that you could get a new Webster's Unabridged Dictionary—something that'll do you some good."

I got the dictionary, and I hope it was a fair exchange, but it didn't seem so then. Nevertheless, Father paid for lessons for me on the old Estey organ, and he occasionally dropped in on my teacher, Ruth A. Jones, to hear how I was progressing in sacred music.

CHAPTER TWO

Songbirds and School Days

MY MUSICAL ambitions received no encouragement at school either. Our teacher surprised us one day by suddenly departing from the recitation and asking the class what we intended to be in life. After a number of others had announced their ambitions to become doctors, lawyers, teachers and preachers, I whipped up my courage and suggested that I wanted to be a musician.

That brought an abrupt end to the questions. A bomb explosion could not have been more effective. With anger flaming in his eyes, the teacher rose, waved his long sinewy arms, and gave me his opinion of the musical profession. Musicians were idlers, dissipated characters, whisky drinkers and rounders. They were social pariahs. Southern white gentlemen, he said, looked upon music as a parlor accomplishment, not as a means of questionable support. Such men should be our examples. To drive the point home he wrote a note to my father and asked me to deliver it.

That evening my father calmly preached my funeral. "Son," he said, "I'd rather see you in a hearse. I'd rather follow you to the graveyard than to hear that you had become a musician."

I did not answer. My father was a preacher, and he was

bent on shaping me for the ministry. Becoming a musician would be like selling my soul to the devil.

Despite his horror of musicians, however, our teacher's hobby was vocal music. Instead of the usual prayers and scripture readings of the morning devotional period, he spent the first half hour of each day in singing and in giving us musical instruction. This was, needless to say, the part of my school life that I enjoyed most.

This teacher was Y. A. Wallace, and he had come to Florence from Fisk University, where he had been a member of the first graduating class. Curiously enough, Professor Wallace had no interest in the spirituals. Though the famous Fisk Jubilee Singers toured the world in his day and created a lasting esteem for these songs, he made no attempt to instruct us in this remarkable folk music. This, however, was just one item in a great catalogue of Professor Wallace's eccentricities.

Villagers and students of both races laughed when he expounded his pet theory that more people die from overeating than from starvation. But Professor Wallace was serious. He believed and practiced what he preached. While we brought our tin pails to school filled with lunches fit for men at hard labor and washed the food down with quarts of milk, Professor Wallace brought his lunch in his pocket. It consisted of a single baked sweet potato, sliced and buttered. At noon he'd walk to the spring—a good place to go with a dry baked sweet potato—and dine in solitude.

At home his taste ran to roasted peanuts, parched corn and dried persimmons. This, while the trees in his yard were heavy with fruit and his kitchen garden flourished. He evidently saw food value in peanuts before Dr. Carver. Professor Wallace had a tight fist, too. His clothes were carefully tailored, but he wasted nothing.

Forty years later I saw him in Florence. He was nearly ninety. His health was sound, and he still carried the same umbrella that had been familiar to me as a schoolboy. Appar-

ently, too, the same bandanna handkerchief had been stuffed
into his pocket, part of it hanging out. Now, however, his coat
was frayed and fastened in the front with a safety pin. He
carried a basket of groceries on his arm. When I offered him
a drink of coca-cola, he declined, shaking his head.

"No, William," he said gravely. "Save your money. When
I go home, I'll make me some molasses water and put a pinch
of soda in it. That'll taste just as good."

Professor Wallace tried to cure me of sketching. Map
drawing was permitted, but I liked to draw people. I enjoyed
duplicating the pictures of popular actresses that we found in
discarded Duke cigarette packages. This angered our teacher
beyond endurance. He resorted to the rod.

My introduction to the rudiments of music was largely
gained during the eleven years I spent under this quaint in-
structor in the Florence District School for Negroes. I began
in the soprano singing section, progressed to the alto and then
shuttled back and forth between the tenor and bass as my
voice cut up and played pranks.

There was no piano or organ in our school, just as there
were few instruments in the homes of the pupils. We were
required to hold our books in our left hand and beat time
with our right. Professor Wallace sounded his *A* pitch pipe
or tuning fork, and we understood the tone to be *la*. If *C* happened to be the starting key, we made the step and a half in
our minds and then sang out the key note in concert. We
would then sound the notes for our respective parts, perhaps
do for the basses, *mi* for the altos, and *sol* and *do* for the sopranos and tenor, depending of course on the first note of the
sopranos. Before attempting to sing the words of any song,
we were required to work out our parts by singing over and
over the proper *sol-fa* syllables. In this way we learned to sing
in all keys, measures and movements. We learned all the songs
in *Gospel Hymns*, one to six. Each year we bought new instruction books and advanced to a point where we could sing

excerpts from the works of Wagner, Bizet, Verdi and other masters—all without instrumental accompaniment.

When I was no more than ten, I could catalogue almost any sound that came to my ears, using the tonic *sol-fa* system. I knew the whistle of each of the river boats on the Tennessee. One whistle, I remember, sounded like a combination of *do* and *sol* in the musical scale. Another seemed to combine *do* and *mi*. By the same means I could tell what the birds in the orchards and woodlands were singing. Even the bellow of the bull became in my mind a musical note, and in later years I recorded this memory in the *Hooking Cow Blues*.

As a child I had not heard of the Pipes of Pan, but pastoral melody was nevertheless a very real thing to me. Whenever I heard the song of a bird and the answering call of its mate, I could visualize the notes in the scale. Robins carried a warm alto theme. Bobolinks sang contrapuntal melodies. Mocking birds trilled cadenzas. Altogether, as I fancied, they belonged to a great outdoor choir.

There was a French horn concealed in the breast of the blue jay. The tappings of the woodpecker were to me the reverberations of a snare drum. The bullfrog supplied an effective bass. In the raucous call of the distant crow I would hear the jazz motif. The purple night would awaken a million crickets with their obbligatos of mournful sound, also the katy-dids, and down the lonely road the hooves of the galloping horses beat in syncopation. I knew the gait of horses by the rhythm of their hooves. As I grew older I added the saxophonic wailing of the moo-cows and the clarinets of the moody whippoorwills. All built up within my consciousness a natural symphony. This was the primitive prelude to the mature melodies now recognized as the blues. Nature was my kindergarten.

We Handy's Hill kids made rhythm by scraping a twenty penny nail across the teeth of the jawbone of a horse that had died in the woods near by. By drawing a broom handle across our first finger lying on a table we imitated the bass. We sang through fine-tooth combs. With the thumb of the right hand interlocked with the little finger of the left, we placed the thumb of the left hand under our chin and made rhythmic sounds by rattling our teeth. We would put the thumb of our right hand on our goozle or Adam's apple, yelling at the time:

> Went down the river
> Couldn't get across
> Paid five dollars for an old gray horse.

Sometimes we were fortunate enough to have a French harp on which we played the fox and the hounds and imitated the railroad trains—harmonica masterpieces. For drums we wore out our mother's tin pans and milk pails, singing:

> Cornstalk fiddle and shoestring bow
> Broke in the middle, jumped up Joe.

Toward the end of my school days Jim Turner came to town. Jim was from Memphis. He had recently been in love with a girl who had done him bad and broken his heart. Love, as everyone should know, is a strange disease. Jim Turner tried to cure his on whisky. Then, when this didn't work, he staggered to the M. & C. depot and made his way to the ticket cage. Putting down a handful of greenbacks, he asked for a hundred dollars' worth of tickets.

"Where do you want to go?" the agent asked.

"Anywheres," Jim Turner said. "Just anywheres."

The agent sold him a ticket to Florence, and our proud little town entertained a genius unawares. That sad-eyed boy, stabbed to his heart by the scorn of a haughty yellow gal, was perhaps the best violin player Florence ever knew. Fortunately his lovesickness and his drinking did him no harm musically. The drunker Jim Turner was, the better he played.

But Jim brought more than just a fiddle and a broken heart to Florence. He brought a glimpse of another world. He organized an orchestra and taught dancing. Those were the days of the quadrille, the lancers, the polka, the schottische, the mazurka, the york, the two-step, the gavotte, the minuet and the varsovienne. The waltz was popular, as was also the rye waltz, a combination of three-four and two-four tempos. Jim Turner knew them all. He talked about Beale Street in Memphis, where life was a song from dawn to dawn. He described darktown dandies and high-brown belles. He recalled the glitter and finery of their latest fashions. Finally, he planted in my heart a seed of discontent, a yearning for Beale Street and the gay universe that it typified.

Meanwhile, without letting my father or Professor Wallace into the secret, I obtained a cornet and commenced to study the instrument. It came about accidentally. A circus became stranded in our town, and its capable white bandmaster was reduced to teaching a colored band in a barber shop. I formed the habit of stopping at the barber shop on the way home from school and peeping through the windows to study the blackboard chart which he had made to illustrate the fingering of the various instruments. At school I would practice fingering on my desk during classes. In this way I mastered the scales and developed speed. This came to the attention of one of the band members, Will Bates, and he persuaded me to buy his old rotary-valve cornet, an instrument with the valves on the side instead of in the vertical position of more modern cornets. The valves were worked by an attachment with catgut strings. It was an odd contraption, to say the least, but since the price was only one dollar and seventy-five cents, payable in installments, we made a deal. At that, however, it took forty years to clear the account, for on meeting Bates again at the end of that time I found that I had neglected a balance which, with interest, had reached the sum of seventy-five cents.

I continued to play with the Florence band until my father and school teacher caught up with me. By then, of course, it was too late to do much about it. The climax came when Jim Turner got an engagement to play at a land sale at Russellville, Alabama. They needed an alto player, so I skipped school and joined them. At that performance I made the acquaintance of a barefoot boy who was following the band, Charles E. Toney, who was to become one of the first Negro judges elected in New York City, and for whose election my family worked although I had been taught since Cleveland against Blaine never to vote Democrat. For the day's work at Russellville I received eight dollars, which seemed big indeed against the three dollars a week that I was accustomed to receiving for hard labor, and I imagined that my father would have a change of heart when I put it in his hand. But the tainted wages impressed him not at all. He refused to forgive me, and my teacher finished up the job by applying the hickory the next day when I returned to school.

There was no holding me now. I attended dances against their wishes, and I sang with a quartet that often serenaded the moon until the wee hours. Shortly afterwards, when Bill Felton, a minstrel man and a singing banjo player, came to Florence and organized a home town minstrel show, I joined up as first tenor for his quartet. I was fifteen at the time and my colleagues told me I looked pretty funny stepping along with the "walking gents" in my father's Prince Albert. We had seen the famous Georgia Minstrels in Florence, and we knew how to make the pivot turns. We were all acquainted with Billy Kersands, the man who could "make a mule laugh," and we remembered his trick of proving on the stage that his enormous mouth would accommodate a cup and saucer. We had seen Sam Lucas and Tom McIntosh walking at the head of the parade in high silk hats and long-tailed coats. We had an idea of how the thing should be done, but I suppose our trouble was lack of experience.

Our minstrels took to the road. In one of the quartet songs I had a solo part which contained the prophetic words, "Take me back home again; let me see it once more." Sooner than I had hoped, this request was granted. After playing a few towns in Tennessee and northern Alabama, the show got stranded in Jasper. Before skipping town, the manager called me aside and took pity on me because of my youth. He gave me train fare back to Florence, but cautioned me not to tell the others that he had jumped the outfit. Instead of taking his advice, however, I divided with the other boys and decided to take my chances with them.

We rode the train till our money ran out. The conductor dropped us near a lonely water tank. From that point we counted the cross-ties back to Florence, stopping periodically to sing or play for buttermilk and biscuits. The home town boys never forgot this trip. They maintained for years that I never sang so well as when we were stranded along the railroad tracks.

This was my baptism. I have been a trouper ever since.

CHAPTER THREE

Wilberforce, Wallace and Wanderlust

THROUGH the years I had been able to stay near the head of the class; had made good marks in mathematics. My teacher had promoted me to the choir of the A.M.E. church of which he was chorister. Through his influence I became secretary of the Sunday School and in doing this work I organized and was made first president of the Epworth League. He induced me to make a political campaign speech while in my teens and appointed me as a teacher in the primary grades in day school. In the midst of these friendly activities something occurred which caused me to question my teacher's attitude.

One day on the way home from school, a youth made a slurring remark to my cousin Josephine which I resented by word of mouth, but the boy in his reply used a brick, the mark of which remains to this day upon my skull. On the following day when I went to school my teacher administered the hickory to me, which was his form of punishment for fighting in public, although I protested that I had done no fighting. This boy did not attend school that day but on the following day he answered "present." All day there was nothing said or done about him. At the close of school the usual "put by your books" rang out from our teacher. "Girls dismissed," and then "boys dismissed." I made bold to go up to the desk and mention to my teacher that he had only reprimanded one of the parties to our fight. He ignored me, being (as I was convinced) afraid of the other boy's father who was always ready to fight anyone. I thereupon rushed out of the door, and when my adversary came out I knocked him unconscious. My teacher sent older boys to catch and bring me back. He whipped me again until my cousin James Brewer and other boys remonstrated, telling him that he had done enough.

The next session I implored my father to let me work at the McNabb Iron Furnace and study at home, my purpose being to earn and save enough money to put me through Wilberforce University. During this year my brother Charles E. was born and conditions came about that changed my plans. The following year I reentered school at Florence. My teacher, possibly remembering old scores, continually kept reminding my father that I would not be able to finish with my class. I had forgiven the boy, but it seemed to me that my teacher, who had been my ideal, had shown a weakness in his character which I could not forget. I could no longer enter the recitations in my former spirit. A rift had opened between us which, despite all regrets, remained. Nevertheless in the final examinations I held my own.

In 1892 I left Florence at the old Memphis and Charleston Depot on a two-coach accommodation train, to take the teacher's examination in Birmingham. I had already had village teaching experience, and I wanted no more.

A summer at the Crittenden Cross Road school at a salary of fifteen dollars and eighty-six cents a month had been far from a bargain to me, especially in view of the fact that school was held for only three months of the year. The next year at Bethel my salary had been twenty-five dollars a month, but I was still not satisfied. I was going to Birmingham. I had not been given much encouragement for this move.

I had finished the district school, but the breach between my teacher and me had grown so wide that he had refused to give me a recommendation for the Birmingham job. My father's displeasure this time was not directed at me. "Sonny, don't mind him," he had said with unexpected sympathy. "If I should teach a boy eleven years and couldn't recommend him, the fault would be mine and not the boy's." Incidentally, I justified my father's point of view in the County Teacher's examination by making the highest mark of any of my classmates and second to the highest of the seventeen white applicants from State Normal College.

W. E. Shaw, son of an A.M.E. minister, who had been transferred to the Birmingham District, had been suggesting through correspondence that I come to Birmingham and try for a position in the city schools. When ambition calls us away from familiar spots, heart throbs bind us closer to them. So it was with me then. I must leave my mother, father and only brother, Charles, then a baby not old enough to talk. Then came my pal, Jim McClure, my friendly rival in books, music, games and girls, also Constant Perkins, whose association gave me the benefit of his wider experience in music. There was Anna Pool, a girl after any boy's heart. She could ride a horse, row a boat and play any game that youth enjoys. There are three letters tattooed on my left wrist—"A. D. S."—the initials of Amanda D. Simpson, which I put on my arm when fourteen years old, and for whom I had arranged a female quartet of *Come and Kiss Me Annie Darling* which she has kept to this day. And there was a next door neighbor's girl, Mary Key, who took the place of a sister, which unfortunately at the time I did not possess. There were my classmates too. These were in my memory chest, but strong as these bonds were and are today, they could not and did not quiet my restless spirit.

So on the day that James J. Corbett won the heavyweight championship from John L. Sullivan, and the newspapers were telling about the death of John Greenleaf Whittier, I left Florence at the old Memphis and Charleston Depot, bound for Birmingham, on a two-coach accommodation train, one-half of the first coach being for baggage, and the remaining half for colored travelers, with the other whole coach for whites. The one hundred and thirty-five mile journey was passed in reading about Corbett's victory and Whittier's death. The part of the news that concerned the poet came in handy when I reached Birmingham. One of the examination questions called for four pages on the life of Whittier. There was no way for me to miss.

After passing the examination, however, I found out that the schools of that city paid some teachers even less than twenty-five dollars a month and considerably less than the pay of a common laborer. Accordingly, I turned my back on that teaching opportunity and took a job at the Howard and Harrison Pipe Works in Bessemer at a dollar and eighty-five cents a day.

Brute strength and plenty of it was required in the pipe works, but I was not very strong. Experience gained at the McNabb Iron Furnace in Florence and lots of brain sweat enabled me to get around this handicap, however. I was a molder's helper. My duties were to temper the sand and hand my molder the articles he needed at the proper time. I saw the husky duskies wearing themselves out running here and there to borrow a blacking sack, a vent rod, a swab pot or a wee nip. To save my legs, I built a locker to contain all these articles. The molder was pleased, and I got along as well as my more powerful companions.

One afternoon when we were pouring off, running with ladles of molten metal, the foreman shouted to us, "Come on here, you niggers, with that iron!" Remembering something my father had told me I promptly set my end of the carrier down. He ordered another man to pick it up.

That night, to my surprise, he apologized and elevated me to work with his son on "big work." We became good friends.

We liked the same books and enjoyed singing the same popular songs of the day, *That Is Love, Down Went McGinty* and *White Wings*.

Everything was fine in Bessemer for a while. I organized and taught my first brass band. A small string orchestra of the town called on me to act as its leader and teach the musicians to read notes. Folks around Bessemer began calling me Professor, and I began to cut a figure in local society. The fact that I could sing and play my own guitar accompaniment did no harm at all, but made me popular with the girls. My cousin, organist in one of the larger churches in Birmingham, arranged for me to play the trumpet with the choir. Altogether, the boom was on, and I was going up. Between these musical activities and my job in the pipe works, I was earning a fair livelihood and beginning to see bright prospects for Wilberforce.

Presently, however, things took a tumble. A panic set in during Grover Cleveland's second administration, and the iron works, steel mills and mines around Jefferson County shut down. The pipe works laid off half of its force and cut my wages to ninety cents a day, payable in scrip designed to be traded in at their commissary. My working time was then reduced to three days a week.

I left Bessemer and returned to Birmingham. Soon the little money I had saved melted, and I began to walk the streets aimlessly. Then one evening I heard a quartet singing in a saloon.

I went in and introduced myself and offered to teach the young singers some arrangements that we used to sing in our quartet back in Florence. They were pleased with the suggestion, and we got together and organized what we called the "Lauzetta Quartet," singing such numbers as *The Dance of the Nixies*. One of the songs that scored wherever we sang was:

GWINE CHOP 'EM IN THE HEAD WITH
A GOLDEN AX

Old Aunt Kate, she died so late
She couldn't get in at the Heaven Gate
The Angels met her with a great big club
Knocked her right back in the washing tub.

Chorus:

Hear dat trumpet sound
Stand up and don't fall down
Slip and slide around
Till your shoes don't have no tacks
Join dat 'lection band
Better join it while you can
If you don't join dat 'lection band
[bass] Whatcha goin' to do wid 'em den, brothers?
[quartet] "Gwine chop 'em in the head with a golden ax."

Then came the announcement of the World's Fair of 1893.
That set us to thinking. Why not go to Chicago? It was true
that I had only twenty cents to my name, and the others had
exactly nothing among them, but money was no holdback
when you could sing. We promptly appointed a time, met in
the L. & N. Railroad freight yards and boarded a tank car.
All that first night the brakeman tried to get rid of us, but we
stayed with him, hopping back on board every time he threw
us off. Finally, at the end of his patience, he dropped us at
Cullman with the threat that the next time he would kick us
off while the train was in motion.

We were a forlorn bunch of boys as we stood beside the
tracks that night and watched the brakeman raise his lantern
and give the engineer the "high ball." Cullman, as all of us
knew, was a town where Negroes were not allowed to stop.
Still, the night was beautiful, remarkably beautiful. There was
a moon, and something prompted us to sing. Our heads together, we hummed and began *When the Summer Breeze
Was Blowing.*

Presently a voice interrupted us.

"Hey there," the brakeman called. "Why didn't you *say* you could sing?" He signaled to the engineer to delay a moment while he invited us into the caboose.

The next morning we reached Decatur and set about to solve the breakfast problem. I sent a boy with ten cents to get a loaf of bread and some molasses with butter stirred into it. We shared this meal at the spring under the old L. & N. bridge.

While we relaxed in the shade, an excursion boat docked a short distance away. A moment later I saw a group of white ladies walking down toward the levee of the Tennessee River with picnic baskets and colorful parasols. I began to think fast. An excursion boat picnic wouldn't be complete without music. Why hadn't those people thought of that? This was their opportunity and ours. I took from my pocket one of the neatly prepared cards that I had written for the quartet before leaving Birmingham and politely presented it to one of the leaders of the group. I don't know just how effective my Spencerian handwriting was, but the woman to whom I showed the card was immediately convinced that they needed music. She passed the suggestion along to other members of her group. The result was that the Lauzetta Quartet was hired for ten dollars.

The steamer went through the old Muscle Shoals canal, and I saw for the first time all the locks of the Tennessee River, locks later to be submerged by the 150 foot Wilson dam and its backwater. At the picnic grounds the ladies of the group brought us bits from their baskets in order that we might decide which of them had the best cook. We began to feel that our quartet was definitely on its way.

Before leaving Decatur a couple of days later we were able to get a letter from an official to a division agent of the railroad. This was almost as good as a pass. It improved our freight train rides from there on, making them safer for us and more entertaining to the railroad men. Meanwhile program appearances, serenades and kindred entertainments, with the small fees, gifts and handouts that went with them, kept us rolling along on our way.

Indeed, so prosperous were we when we reached Columbia, Tennessee, that I bought a new pair of Plymouth Rock pants and stepped out of the barrel. The quartet sang at the Reverend Gilmore's Baptist Church and we had time to accept a few social bids and get out among the local high-browns.

After Columbia, however, there was a different story. We reached Chicago exhausted and pretty well on our uppers. We had ridden rods and slept in box cars. We had traveled blind baggage. Once a man had given us a suspicious ride. He had put us on a train at Hopkinsville bound for a small Illinois town. When we reached the destination, he explained that he was being paid so much a head for every Negro he induced to come to that town to work in a gravel pit. He didn't care whether or not those he sent there stayed. His fee was earned as soon as we got off the train.

Experiences like these detained us but they did not turn us from our purpose. We refused to turn back. Our heads were set on Chicago and the Columbian Exposition. We were determined to sing our way to the World's Fair. But we reached the goal only to have our hopes dashed. The Fair had been postponed for a year.

We decided to head for St. Louis. Perhaps we would find better luck in that gay capital of the sporting world, soon to become the cradle of ragtime. We guessed wrong, of course, for St. Louis was hard hit by the panic. Quartets had come there from all parts of the country, and many were suffering. Our boys failed to find other work to which they might turn their hands. Hard times got us at last. We were forced to disband.

I found a job in the Elliot Frog and Switch Works in East St. Louis, but when I had worked two weeks a colored contractor cheated me out of my wages. Worse still, a plague of lice overtook me. A swiper from the race tracks saw me standing on Eads Bridge throwing my infested shirt and underclothes into the muddy river and thought that I was contemplating suicide. He offered to let me sleep on the hay in a horse's stall at the St. Louis race track. I accepted with thanks, and helped him rub down his horses.

Still there were worse nights ahead. I slept in a vacant lot at Twelfth and Morgan Streets, a lot I shared with a hundred others in similar circumstances. I slept on the cobblestones of the levee of the Mississippi. My companions were perhaps a thousand men of both races. At other times I slept in a chair in Victor's poolroom, and I shall never forget the pop-calls of policemen dropping in to catch vagrants.

Their test for vagrancy was unique. If a man fell asleep in a poolroom chair, he was picked up. Thus the officer's problem was to catch his victim nodding. "Foot-working" was the usual criterion. Either your feet had to be swinging or moving or your eyes had to be open when the policeman entered the room. Otherwise you were a bum. I am glad to say that my feet were always working at the proper time even though I was fast asleep when the officer entered, so the boys told me. Some odd, subconscious instinct made my feet move at the approach of the dreaded steps.

My brother Charlie encountered a similar situation in St. Louis some time later and tells how a one-eyed man solved the problem. Most of the down-and-outers had a way of pulling their hats over their eyes so as not to attract attention to their eyes. This one-eyed fellow, however, covered only his left eye. His right eye, which happened to be glass, he left exposed; and since it remained wide open when he slept, he was always safe from suspicion.

Two popular songs grew out of the brutality of the police in those days, *Brady, He's Dead and Gone* and *Looking For the Bully*. Policemen carried nightsticks about a yard long.

They had a way of hurling these at the feet of fleeing vagrants in such a way as to trip the fugitives. One frequently heard of legs broken in this way. Even more serious injuries sometimes resulted.

One night, in my destitution, I stood outside a white saloon, attracted by the music of a singer who accompanied himself on a guitar. I stopped to listen because the song was *Afterwards*—the second verse had always appealed to me.

> Sometimes my heart grows weary of its sadness,
> Sometimes my life grows weary of its pain.

Moved suddenly by the familiar tune, I forgot that I had no shirt under my coat, that I was a miserable sight and that I should have been unwanted in that place under any circumstances. After a moment's hesitation I ventured inside. At first the bartender was inclined to be rough. When he found that I too could play the guitar and sing that song as well as other songs, he changed his tone. When I had finished a second selection, the crowd in the saloon took up a collection, gave it to me, and invited me to come and sing often. I did not accept the invitation, but I did buy a change of clothing.

I have tried to forget that first sojourn in St. Louis, but I wouldn't want to forget Targee Street as it was then. I don't think I'd want to forget the high-roller Stetson hats of the men or the diamonds the girls wore in their ears. Then there were those who sat for company in little plush parlors under gaslights. The prettiest woman I've ever seen I saw while I was down and out in St. Louis. But mostly my trip was an excursion into the lower depths. I would not want to forget the Great Western Band.

Still, I have always felt that the misery of those days bore fruit in song. I have always imagined that a good bit of that hardship went into the making of the *St. Louis Blues* when, much later, that whole song seemed to spring so easily out of nowhere, the work of a single evening at the piano. I like to think that that song reflects a life filled with hard times as well as good times. I could have returned to Florence. I wasn't compelled to sleep on cobblestones. Every night my soul, I think, occupied clean sheets on a good bed in Florence, but nevertheless I had a stone for a pillow. I would hear an inner voice saying, "Your father was right, your proper place is in Wilberforce studying for the ministry." Professor Wallace's words, too, were remembered: "What can music do but bring you to the gutter?" How true. In fact, I was a prodigal son and there were few husks to eat, but when I would decide to arise and go to my softer bed in Florence, another voice would say, "No! What will you be returning to but a chorus of 'I told you so's'? You will be advancing under a flag of truce and that flag will not be a white one, it will be yellow. No," this voice would repeat, "you will fight it out in spite of your adversities."

Whatever the hardships, Orpheus did not desert me and melody sounded a requiem to the blues. Yes, music cheered me on and played an accompaniment to many hard knocks. It matriculated me in a school not as ethical as Wilberforce, but surely a more effective one, known to all who have become victims of the wanderlust.

CHAPTER FOUR

Mahara's Minstrel Men

MY FATHER always held that it's better to be born lucky than rich. When I left St. Louis, I began to think that maybe there was something in this philosophy after all. My luck changed suddenly. Hitting the road again, I hoboed my way to Evansville, Indiana. There, shambling listlessly through the town under a broiling sun, I came upon a gang of men repaving Fourth Street. As a matter of habit, I went to the boss and asked for a job. He nodded favorably and took me on.

For the first half day I worked on an empty stomach. At noon when we knocked off for the lunch hour, the other men all made a big dash for a nearby restaurant. The boss noticed that I lingered behind.

"What's the matter, Bo?" he asked. "Ain't you hungry?"

I don't know what I told him, but it must have been eloquent enough. He went into his pocket, brought out a two-bit piece and flipped it to me. The beanery advertised good meals for fifteen cents. Surely the worm was turning, but not turning a minute too soon. Already, as the old T.O.B.A.[1] comedians would have said, my stomach had commenced to think my throat was cut.

Later the same boss detailed me to a cooler spot in the shade of an apple tree where dirt was being dumped near Water

[1] Theatrical Owners Booking Association.

Street. There the work was lighter. Under the influence of agreeable food and good treatment I began to feel like myself again. I looked about and found that eight of the men on the job were from my home town. We promptly gravitated together, pooled our expenses and managed to live on a dollar a week apiece. The work on Fourth Street lasted only two weeks for me, however.

When you're up on your luck, one thing just seems to lead to another. In Evansville, for example, I found several brass bands—Warren's, Schrieber's and the Hampton Cornet Band. —and naturally I was on hand for all their parades and concerts. More than that, I stuck my head into the rehearsals of the Hampton Band, and before I knew it, I was playing with them. The next thing I knew people were talking about my playing.

Cyrus Taylor of Henderson, Kentucky, heard the talk and engaged me to play for one of those richly colorful barbecues for which the Southern aristocracy was once famous. The wage was eight dollars, but I cherish the day for another reason. In the small churches in the country the old folks liked to sing about the time when they got religion. Well, I learned what it was to come out of the wilderness too. I had my change that day in Henderson. But mine was a change from a hobo and member of a road gang to a professional musician. The dove descended on my head just as it descended on the heads of those who got happy at camp meeting. The only difference was that instead of singing about the New Jerusalem my dove began to moan about high-brown women and the men they tied to their apron strings.

Many things happened in Henderson, and all of them seemed to work out to a purpose. A young man named A. O. Stanley danced at the barbecue. Later he became a United States Senator. Carl Lindstrom, the twelve-year-old child prodigy, cornet soloist in the famous Gilmore Band of which John Philip Sousa had been a member, heard me play and came and ex-

4

changed observations about the instrument he and I both loved. I joined a band under the direction of the brilliant David P. Crutcher. Most important of all, I met Elizabeth V. Price.

Altogether Kentucky seemed as fresh and green and full of music as it had been in the age when leaves were born. The sky was a deep, fathomless blue. In every tree and hedge a bird sang. Moreover, she was beautiful, this Elizabeth Price. I couldn't pull myself away. Eventually she became my wife.

A German singing society of several hundred voices was one of the glories of Henderson at that time. I was so impressed by the work of Professor Bach, their director, that I angled for a janitor job in their Liederkranz Hall in order to study the professor's methods and at the same time hear the men sing. In this way I obtained a postgraduate course in vocal music—and got paid for it.

Of course I wasn't content to remain at a distance. Before long I was doing odd jobs around Professor Bach's house, winning my way into his good graces and hungrily snatching up every musical crumb that fell from the great man's table. Bach was not only an accomplished teacher and director. He had also written several successful operas.

All of this, as I now see it, was leading to the big moment that was presently to shape my course in life. It came on August 4, 1896. On that day I received a letter from Elmore Dodd, a young musician with whom I'd played in Henderson and Nashville. He had left our band to join Mahara's Minstrels. His letter requested me to come to Chicago for rehearsal and to play cornet with band and orchestra. The salary was only six dollars a week plus "cakes," for the country was still deep in a depression, but there would be a chance to travel and, better still, an opportunity to rub elbows with the best Negro musicians of the day. On August 6th I joined W. A. Mahara's Minstrels at the Winterburn show-printing office in Chicago. We opened at Belvidere.

My picture at nineteen, in Hampton Cornet Band, Evansville, Indiana.

It goes without saying that minstrels were a disreputable lot in the eyes of a large section of upper-crust Negroes, including the family and friends of Elizabeth Price, but it was also true that all the best talent of that generation came down the same drain. The composers, the singers, the musicians, the speakers, the stage performers—the minstrel shows got them all. For my part, there wasn't a moment's hesitation when I received Elmore Dodd's letter. I took it for the break it was. The cards were running my way at last.

In the show itself my luck held up marvelously. The bass violin player quit. I took over, and my salary was raised to seven dollars a week. Someone observed that the show needed a better quartet. I trained one, and another raise followed. Meanwhile I laid away the old J. W. Pepper silver cornet that had replaced my earlier Conn & Dupont, bought a spanking new C. G. Conn gold-plated trumpet and began practicing like an archangel from four to six hours a day. Soon I was on the stage in the olio, a recognized cornet soloist. Up again went my salary—way up. At odd times I arranged orchestrations for some of our featured singers and discovered the strange, indescribable thrill of hearing my work played by a good orchestra.

Then McKinley was elected and prosperity made the turn. I bought smart outfits, one being a suit, hat, watch fob, umbrella strap and spats, all cut from the same bolt of rich brown cloth. Also, a couple of diamonds. Dressed to kill, I became a figure on the Avenue. The musical press began to throw roses in my direction.

That was just the beginning. After the first season with the Mahara Minstrels I received a letter from the management saying that they had decided to carry two bands with the show during the coming year. This enabled them to offer me the leadership of a band which would consist of thirty pieces in the parades and of forty-two in the night concerts. Naturally a bright uniform, golden epaulettes, and a gleaming silk topper were included. It was too good to be true.

Encyclopedists and historians of the American stage have slighted the old Negro minstrels while making much of the burnt cork artists who imitated them. But Negroes were the originators of this form of entertainment, and companies of them continued to perform as long as the vogue lasted. Mahara's outfit, like the Georgia Minstrels, the McCabe and Young Minstrels, and the Hicks and Sawyer Colored Minstrels, was the genuine article, a real Negro minstrel show. Our show, like most of the others of its type, was under white management.

Life began at 11:45 A.M. in a minstrel company. At that time the manager of the parade blew his whistle in the theatre, ordering "all out." The order of things would be varied slightly if the train reached the city late. In such a case we would dress in our private Pullman car and commence the parade from the railroad tracks. Either way we were sure to find a swarm of long-legged boys on hand, begging for a chance to carry the banners advertising the show—the same young rabble, perhaps, that invariably swept down upon the circus with the offer to water the elephants in return for free tickets.

The parade itself was headed by the managers in their four-horse carriages. Doffing silk hats and smiling their jeweled smiles, they acknowledged with easy dignity the small flutter of polite applause their high-stepping horses provoked. After them came the carriage in which the stars rode. The "walking gents" followed, that exciting company which included comedians, singers and acrobats. They in turn were followed by the drum major—not an ordinary drum major beating time for a band, mind you, but a performer out of the books, an artist with the baton. His twirling stick suggested a bicycle wheel revolving in the sun. Occasionally he would give it a toss and then recover the glistening affair with the same flawless skill.

The drum major in a minstrel show was a character to conjure with; not infrequently he stole the parade. Our company had two such virtuosi; in addition to twirling their batons, they added the new wrinkle of tossing them back and forth to each other as they marched.

Finally, distributed at intervals from one end of the parade to the other, there were the boys with the banners. Each banner described one outstanding feature of the colossal spectacle.

The band played marches as this procession paraded the principal streets of a town. Curiously, we made few concessions to low-brow taste in our selection of music. We used the heaviest works of W. P. Chambers, C. W. Dalbey and C. L. Barnhouse; even the stiff composition *Alvin Joslin* by Pettee was not beyond us. It was only when we were lip-weary that we eased off on the light, swingy marches of R. B. Hall and John Philip Sousa.

The procession circled on the public square, and the band played a program of classical overtures plus a medley of popular airs for the throngs that assembled there in the open. *Brudder Gardner's Picnic* (a selection containing the gems of Stephen C. Foster) was always in order. Special features like trombone, piccolo or clarinet solos were interspersed among our numbers. Usually too we included a comic act such as a trick bicyclist made up as a tramp or an interlude by the lanky D. C. Scott, a "natural-born reacher," in his slapstick get-up. And here, finally, was the place for the oratorical gifts of the remarkable George L. Moxley whose business it was to sell the show to the natives.

Another parade with music brought us back to the theatre. For the remainder of the afternoon our time was our own— and did we flirt—but at seven-thirty we played a program of classical music in front of the opera house. In all probability, we would pull the "Musicians' Strike" out of our bag of tricks. During this well-rehearsed feature each musician would, when his turn came, pretend to quarrel with someone else and quit the band in a huff. When, to the dismay of the innocent yokels, the band had dwindled to almost nothing, a policeman who had been "fixed" and planted at a convenient spot would come up and ask questions. This would lead to a fight between some of the remaining musicians, and the officer would promptly arrest them.

The crowd could be depended on to express its disappointment in strong language. "Just like niggers," they'd groan. "They break up everything with a fight. Damn it all, they'd break up Heaven." During these recriminations we would spring the old hokum. The band, having reassembled around the corner, would cut loose with one of the most sizzling tunes of the day, perhaps *Creole Belles, Georgia Camp Meeting*, or *A Hot Time In the Old Town Tonight*, and presently the ticket seller would go to work. Our hokum hooked them.

Inside the opera house the curtain rose on a conventional orchestra of fourteen players sitting high on an elevated platform. Before the orchestra sat the two brilliant semi-circles of performers. The first was occupied by the featured soloists; the second, by singers and others later to take part in the olio. Immediately upon the rise of the curtain this entire group burst into song. And what singing it was! Anyone who ever followed the old minstrel shows of the last century will bear witness to the quality of the ensemble singing of these amazingly well-trained groups.

Old-timers will remember as well what followed. Following the curtain music, the interlocutor entered togged in blue silk and lace à la knickerbocker and introduced the comedians. A thrill that the present generation may never know waited only for this individual's trite but magical words: "Ladies and Gentlemen, we've come out tonight to give you a pleasing entertainment. With bones on the right and tambourines on the left we'll proceed with the overture. Gentlemen, be seated!" That gave the end men their cue, and they promptly joined the grand ensemble, beating tambourines and rattling bones while they made faces, pantomimed and otherwise laid the spectators in the aisles with their tomfoolery.

It is interesting to recall that our sopranos and altos in the minstrel chorus were men, but that was no handicap with men like Dicky Lewis and William Burton in our company. They could hit top C like women. Our tenors and bassos were equally capable. Sloan Edwards, the big basso, had no trouble getting down to double B flat. Any of our top tenors, when they were soaring, could bring a mist to the eyes.

That was as it should have been. Tenor singers in those days had peculiar responsibilities. Everyone knew that there were those who came to a minstrel show to cry as well as to laugh. Ladies of that mauve decade were likely to follow the plot of a song with much the same sentimental interest that their daughters show in the development of a movie theme nowadays. The tenors were required to tell the stories that jerked the tears. For this purpose they had at their disposal such songs as *She May Have Seen Better Days* or *Just Tell Them That You Saw Me*. If he failed to do this, he was simply not first string by minstrel standards and could expect to be replaced by a better man.

A memorable figure in and out of the show was our interlocutor, George L. Moxley. Upon occasion he passed for white. Handsome, prematurely gray, he wore a silk stove-pipe hat and liked to pose as a theatrical owner. Moxley often refused his salary, preferring, as he would say with a cavalier gesture, to just keep four-bits in his jeans and live off his wits. It sounded somewhat like a boast, but Moxley never failed to make it good. On top of that, he saved the management untold sums of money by his smooth talk at such times as the boys or the boss got into trouble. White in appearance, Moxley was by birth and at heart a Kentucky Negro.

More than once I have seen Moxley walk into a fine restaurant flat broke, order a two-dollar meal and then borrow three dollars from the proprietor "to make the bill an even five dol-

lars." Then there was the night at Billings, Montana. We had
been traveling through the Black Hills by stagecoach and had
seen cowboys occasionally ride up to a bar and recklessly buy
drinks for the house. By the time we reached Billings, Moxley
was ready to show the natives something. Money flowed in
large dimensions in that part of the country. You saw no
nickels or dimes and few quarters in circulation. This did not
intimidate Moxley. Empty of pocket and on his wits as usual,
he set up the house, and told Wild West stories. His poise had
never been more magnificent. The crowd responded glee-
fully, and presently everybody was royally tight and some
blowing or winning dollars by the thousand. Eventually the
house made the mistake of presenting Moxley with a bill for
his initial treat. Moxley showed surprise, but he was not too
shocked to convince the bartender that instead of owing the
house, the house owed him a substantial commission for the
business he had stimulated. Of course the bill was forgotten.

Moxley had gathered a great store of theatrical anecdotes.
He had been around and learned the ropes. I always enjoyed
listening to him talk. Recently, in response to a letter of mine,
he wrote me from Martinsburg, West Virginia, giving some
of the details of his career before and after the years we spent
together in the Mahara Minstrels. Here is part of his letter:

"I began singing to the public in my 13th year at the Philadelphia Centennial of 1876. Then, for two years, I was with Tony
Pastor in the theatre he made famous in New York. I appeared
also at the Castle Gardens with many others. The public knew me
as George L. Moxley, the 'Cuban Tenor Solo Singer,' and considered me as white as any foreigner is expected to be. This made it
possible for me to get in all shows.

"Then for several years I was with Alice Oates and the Alice
Townsend Company in burlesque. I met Sam T. Jack at Haver-
hill, Mass., and helped him put the celebrated Creoles together.
Irving Jones worked with me in the Creole show and I introduced
him to his wife in Louisville. In 1888 at the Buckingham Theatre
at Louisville I was consulted by Whalen and Martelle relative to

routining their shows. I joined the Ed. F. Davis English Concert
Co., and we toured through New York State and Canada.

"Then for several seasons I helped arrange programs for the
Mardi Gras at New Orleans. I lectured on Jim Kee, the educated
horse. I made announcements at the Omeramagrau Exposition * at
Omaha. In 1894 I joined W. A. Mahara, called the first rehearsal
at Chicago and was with him 12 or 14 years. . . . Ben Hunn, Sam
Lucas and his wife and Burn Hawkins, Ted Pifer and Dora Dean,
the first woman to do the cakewalk, were all with us in Sam T.
Jack's Creoles. John W. Isham was agent. Met the Hier Sisters in
Boone, Iowa, and Lamden Jubilee Singers at St. Louis in 1887.
Sisseretta Jones, the 'Black Patti,' entertained me in Fargo in '97.
I was then on business for W. A. Mahara.

"I met Tom Mackintosh, Billy Kersands, Charlie Housley and
Bowhee Brothers, the dancers, at Bay City, Michigan, in 1882.
They were with Jack Haverly's Minstrels. Queen Victoria had
recently given Billy Kersands the big diamond cluster. . . . I don't
remember the town in Michigan where we buried dear little Gene
Brewer. I read the Bible and led a sacred hymn, if you remember.

"I worked with several ofay [white] outfits in my time without any trouble. W. A. Mahara was the only Minstrel Company
I traveled with, but I put on an Elks' Minstrel once in Shreveport
and one in Dayton, both ofays. They would have hung me in
Shreveport had they known that I was colored, and the same is
true in plenty of other places.

"I forgot to tell you that I first met Williams and Walker in an
upstairs 'Beer' theatre in San Francisco. They were singing and
dancing between the tables. I did not know them but we became
acquainted and I advised them to go to a better place in a basement. I first met Ernest Hogan in Cripple Creek, Colorado, singing in a beer saloon. He had written one verse of *All Coons Look
Alike to Me*, and he read it to me. I worked with William A.
Brady at the Auditorium Theatre in Chicago.

"I put in one season in Texas telling fortunes and all that goes
with it. I was 70 years old December 17, 1935. Born in Kentucky,
I was reared in Ohio and Chicago. I couldn't read or write at the
age of 13 when I started out."

The star of our show was not Moxley, however, but "Clever
Billy Young." Beau Brummell of the first magnitude, Billy

* This was the Trans-Mississippi Exposition . . . 1898.

also qualified as a gentleman. Born in Kentucky, he claimed as well a gentleman's privilege when Rye or Bourbon was in question. Billy had come to our company by way of the McCabe and Young Minstrels. W. A. Mahara had been an advance man for Young around '88, during the days of the Young-McCabe tie-up. The following year the cards were shuffled most interestingly. Dan McCabe headed his own show. Billy Young went to work for Mahara. Show business has always been the same in some of its aspects. The dog-eat-dog equation goes back even further than I can remember.

The word "clever" definitely belonged in Young's billing. He was an all-round man if there ever was one on the stage. Equally talented at dancing or singing, comedy or tragedy, Billy was, in my opinion, the daddy of them all in his line of work. Back in the McCabe and Young shows he had featured and popularized the dramatic song *I Belong to the Upper Ten; You Are the Lower Five.* In our company his long suit was *Elegant Barney*, a sure-fire number in which he imitated the well-known Broadway favorite, Barney Fagan. He was good in his own *Flower Song* in the first part, and he was better in his *Wine Song* in the finale. In each of these Billy wound up on a high note which he held endlessly, it seemed, walking around the semi-circle and back to his seat still holding the high note while the house came down with stormy approval. He brought out the best in our chorus too. I shall never forget the support we gave him when he sang Chauncey Olcott's *My Beautiful Irish Maid.* Yes, clever was the word for Billy Young. Give him his Bourbon and a spot on the minstrel stage, and he'd take up the curtain with the best of them.

When Billy appeared for his specialty in the olio there was always a moment of uncertainty in the orchestra. We never quite knew what he might say or do. A Dutch gag probably indicated a German song, and we might usually expect the same sort of hint for an Irish, Scotch or Negro number, but there was always Billy's liquor to be reckoned with. He gave

us the eternal jitters, but still the show never suffered. We
learned to keep step with his quick changes.

Billy's saving grace was his gift as an improviser, his inspired ad libbing. There was a night in Helena, Montana,
when this very nimbleness proved to be a two-edged sword,
but nobody complained too much. Three sheets in the wind
and tottering visibly on the stage, Billy began:

> When a Russian is smoking, he's thinking
> When a German gets drunk, he's drinking.

Several too realistic gulps and burps followed, and during the
moment's pause the people in the audience had to hold their
sides to keep them from splitting. Billy hesitated, his timing
still a thing of beauty, then repeated:

> When a Russian is smoking, he's thinking
> When a German gets drunk, he's drinking.

This time, however, the pause was slighter; Billy had found
his thread and was ready to sail ahead triumphantly:

> But when a colored man gets warm in the summertime
> Well—use your own judgment.

To all appearances this bit of doggerel was a bull's eye. It
went over like a cannonball. But a local colored lawyer, sitting in the audience with his white wife, failed to see the joke.
The eyes of the audience suddenly turned upon him. The
couple were humiliated and bitterly resentful. Before we left
those parts, Mahara had to settle a damage suit, deducting the
amount from Billy's already overdrawn salary. But, as I've
said, the management didn't mind. Crowds pay good money
for the unexpected. And they knew, as we knew in the orchestra, that the unexpected is what they were sure to get when
Billy Young appeared.

Billy was also a mighty man with the ladies. His popularity

extended from Avenue A to the Tenderloin. When carriages waited after the show, we understood. When the harness was silver-trimmed and flunkies sat on the front seat, we knew Billy was headed for the bright lights. If soft eyes gleamed from the shadows of a cab that gave forth rich perfumes when the door swung open, we took the hint; we knew why the lights were then of a different shade. Billy was going where he couldn't be followed. We heard it said that there were locks on exclusive doors that admitted no hat, however high, while Billy remained. Billy's exploits became a legend among minstrel men of our day.

Another ace with our company was Leroy Bland, a female impersonator whose real name was Johnny Stone. He had adopted Bland as a stage name because of his admiration for the composer of *Carry Me Back to Old Virginny*. Leroy introduced me to James Bland in Louisville in 1897. I remember still the thrill it gave me to shake the hand of this truly great minstrel who wrote and featured *In the Evening by the Moonlight, Climbing Up the Golden Stairs, Oh Dem Golden Slippers* and other songs that attained a place in American music second only to the work of Stephen Foster in the same field.

Even the musical world had forgotten James Bland completely. Some learned with surprise, others dismay, that he was a Negro composer. His sister, Mrs. Irene B. Jurix, still lives in New York's Harlem. I little dreamed that day in Louisville that I'd live to participate with a small group of others in bringing the nameless grave of the composer to the attention of a forgetful world.

Leroy had a partner, Dan Avery. Mahara took the pair on when they were "picks." They had a good act, these two, but Dan later joined one of our rivals, the Georgia Minstrels. He made good with them and then went to New York and enjoyed a long popularity in the vaudeville team of Avery and Hart.

Sudden, stark tragedy sometimes darkened our minstrel days. There was Louis Wright, for instance, who played a trombone in the boys' band. Later, though still in short pants, he was elevated to my division. An unusually talented musician, this slim, sensitive boy resented insult with every fiber of his being. He would fight anyone any time and with any weapon within reach. In our company we understood his fierce pride; we knew how to treat him.

Later, however, when the Georgia Minstrels lured him away from us, he didn't fare so well. They were in a Missouri town and Louis, on the way to the theatre with his female companion, was snowballed by some white hoodlums. He retaliated swiftly, laying down a blast of curses.

That night a mob came back-stage at the theatre. They had come to lynch Louis. In his alarm the sharp-tempered boy drew a gun and fired into the crowd. The mob scattered promptly, but they did not turn from their purpose. They reassembled in the railroad yards, near the special car of the minstrel company. This time their number was augmented by officers. When the minstrels arrived, the whole company was arrested and thrown into jail. Many of them were brutally flogged during the questioning that followed, but no squeal was forthcoming. In time, however, Louis Wright was recognized. The law gave him to the mob, and in almost less time than it takes to tell it they had done their work. He was lynched, his tongue cut out and his body shipped to his mother in Chicago in a pine box.

One day in a Texas town I began to think that my turn was next. While playing a cornet solo in the public square during the noon concert, I suddenly turned around to discover a rifle pointed at my eye. I ignored the threat, playing as if nothing was happening. A few moments later, the drums rumbling as we began the march back to the theatre, a gang of cowboys appeared and began roping our walking gents with their lassos. A swarm of rowdy boys joined in the fun and threw rocks down the bell of the big bass horn. Then the kids turned on the drums. They pelted our drums so vigorously the noise sounded like the rat-a-tat-tat of a machine-gun. I was furious and stoutly refused to play a note during the parade. We marched faster than usual, but we kept our ranks. Later, Mahara complimented me warmly for keeping the parade in formation and refusing to play.

There was also the night in Texas when local bad-men boasted that they would break up our show just for the devil-ment. The rangers, mortal enemies of these prairie rowdies, got wind of this, however, and one of them showed up in time to put a crimp in these plans. The rangers, it seemed, had the eagle sign on the Texas toughs. One of them could, and sometimes did, rout a hundred bullies at a time.

Orange was the Texas town we dreaded most. Whenever it became known to the home town mob that our show was routed their way, they would sit up all night waiting for the train to pass. Their conception of wild, he-man fun was to riddle our car with bullets as it sped through their town. Our strategy was to extinguish the lights and lie quietly on the floor. Fortunately none of our company ever got killed during these assaults.

The management of our two minstrel companies was rough and ready too. It consisted of three Irish brothers, William A., Jack and Frank L. Mahara, the fightingest triumvirate of Irishmen that ever hoodwinked the railroad company. Jack won his spurs in the days of the Dalton gang. He was riding with a number of other passengers on a Texas train when the outlaws came aboard and ordered everyone to his knees. Jack obeyed, along with the others, but he stayed down only long enough to whip out his gun and open fire. In the exchange a bullet plowed a furrow in his skull. Later an operation was necessary, an operation in which he lost two inches of his skull. But this did not break the Mahara fighting spirit. Jack remained a gamecock to the last.

His brother W. A. went in for a touch of glamour. W. A. wore three diamond rocks in his shirt front. They sparkled like headlights. They were said to have cost him three thousand each. Big money in those days. The boys would say W. A. was the kind of manager who doesn't care a damn whether the show is good, bad or indifferent so long as his show made money. Performers sometimes spoke of his outfit as a finishing school. When it was left to W. A., anybody who had something to offer could get a job with the show, provided the price was right. He liked a big company. His average roster was sixty men. At the same time he took pains to see that no train conductor ever found more than forty when he collected fares.

I was with Frank's outfit in 1903. Frank was a different pair of sleeves. He had a passion for detail. He required that everything be just right. For him the minstrel show was not just a fabulous mine of profits but a company of human beings each of whom required personal consideration. The music, the uniforms, the program and the talent, even the food he bought and the Pullman car in which we traveled, had to be the best obtainable. He also saw to it that our Pullman had a hidden compartment under the floor like W. A.'s, a compartment which we came to call the "bear-wallow" or the "get-away." In this secret hold we carried reserves of food, not to mention a small arsenal. One night in a Tennessee town it contained me.

The town was Murfreesboro, the same town in which my old Grandpa Handy had been ordained to preach the gospel back in '65. Our car, as usual, had been switched down to the railroad yards. There dinner was in progress when two of our performers who had been carrying chips on their shoulders a long time got up and started a nasty brawl. This was the cue for Will Garland to take a hand.

Will, it happened, in addition to being our tenor singer and tuba player, was quite some shakes as an athlete himself. From his home in Keokuk, Iowa, he had brought along a set of boxing gloves, and now he cautiously suggested that the soreheads settle their grudge in a bout with the gloves. The offer was accepted, and the rest of us abandoned dinner to surround the scrappers and egg on our favorite in the contest. The battle got under way with both men pumping leather like seasoned pugs. Excitement was rising to a climax a few moments later when, apparently from out of nowhere, a white ticket agent with a coupling pin in his hand suddenly shoved his way through the crowd. He raised the heavy iron and aimed it at the head of one of the boxers.

A gory tragedy was in the making and would have been accomplished had I not been standing where I could intercept the blow. I sprang forward, caught the man's hand and wrested the iron backwards. I failed to disarm him, however, and a second later when he regained his balance, he turned on me. This time Will Garland grabbed him from behind and pinned his arms to his sides. That was all I wanted. I savagely rubbed my fist in the helpless fellow's mouth. "You just wait here till I come back," I concluded melodramatically. Then I rushed away angrily.

Of course I was bluffing. I had no intention of coming back, but I must have acted my part well. The railroad man assumed that I'd gone for a pistol, and when Will Garland released him, he broke and ran to the station and hid. Meanwhile, I crawled into the "get-away" and waited for times to get better.

Some time later I heard the sheriff and his posse searching our car. Mahara was with them. He pretended to be angry enough to chew nails. I could hear his voice tremble with rage as he told the Murfreesboro sheriff and his men that I had better sense than to come on that car again after what I'd done. He left no doubt that he would make even shorter shrift of me than the sheriff intended, once he got his hands on me. This pleased the sheriff. He and his men gave up the search of the car and went out to scour the countryside. Many times I have had to use such native wit or suffer for the lack of it.

It was not long before the wrath of God was on us again, and we stood in pressing need of all the mother wit we could muster. Cricket Smith was the cause, the same Cricket Smith now remembered as the trumpeter of the Ford Dabney band that played on the Ziegfeld roof. In Austin, Texas, Cricket was stricken with an ailment that a local physician diagnosed as a "slight skin infection." Truth to tell, however, Cricket's ailment was no skin infection and it was far from slight.

Mrs. Handy was with me at the time. She had joined me at Houston for a short visit. When we left one of our two Pullman cars in that city and proceeded to Austin and Tyler for one-day stands, I prevailed upon her to go with me, explaining that while the car would be crowded, we could get comfortable lodging with good families in each city. She agreed, against her better judgment, and we moved on to Tyler. The train arrived late, and she remained in the car during the morning parade. Cricket was excused in order to visit a doctor. Things seemed to work out well enough for a while, but I can tell you now that the witches' caldron was boiling even then.

We had reached the public square and commenced the noon concert when an excited doctor arrived on the scene, waving his arms wildly.

"Stop! Stop it!" he cried. "Stop this damn music." I turned in alarm. The members of my band began to look foolish and unnecessary. Presently, turning to the assembled crowd, the doctor added, "Ladies and gentlemen, these niggers have got the smallpox. If they don't get out of town—and that right quick—we'll lynch them all."

The effect was electrical. Stunned for a moment, we quickly regained our wits well enough to fall into step with the rat-a-tat-tat of George Reeves' snare drum and commence a double-quick to the car. In another jiffy an engine was hitched to

5

our car and we were taken to a siding on the outskirts of the town. County officers came a short while later to inform us that the appearance of one more case of smallpox among us would be the signal for them to burn the car and carry out the doctor's lynching threat with regard to the rest of us, men and women.

Our difficulties immediately multiplied. No provision had been made for the luckless Cricket, and no food, water or sanitary arrangements were made for the rest of us. We might have hit bottom immediately had it not been for a couple of seventy-gallon tanks of water and the ever-handy food reserves in the "bear-wallow." W. A. Mahara made it a point always to prepare for the worst while hoping for the best.

During our enforced idleness, something told me to brush up on my shooting. In addition to the arsenal in the bottom of the car, I had my own private collection of arms, a Winchester 44, a Smith and Wesson and a Colt revolver. The S. & W. had been bought especially for my wife, and during the lull I tried to teach her to shoot it. This proved to be a waste of time. She was too nervous to pull the trigger. At any rate, I built a fortress of cross-ties, and this became our protection by day as well as a bed by night.

We decided immediately that there would be greater safety, considering the tenseness of the situation, in sleeping in the open than remaining in the car. This met no opposition, but it led to a greater problem. Guards were thrown around our concentration camp. By sundown some of us began to be disturbed about the lack of privacy. We requested the guards to allow our women to walk the tracks down to the nearby woods. This was denied. Will Garland got his fighting clothes on immediately. He was in the midst of a romance with Nettie Goff, our lady trombonist, and he was willing to pit his gallantry against any opposition. My blood boiled too. Will and I grimly raided the arsenal, took positions and calmly instructed the women to take their walk. We invited the guards to oppose us, if they dared. They didn't. As a matter of fact, their attitude softened after that. Some of them actually became friendly.

But we found a more substantial friend in a local merchant named John Brown. Less militant than the hero of Harpers Ferry, whose name he bore, Mr. Brown was nevertheless a solid sender where we were concerned. After we had been quarantined a few days, he secured orders from the county to supply us with sow belly, beans, cornmeal and molasses. In conformity with his orders he made out bills for this type of provision, but actually he was a sensitive man who understood that we were not accustomed to this sort of food. While this may have been the diet the townsfolk had been in the habit of supplying their field hands, it was certainly not the grade of food that W. A. Mahara provided for his minstrels. Accordingly, while not offending local sensibilities, Mr. Brown used his own judgment in filling the orders.

One meets men like John Brown even in unfortunate circumstances. They help to shape in us a better opinion of mankind. In this case, as our acquaintance grew, we formed the habit of tossing money to our benefactor with the simple request that he bring the "correct ingredients." The guards blinked in puzzlement, but they did not guess that what we wanted was beer or whisky. Mr. Brown understood. Sometimes he surprised us with unexpected delicacies. Our internment, thanks to him, became almost endurable.

Before it was over, smallpox claimed fourteen victims among our number. Meanwhile the authorities gave us plenty of air. They never came close enough to the car to check on the spread of the disease. I suppose they were just being smart and taking no chances, but this was where they outsmarted themselves.

During the afternoons I got the band together and played a concert behind our barricade. The townsfolk, as usual, swarmed around like flies drawn to a molasses drop. In the midst of the musical program big Gordon Collins came on with a stunt that left the folks limp from laughing. Two hundred and eighty pounds of brown meat, Gordon would leap high into the air, thrust his legs before him and come down with a whosh on his mighty buttocks. He was well-cushioned by nature, and no calamity resulted for the big boy. Moreover, the spectators thought it was tremendous. He would follow his leaping act with humorous songs. These got the crowd too. But entertainment was not our underlying aim on these occasions. Gordon was not bruising his bottom just for fun.

This performance was repeated several times. Then one evening we decided that the time was ripe for action. While the guards were holding their sides as they laughed at Gordon, a number of our company repaired to the car. There the fourteen sick men were quickly dressed in women's clothes. Each was provided with sufficient money to get him out of Texas and to some city where the benefits of a hospital might be enjoyed. All of us knew what was going on—we had been plotting it for days—but all could not take a hand in the actual business. The show had to continue. Still, out of the corner of my eye, I watched the would-be females make their way down the tracks while Gordon leaped higher and higher and bounced harder and harder. And through it all the band played in the gathering dusk. Finally the last of our friends disappeared in the woods.

Will Garland was among them. After our reckless challenge to the guards who refused to let the womenfolk take their walk, he too had fallen a victim of the contagion. This little misadventure, together with others that went to make up life with Mahara's Minstrels, may have soured him. He went to England soon afterwards and produced shows that traveled throughout Europe, but he never returned to America. Others went to France, Germany, Russia and Egypt, where they remained. Perhaps they found it hard to erase from their minds the nightmare of those minstrel days.

Publicity has saved many a show, but it killed ours. We were literally "as welcome as the smallpox" in those parts, and nobody could accuse our managers of failing to catch a hint. We jumped all the way to the Atlantic coast. There, awaiting proposed bookings in Cuba, we passed the time wildcatting through Georgia and Florida. Meanwhile all our smallpox victims had rejoined us in good health.

The weather was diamond-bright during those months—December 1899 and January 1900—and our company tried to imagine what the real tropics might be like. My wife, who was still with me, began to be fed up with the hardships of the road. When she learned that her steamer fare and hotel bills in Cuba would have to come out of my own pocket, she decided to return to Henderson. I had to argue mightily to change her mind. Eventually, of course, I carried my point, insisting that two could live as cheaply as one and that, more important still, there might not be another chance to visit Cuba soon. So, having compromised, we set sail from Tampa via Key West.

When we entered the harbor at Havana, the morning sun was rising and the splendors of a thousand abalone shells were flashing through the mist. In the foreground loomed the gray ramparts of Morro Castle and Fort Principe. Beyond the shimmering water an amber city seemed to emerge from a purple sea where the Prado, boulevard of dreams, came into view. Somehow it seemed more like a garden than a thoroughfare.

Suddenly I discovered tears in Mrs. Handy's eyes as we stood at the rail. What if she had carried out her original intention and returned to Henderson! Just see what she would have missed! For once I was right, unmistakably right. This was much too marvelous to miss at any cost. Tank towns and ruffians, smallpox and Jim Crow coaches were all forgotten in the twinkling of an eye. Shadows left the breast and flew away.

While entering Havana harbor we passed an historic relic, the wreckage of the battleship *Maine*, with nothing visible but an iron mast, pointing at the sky with a corroded finger, and swept by waves which suggested troubled days. Inspired by a patriotic feeling I contrived to secure a bottle of sea water there, which we kept for years in an honest endeavor to remember the *Maine*.

February in Havana was like August back home. Indeed, so intense was the heat of those February days that we had to change our noonday parade to five o'clock. Moreover, the streets of the city were certainly not made to order for a minstrel parade. Calle de Obispo, in the heart of the business section, was narrow enough to dispute the passage of two carriages unless they were handled by skilful drivers. The sidewalks were in proportion and offered no place for the cheering crowds to which we were accustomed. Still the boom of our drums and the tantaras of our brasses were not wasted. Nothing is ever lost. If the thin line of spectators that lined the narrow walks was disappointing, the throngs on the balconies more than compensated.

Overhead, behind the wrought iron bars of their balcony windows, Cuban señoritas smiled. For a moment I was mesmerized by the hocus pocus of lovely dark eyes, red roses and fingers that threw kisses. I took it that my well-cut maroon uniform, my bright buttons and gleaming gold epaulettes were not entirely ineffective. I fancied that in their own language soft voices were saying, "Ah, do it, Mr. Handy!"

Our parade paused before the American Legation to serenade General Luke E. Wright. The Governor-General was so pleased he took time to address a written note of thanks and congratulation to the band.

While in Havana I bought a copy of the Cuban *Hymno*

Bayames, and arranged it for my band. Later, when we played
it on the Prado, one of the natives became so excited he took
my cap and tossed it high into the air, a gesture which reminded me of the way Confederate soldiers tossed their own
hats whenever we played *Dixie* for them. Surely, I began to
think, music needs no interpreter when it speaks. For those
who employ this language Bali and Broadway blend in world-
old ways.

The music of the island intrigued me. I never missed the
concerts of the one-hundred-piece Havana Guards Band.
More often I sought out the small, shy bands that played behind closed shutters on dark out of the way streets where the
passion flower bloomed in the heart of the night. These fascinated me because they were playing a strange native air, new
and interesting to me. More than thirty years later I heard
that rhythm again. By then it had gained respectability in
New York and had acquired a name—the Rumba.

After the show in the evening, feeling very correct in suits
of tropical drill, small groups of us sat for hours over tall
drinks in a leaf-fringed establishment where ladies and gentlemen mingled and refreshments ranging from sodas and ices to
wines and whiskies were served. We were astonished to see
ladies of quality seated in boxes ordering hard drinks and
smoking cigarettes. Eventually, of course, this custom reached
Broadway and points west and south, proving, as the old folks
would say, that "the sun do move." But at the time of our visit
Americans were just beginning to visit Havana in numbers. It
would be hard to say from this distance which country prof-
ited most from the consequent interchange of ideas and
customs.

Mrs. Handy and I passed the golden days driving about the
city and into the country. We browsed in the curio shops
buying odd fans, old coins and quaint jewelry. We visited the
historic fortresses; drove out to the coffee and cocoanut and
banana plantations. We promenaded with the gay throngs on

the Prado. But the daily expense of our carriage, coachman and footman included, was only forty cents. Two *could* live as cheaply as one.

For some reason, however, Mrs. Handy suddenly lost her taste for Cuban cuisine. Later, when we found an American restaurant run by a Chinaman, she discovered that the food there tasted no better. I began to lose my patience. It didn't seem to me reasonable that anybody should turn up his nose at the sort of fare we were enjoying. "Women, women, women," I complained. "They just won't do." I became more tolerant, however, when I learned that I was destined to become a father. All was forgiven.

I'd have excellent reason to remember the perfumed influence of sultry Havana.

CHAPTER FIVE

Work Is the Measure of Worth

MAHARA'S MINSTRELS played northern Alabama after our return from Cuba, and my father, hearing that we were near,
came over to Huntsville for the performance. For him this
was a monstrous violation of principle. Not since he was a
young man had he attended a show of any kind. At that time
he had listened with great interest to a barker who promised
that those who ventured inside would see and hear something
they would never forget. My father, thirsting for knowledge,
paid his hard earned money and entered. Inside the tent a
tobacco-chewing bumpkin stood on a platform whittling a
pine stick with a jackknife. "Gentlemen," he muttered as he
cut, "always cut from you. If you cut from you, you will
never get cut." Over and over again he repeated the line,
whittling stupidly as he muttered. My father felt not only
duped but vastly insulted. He never forgave the barker, the
whittler or the show business. I knew therefore, when he
came to Huntsville for our performance, that his conscience
was taking a frightful beating.

During the band concert a crowd surged around us. The
air was filled with honeyed words. There was little doubt that
they liked us enormously. In the midst of the excitement I
heard my father telling folks around him that the leader of the

band was his son. He chuckled as he said it, and I could see that he was about to burst with pride.

That night he attended the show, and when the curtain fell, he grasped my hand and repeated words that have burned in my brain through the years. He said, "Sonny, I haven't been in a show since I professed religion. I enjoyed it. I am very proud of you and forgive you for becoming a musician."

The next day the show moved on to Florence and I made ready to paint the town and greet old friends. They, in turn, received us with open arms. Professor Wallace watched my every movement and lost no opportunity to express his approval of what I had accomplished. Even more effusive was Willie Brown, leader of Florence's white band. He sent our band a huge bouquet and followed this with cases of beer, wine and assorted liquors. To cap the climax, he brought me his gold cornet and requested that I play my solo on it in the band concert.

Years earlier, when I had just bought the old rotary-valve horn for a dollar and six bits, Brown had told me with cutting frankness that I was wasting my time and money. I could never learn to play the cornet, he argued. My lips were too thick. Negroes, in his opinion, should stick to the banjo and guitar. His words made only a slight impression on my mind, for I took the advice to be no more than the usual smallness one meets all along the line. I had ignored and almost forgotten it. After the return to Florence it gradually dawned on me that there had never been any question of the man's sincerity. He seemed more than glad to atone for his miscalculation.

While enjoying my friends I had to call the hand of a certain comedian in our company, a two hundred and fifty pound bully who had been giving me lots of trouble ever since the quarantine in Texas. During the smallpox layover this fellow had touched me for money. Later he had used the loan as a means of bulldozing me, daring me to ask for it and boasting to the others of his highhanded doings. In Montana the comedian had interrupted a band rehearsal to leap from the stage and threaten to jump my old friend Jim Turner. I spoke up sharply in Jim's behalf. This infuriated the bully and he turned to swing on me. Mahara came up and caught him but I went directly for my gun. During the remainder of the rehearsal I kept it plainly exposed.

A legend promptly went abroad in minstrel circles, a legend to the effect that I always laid my gun on the desk during Mahara's band rehearsals. This, obviously, was something of an exaggeration.

Back in Florence now, when he moved my trunk out of a dressing room and substituted his own, I ordered him to put mine back. He did, but the performance galled him. That night the big boy and his liquor came down Tennessee Street roaring like a lion. He passed my aunt's house swearing to the stars that he was going to kick me off the train when I came aboard. Suddenly devilment entered my head. I went to the street, shouted his name loudly, and fired a shot into the air.

He picked up his heels and flew. Policemen came to investigate the shooting. I told them how long the fellow had imposed on me, and they arrested him. Very soon afterwards the comedian himself sent for me. When I reached the jail, I found a changed man behind the bars. Dead sober and humble as a lamb, he wanted only to repay his debt and to request me not to appear in court against him. I agreed readily, and we forgave and forgot, but I quit the show.

Florence was quiet, comfortable and just a trifle dull after Mahara's Minstrels. But on June 29th this dullness disappeared for me because our first child Lucile was born. Jim Turner and I got together again and organized a small orchestra. A week or two passed. Then we accepted an invitation to play for a school closing in nearby Sheffield, and I contributed a cornet solo. The guest speaker was W. H. Councill, President of the Agricultural and Mechanical College located at Normal on the outskirts of Huntsville. Professor Councill no doubt had noted the furor created by our minstrel band in Huntsville, and now, having heard my playing with his own ears, engaged me to take charge of band, orchestra and vocal music at the A. & M. College.

In September 1900 I began the life of a faculty member on the campus. They listed me as teacher of elementary English since the budget did not provide for a musical director—and my duties included in addition to band, orchestra and vocal instruction, supervising study hours, assisting in Tuesday night prayer service, teaching in the College Sunday School and playing in or conducting the chapel choir. But I fell into the rhythm of things easily and might have been there till now had it not been for an odd new vogue called "ragtime."

To understand what happened at A. & M. it is necessary to know Professor Councill. Councill was one of the first important figures in Negro education in the South following the Civil War. A colorful and eloquent man, he introduced industrial education at A. & M. six years before Booker T. Washington established Tuskegee. He was a Democrat and Democrats were in disfavor with most Southern Negroes. Councill had served the state as a Republican until 1875 when he wrote thus:

"If you do not now make friends and unite with the white people among whom you live, on all questions touching our civil and political welfare, you will regret it in time to come. It will not be 25 years before the white people of this country (the South) if they have found that you go en masse against them right or wrong, on all political questions, will come into power and take from you the ballot which you continue to cast against them. The Republicans will grow tired of you, and seek to unload the Negro element, and like the bat which was disowned by the beast and not recognized by the birds, you will find favor with neither Democrats nor Republicans."

He sold the idea of educating Negroes to a somewhat reluc-

tant South, and he made successful appeals to Northern phi-
lanthropists for the funds necessary to carrying on this work.
He was frank and direct in his addresses, chastising both Negroes and whites upon occasion and sometimes not bothering
even to sugar-coat the pills. Still they all loved it, and Councill
built his school.

In those days the strategy was to show Southerners that the
aim was not so much to lift the Negroes socially but to make
better cooks, nurse maids, mechanics and share farmers of
them. Thus the real benefit would come to the whites. With
this sort of logic to chew on, the authorities were sometimes
willing to suffer the existence of a school for the blacks, but
not always. Night raiders set fire to Councill's school at one
time and burned the buildings to the ground. This act only
fired the president to greater eloquence. He went on a speaking tour. Money poured in from friends in all parts of the
country, and the school, phoenix-like, rose from its ashes.

Councill was favorably known abroad. In England he had
been presented to Gladstone. The King of Belgium was personally interested in him. He had lectured in Rome and traveled in Europe, Asia and Africa.

I admired the way Councill took the state of Alabama to
task when it threatened to trim the annual appropriation to
the school from four thousand to two thousand dollars a year.
He showed them how much money the institution spent in
the town of Huntsville, how it employed twenty-six teachers
and generally proved itself an asset to the community. Then
he chided the politicians who could pay a ten-thousand-a-year
salary to one white college president while showing themselves so small as to renege on the paltry four thousand they
had appropriated to a whole Negro institution. I gave him
credit for handling this sort of problem in such a way as not
to antagonize greatly those who really had the destiny of the
school in their hands. In many ways Councill was a remarkable man. Where music was concerned he was a stickler for

the classics—both in music and in literature. Since he was deeply religious he loved the best forms in sacred music.

Clorinda, the musical show written by Paul Lawrence Dunbar with music by Will Marion Cook, clicked on Broadway and *Darktown Is Out Tonight,* its hit number, swept the country. Folks began whistling Ernest Hogan's songs on street corners and in barber shops. I did a little whistling on my own part, but these songs were ragtime, and ragtime was not respectable. In some quarters it was condemned because of its Negro origin. In others it was damned because it cut down the sales of the more sedate music. It was charged that even the mandolin and guitar arrangements of Sousa marches suffered in competition at music counters. To avoid the opprobrium that dogged the feet of composers who lent their names to the taboo stuff, Cole and Johnson wrote *Didn't He Ramble* under the nom de plume of Will Handy. But if it had been signed by Gabriel, Councill wouldn't have liked it any better.

In this school, like many others, there seemed to be an unwritten law against American music and any inferior song of foreign origin was considered "classical." I noted this superficiality. *Ben Hur Chariot Race March,* though written strict tempo, was played with a tinge of ragtime. It was in the blood. However, music with classical titles got the favorite spot in programs. With my band I rendered a program one evening in the chapel. But I had a secret plan to include a stirring ragtime number, *My Ragtime Baby,* which our minstrel band had featured. It was written by a Detroit Negro, Fred Stone. I rewrote this high stepper and programmed it *Greetings to Toussaint L'Ouverture* so that the manuscript sheets would create the impression of classical music without changing a note of the original. It did the trick. The students couldn't sit still, nor could the teachers. The president himself patted his feet. At the conclusion he remarked, "My, my, what a delightful program. Mr. Handy is the best band teacher we've had since the days of Mr. Still." (He was referring to the father of

William Grant Still.) "Let's have *Greetings to Toussaint L'Ouverture* once more." I was only too happy to comply with this request, but explained how I had tricked them and made them appreciate the potentialities of ragtime by giving it a high-sounding name.

It's easy to see from this distance that from the time I began seriously fighting for American music I was on my way out of A. & M. College as musical director. I had been making a financial sacrifice to remain there and had begun to feel that I had outlived my usefulness. Councill, on the other hand, must have sensed my trend and grown increasingly uneasy.

Near the end of my second year I was assigned to take an inventory and make an appraisal of every building on the campus, the farm and livestock and contents of every room. The assignment was an odd one for a musical director. On the chapel wall was a motto: "Work Is the Measure of Worth." I performed my assignment, but accepting the philosophy the motto expressed, I decided that I was worth more than the forty dollars a month I had been receiving for my services and lost no time in handing in my resignation to take effect if increase in salary were not forthcoming.

The president graciously handed the matter to a committee —Mrs. H. E. Archer, Miss Willie A. Simmons and the Reverend J. J. Scott. First a check-up on my work was required. The committee, packed in my favor, reported that students of the school had never before shown such a marked interest in music. In spite of this good word, however, I was made to understand by the faculty that an unbudgeted musical director was lucky to get even forty dollars. It was not their fault, one pious teacher remarked, if I were not capable of earning more. I told him I was a two-hundred-dollar-a-month man in a forty-dollar job. There seemed to be some doubt. I resolved to show them.

The next week I ran an ad in the *Indianapolis Freeman*, a popular Negro newspaper of the day. A flood of mail came in answer. Among the letters were two envelopes with pictures of sliced watermelons on the outside. The melons had big black seeds which, examined closely, proved to be the pictures of various Negro minstrel stars. These letters were from the Maharas. Each contained an offer: fifty a week—come at once. So I accepted F. L. Mahara's offer.

My increased mail attracted attention, and Councill began to suspect something. Apropos, he delivered a chapel lecture on Negro minstrels. The tone of his remarks was sarcastic and derisive in the extreme. When he had finished, he called upon all the teachers to express their opinions of the profession with which I had been associated. Each teacher took his cue at the proper time, rose and spoke briefly. They used a variety of words, but in effect all said, "Me too." I refused to let them have it entirely their own way, and asked permission to say a word in behalf of the men I loved. Before it was over I found myself making an impassioned defense of my former associates. The minstrel show at that time was one of the greatest outlets for talented musicians and artists. Some of them were paying for education of brothers and sisters, some taking care of aged parents, others supporting their own families, but all contributing to a greater degree of happiness in the entertainment world. "If morning stars sing together," I concluded, "who shall say that minstrel men may not lead parades through pearly gates and up streets of gold?"

The students gave me a big hand. Many of the teachers congratulated me at the close of the service. Councill stood apart, silent and grim. He appeared to be convinced that he had guessed right, that I had actually received new minstrel offers and that I was on the verge of accepting them. He looked disappointed and sad. Suddenly I lost my bitterness. I had no further wish to show up those who had derided the minstrels. I found no pleasure in adding to the burdens of the lonely man who was trying so hard to keep his school going against great odds. Perhaps it was not his fault that we didn't see eye to eye. Perhaps he was too worried about the threatened withdrawal of the state's small appropriation.

At any rate, the next season saw me back with Mahara again, and James Wilson, cornetist in our minstrel band, became musical director at A. & M., a position he has held almost forty years. Two years at the A. & M. College had broadened my horizon and introduced me to problems which had my complete sympathy and to persons well worth knowing. It had given me for the first time a home of my own. It had seen my family increased by the birth of my second daughter, Katherine. On leaving Normal I could not help but feel that the tough assignment given me by Professor Councill, whose motto was "Work is the measure of worth," had the same underlying purpose as the one in which my father put the plow-lines in my hands and said, "The work won't hurt you."

Only one more year of trouping remained for me before the twilight of the minstrel era descended upon that distinctly American form of entertainment. It was a short year too, filled with incident, growth and development.

In Chicago I picked up a quartet of saxophones who made the parade with us when we played Joliet, Illinois. I was featuring *The Holy City* as a cornet solo and these saxophones contributed wonderfully to the religioso. That night I went to the box office and invited F. L. to come out and listen to my band concert with its remarkable reed section, only to find that my quartet of saxophones had left us. I had inadvertently neglected to record their names, but twenty-five years later I met one of them, Nappy Lee, in New York. He told me then why the four homesick boys had gone back to Chicago.

Gone was my dream of scoring a sensation with a daring innovation, but I continued to encourage the use of the instruments. Five years before, I had bought a tenor sax for myself, but W. N. P. Spiller, our alto horn player, appropriated it mostly for his own use. This was the genesis of "The Musical Spillers," a headline vaudeville act of later years.

We played many cities in competition with other shows just as we had done years before. While in Portland, Oregon, the Georgia Minstrels, best known of all the Negro companies, was showing. They came to our show. Back stage I met their peerless end men, Neil Moore and Bobby Kemp, along with Jim Crosby the diamond-studded comedian. Also in the group were Robert Leach of Mississippi and Lorenzo Tio, Sr., of New Orleans, first of the top-notch clarinetists of our race.

Before the time of Leach and Tio, Europeans and Mexicans played the clarinets in Negro bands where these instruments were used at all. The only clarinet in the Mahara band at the time I first joined it was played by an Englishman named W. R. Rowe. The instrument was a strange yellow affair with seven keys. By the time of my last year with the band, however, we carried a complete clarinet section. Among our players was Wilbur C. Sweatman, later to become a figure in vaudeville as a one-man trio. Sweatman had a stunt of playing three clarinets at the same time, each instrument following separate notes in three-part harmony. Horace George, clarinetist with our outfit, followed in Sweatman's steps and did the same stunt. But the ace of the reed players with us in the Mahara days was Fred Richardson. That boy was chained lightning on a clarinet. Joe Ricks was our flute and piccolo soloist. Piccolo Jones was featured with the Georgia minstrels.

Credit is due the army bands for training early Negro clarinetists as well as Negro bandmasters. We had a former 9th Cavalry man in the cornet section of the Mahara band. He was George A. Swan, and I was early impressed by his military bearing. Back in 1896 Swan had introduced me to some of the bandmasters and military musicians along the way. At Fort Robinson, Nebraska, he took me out to meet his old

German bandmaster, Herr Gungl. I joined the men in rehearsal and for the first time caught the effect of a complete clarinet section in a band. Swan and I visited the 10th U.S. Cavalry at Fort Missoula, Montana, and marveled at the spic and span cavalry band on horseback—all Negroes except the English bandmaster. Horses maneuvered at the sound of the bugle, instruments flashed in the sun, stirring music echoed and re-echoed across the plain. The pageantry of the scene won me. I wanted to join up then and there, but yielded to persuasion and remained with the show. But many minstrel men joined army bands and the army bands in turn gave to the minstrels better musicians. Everything was on the upgrade musically speaking. Lieut. Walter A. Loving, Negro bandmaster of the U.S. Philippine Constabulary band, had been engaged for the St. Louis World's Fair and a tour of the continent. This inspired many bandmasters to enter service in the army just as N. Clark Smith, bandmaster at Tuskegee, had previously done, blazing the trail for Lieut. F. L. Drye and others. Our old trombone soloist, Fred Simpson (the musical team of Simpson and Pittman) donned the uniform as bandmaster for the 15th Infantry in New York.

Three other individuals fix themselves in my minstrel day memories. One was a cornetist, the second a cook, the third a man with an amazing birthmark. Each of the three had about him an air of mystery.

The first followed along behind our band in Council Bluffs, Iowa. He was a dark, handsome man, but noticeably shy and bent on attracting as little attention as possible. I couldn't imagine what he was up to. No words were exchanged. He simply followed, watching and listening intently, as if he had been employed to shadow me.

That night I saw him again. He was at the Omaha Exposition then, blowing a horn in such a manner as to suggest that he might have been Gabriel's right-hand man. After the show we met. He was P. G. Lowery, a cornet virtuoso in a great list of fine cornet soloists our race has produced and is still producing. He had made his name with P. T. Wright's Nashville Students. He had trailed our band in Council Bluffs to spot and hear me play. That night we got together and took each other's measure like a pair of gamecocks in a crowing match. I called for a number, and he gave it to me with plenty of gravy and dressing. He named his terms, and I came back with my Sunday best. From that day my great ambition was to outplay P. G.

Another year passed, and P. G. wrote an article for the *Indianapolis Freeman*. Someone else, it seemed, had wanted to know who was the best cornetist of the race. "For high notes," Lowery replied, "Elmore Dodd on the Eb cornet. Low notes and broad tone: Harry Prampin. But W. C. Handy's street work is smooth, his triple-tonguing is brilliant, and he certainly plays a song to suit me." P. G. was being overgenerous. The palm was his.

The second individual who puzzled me made no musical pretenses. He was a Japanese who came aboard our car looking for work. A new chef was not unusual. We had seen every kind, black, white and grizzly. At the moment we had been complaining violently against an Irishman who couldn't cook a lick. Mahara was inclined to agree with us, and when the strange Japanese showed him the point where he could save the management from twenty-five to fifty percent weekly —provided, of course, the cook received his share of the saving—Mahara took him up on it. He made it plain to the little Oriental that the minstrels would have to be satisfied. With characteristic politeness the small brown man assured F. L. that he would take that chance.

We were satisfied with the new cook—eminently satisfied. He could turn out an old-time, down-South meal that Aunt Jemima wouldn't be ashamed of. The next day, perhaps, he would come back with a rare Japanese dish. At the same time he made good on his promise to save the management money.

Within a very few days it was perfectly plain that the Japanese cook was in solid with all concerned.

In the evenings when I returned from the show, I always found him reading, and I noticed that his books were not all written in the same language. It was hard to tell just how many languages he had at his command.

His name was Louis Hondi. The last name was almost indistinguishable from mine when spoken, and this seemed to dispose him favorably toward me. When we stopped in cities where there were Japanese communities, he would take me with him as his guest. He covered the Pacific coast with us and returned as far as Chicago. When we parted there, he confided to me that he was an officer of rank in the Japanese Army.

The last of these three individuals might well have stepped from the pages of the *Arabian Nights*. He gave me cold chills. He joined our show at La Crosse, Wisconsin, a violinist and alto player. His eyes were deep-set and filled with weird shadows. His name was William Malone, and he had been earning his salt by playing up and down the old Streckfus line between St. Paul and St. Louis. A kindly, self-educated boy, I prevailed upon him to join our show, and he and I became berthmates. Then it was that I discovered his unearthly affliction. Periodically during the night a strange, tortured sound would escape his lips. I cannot describe the sound. It was as if the woe of the entire world was suddenly rolled upon the lonely young man. Over and over again, as long as he slept, this moan was repeated. I was so disturbed I asked him if he were aware of it. He assured me that he was and gave me his own explanation.

Back in Reconstruction days his father had been active in Mississippi politics. The Klan set about to clip his wings. They hounded him with threats. They sent him notes signed with blood. Often hooded men sprang from the thickets and attempted to pounce upon him. The poor ex-slave tried hard to stand his ground, but the odds were great. As fear grew, he formed the habit of sleeping beneath his cabin floor. Alone in the tiny room above, his young wife cried herself to sleep. From one night to the next they lived in mortal anguish of what might happen to the man, the wife and the child that was waiting to be born. Eventually all three escaped safely to Washington, but the infant was marked for life. This, Malone explained, was the cause of the low moaning that I heard so often. He was the child of that harassed pair.

The boy's own life had been equally tragic. He had married a Mississippi girl whose parents and grandparents persuaded her not to follow him out into the big, hazardous world beyond their crossroads. Malone went alone to make his way. Two children were born of his infrequent returns, but the young father saw them only rarely. With Mahara's show he grew more and more unhappy. Then one day in Wyoming he jumped the outfit. For eleven years he was believed to be dead. His wife had collected his insurance and married again. Some property he owned had been turned over to the children.

Much later I found the name of a William Malone on an old envelope in a wastebasket in Memphis. It looked like his handwriting yet I couldn't believe my eyes. However, I wrote him inquiringly. He answered promptly. He was the old friend we all mourned dead. He came to Memphis at my invitation and joined the very different kind of band I was directing then. After moving to New York he made a tour of the South with my band. On returning to New York I received a letter from Memphis inquiring about William Malone, the boy who had written expressing the belief that this was his father. Malone went to Memphis and brought his son and daughter back with him. In 1934 he invited me to dine with the family in their new home in Newark. While this engagement was pending, the end came for William Malone and his strange habit of crying in his sleep.

Right here, perhaps, I should ring down the curtain on
Mahara's Minstrels. My association with them had made of me
a professional musician and a bandmaster. It had taken me
from Cuba to California, from Canada to Mexico. It had
shown me almost every river and mountain, every city and
state that my geography book had taught me to name. It had
thrown me into contact with a wistful but aspiring generation of dusky singers and musicians. It had taught me a way of
life that I still consider the only one for me. Finally it had
brought me back, after trying days, into the good graces of
such home folks as my father and the old school teacher. The
time had been well spent.

If I could bring back those times just once, however, I
think I could set up an all-star show that even the generation
of today couldn't deny. This is how I'd do it.

I'd bring the company to blasé Broadway. The first drums
would rumble at noon as I led my forty-five men down the
Great White Way. Their heads high, their feet nimble, I'd
pour them into Times Square playing *Bill Bailey Won't You
Please Come Home*. We would stop before the Winter Garden, and my concert would begin—no, not with *St. Louis
Blues*—with Sousa's *Stars and Stripes Forever*.

That evening, in the second part, as nine trumpets bleated
the trebles and seven trombones rumbled the glissandos of
Cotton Blossoms I would secretly challenge all comers to beat
the effects. I'd give a pretty to the ear that could forget them.
Presently I would bring George Moxley before a loud-speaker
with the simple instruction to get them told. Behind us, as the
superb Moxley strutted his stuff, the lobby of the theatre
would be lit up with W. A.'s diamonds. Frank Mahara would
occupy the ticket cage. Looka here, looka here!

Inside, as the last seat was snapped down in the balcony and
the S.R.O. sign was being put in place, my curtain would begin to rise. It would disclose a pyramid of sixty men, "Sixty,
count 'em!" With Moxley, the interlocutor, seated in the cen-

ter and Billy Young, George Tichenor, Gordon Collins, Lew Hall, all-time end men, premiering on the flanks, you'd feel a strange enchantment creeping over you. The show would be definitely on.

From the circle you'd hear songs that should never have been forgotten: *Night Bird's Cooing, Song That Reached My Heart, That Is Love, Across the Bridge He Goes, Little Empty Stockings on a Christmas Night, Bye Bye, Baby, Bye Bye, Gwine Back to Dixie, When the Robins Nest Again, Six Feet of Earth, Her Own Boy, Jack, Mottoes on the Wall, Picture 84, In the Baggage Coach Ahead,* and *My Dad's the Engineer.*

In the olio I would use modern blackouts to snap up such sketches as *Book Agent, You'll Like the Place, Clam Seller,* and *The Laudophone.* Then when the show was over I would let the curtain descend as Julius Glenn, Will Garland, Simon Epps and the handsome basso Jack Johnson, against the soft humming of sixty men, were singing Pensuti's *Goodnight, Beloved, Goodnight.*

CHAPTER SIX

Mississippi Mud

SUMMER RETURNS. A blistering sun beats down upon a gang of black section hands during the late nineties. They are working down in Mississippi, laying the railroad tracks for the Yazoo Delta line between Clarksdale and Yazoo City. Their hammers rise and fall rhythmically as they drive the heavy spikes and sing "Dis ole hammer killed John Henry, won't kill me. Dis ole hammer killed John Henry, won't kill me."

For - ty - one days   *Huh! is for-ty - one dol - lars,
Huh! For - ty - one days   Huh! is all Ah want.

* Grunts as hammer falls.

A locomotive, following the progress of the men, is steaming idly on the track. The letters "Y. D." are painted boldly on its coal car.

A traveling salesman comes up the embankment, mops the sweat from his face, shifts a chaw of tobacco from one bulging red cheek to the other, and says:

"Hey, boy. What in tarnation does that there Y. D. stand for?"

71

A Negro straightens up, rubs the kink out of his back and begins to scratch his head in obvious puzzlement.

"H'm," he ventures slowly. "Yaller Dawg, I reckon."

The stranger's eyes twinkle. He cackles softly and walks on down the track. "Yaller Dawg," he repeats under his breath. "That's pretty cute, hanged if it ain't. Yaller Dawg. Gee whiz, that's a good one." The Yazoo Delta R. R. was christened The Yellow Dog.

This story was circulated and the idea spread until one branch of the Yazoo Delta was known as the North Dog. For reasons equally suggestive, the fast, direct train from Clarksdale to Greenville was known as the Cannon Ball, while its slow-time, round-about companion between those points was called the Peavine. Negroes had nicknamed all these roads.

During my last year with Mahara's Minstrels I little guessed that I would shortly know every foot of these lines by heart. At no time did I even dream that the Mississippi delta would presently become my stamping grounds, but that is exactly how it worked out, and I know now that it was the best thing that could ever have happened to me.

The year was 1903, and the outfit was in Michigan when the decision was made. A Michigan town had offered me an opportunity to direct its municipal band, composed of white musicians, and I was slowly making up my mind to accept. While this decision was pending, I received a letter which contained an offer to direct a colored Knights of Pythias band in Clarksdale, Mississippi. There was little comparison between the two propositions, as I saw it. The Michigan thing was miles ahead, more money, more prestige, better opportunities for the future, better everything I thought. Yet, for no good reason that I could express, I turned my face southward and down the road that led inevitably to the blues.

Perhaps my friend Jim Jordan turned the trick. A former pupil of mine in the Corinth, Mississippi, band, Jim actually sold the Delta city to me. Earlier, it seems, he had sold me to the town folks. I bowed to his persuasion and gave my word to the managers of the Southern band. A few days later a cashier's check, drawn on the Planters Bank and signed by an S. L. Mangham, came to cover my expenses to Clarksdale. I stuffed the check into my pocket, having no immediate need for it, and began packing my duds.

In Clarksdale a few days later I entered the Planters Bank. A guard directed me to the cage of the assistant cashier and there I saw something I had never seen before in all my travels. A Negro stood at the window of that Southern white bank handling foreign and domestic drafts. Still blinking and wondering whether or not I was awake, I approached the window. "I have no one to identify me," I apologized, slipping the check through the cage.

He gave me a suave smile. "My name is your endorsement," he said quietly. "You will find it on the other side."

He was S. L. Mangham, assistant cashier. More important still, he was a clarinet player in the band I had come to direct. The local businessmen and bank officials called him Stack; they swore by him, coming and going. Whatever Stack promised, they said, he delivered. I found that he was held in equal favor by the band. Stack never left the platform when we played for dances. He never took a drink, and he never got excited. Nothing upset him. I cannot recall ever having seen his name or picture in a newspaper, yet Stack was a power in the town. He remained with the bank for thirty years and until it closed its doors. Mangham developed a peculiar type of paralysis and had to wear an iron truss to keep his head from turning around backwards, but now the truss is not necessary.

The band which I found in Clarksdale and the nine-man orchestra which grew out of it did yeoman duty in the Delta. We played for affairs of every description. I came to know by heart every foot of the Delta, even from Clarksdale to Lambert on the Dog and Yazoo City. I could call every flag stop, water tower and pig path on the Peavine with my eyes closed. It all became a familiar, monotonous round. Then one night at Tutwiler, as I nodded in the railroad station while waiting for a train that had been delayed nine hours, life suddenly took me by the shoulder and wakened me with a start.

A lean, loose-jointed Negro had commenced plunking a guitar beside me while I slept. His clothes were rags; his feet peeped out of his shoes. His face had on it some of the sadness of the ages. As he played, he pressed a knife on the strings of the guitar in a manner popularized by Hawaiian guitarists who used steel bars. The effect was unforgettable. His song, too, struck me instantly.

Goin' where the Southern cross' the Dog.

The singer repeated the line three times, accompanying himself on the guitar with the weirdest music I had ever heard. The tune stayed in my mind. When the singer paused, I leaned over and asked him what the words meant. He rolled his eyes, showing a trace of mild amusement. Perhaps I should have known, but he didn't mind explaining. At Moorhead the eastbound and the westbound met and crossed the north and southbound trains four times a day. This fellow was going where the Southern cross' the Dog, and he didn't care who knew it. He was simply singing about Moorhead as he waited.

That was not unusual. Southern Negroes sang about everything. Trains, steamboats, steam whistles, sledge hammers, fast women, mean bosses, stubborn mules—all become subjects for their songs. They accompany themselves on anything from which they can extract a musical sound or rhythmical effect, anything from a harmonica to a washboard.

In this way, and from these materials, they set the mood for what we now call blues. My own fondness for this sort of thing really began in Florence, back in the days when we were not above serenading beneath the windows of our sweethearts and singing till we won a kiss in the shadows or perhaps a tumbler of good home-made wine. In the Delta, however, I suddenly saw the songs with the eye of a budding composer. The songs themselves, I now observed, consisted of simple declarations expressed usually in three lines and set to a kind of earth-born music that was familiar throughout the Southland half a century ago. Mississippi with its large plantations and small cities probably had more colored field hands than any other state. Consequently we heard many such song fragments as *Hurry Sundown, Let Tomorrow Come,* or

> Boll Weevil, where you been so long?
> Boll Weevil, where you been so long?
> You stole my cotton, now you want my corn.

Clarksdale was eighteen miles from the river, but that was no distance for roustabouts. They came in the evenings and on days when they were not loading boats. With them they brought the legendary songs of the river.

> Oh, the Kate's up the river, Stack O' Lee's in the ben',
> Oh, the Kate's up the river, Stack O' Lee's in the ben',
> And I ain't seen ma baby since I can't tell when.

WHEELBARROW SONG

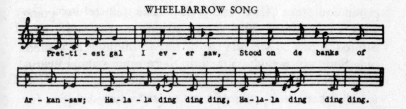

At first folk melodies like these were kept in the back rooms of my mind while the parlor was reserved for dressed-up music. Musical books continued to get much of my attention. There was still an old copy of Steiner's *First Lessons in Harmony*, purchased back in Henderson for fifty cents. While traveling with the minstrels I had bought from Lyon and

Healy a copy of Moore's *Encyclopedia of Music*. For a time books became a passion. I'm afraid I came to think that everything worth while was to be found in books. But the blues did not come from books. Suffering and hard luck were the midwives that birthed these songs. The blues were conceived in aching hearts.

I hasten to confess that I took up with low folk forms hesitantly. I approached them with a certain fear and trembling. Like many of the other musicians who received them with cold shoulders at first, I began by raising my eyebrows and wondering if they were quite the thing. I had picked up a fair training in the music of the modern world and had assumed that the correct manner to compose was to develop simples into grandissimos and not to repeat them monotonously. As a director of many respectable, conventional bands, it was not easy for me to concede that a simple slow-drag and repeat could be rhythm itself. Neither was I ready to believe that this was just what the public wanted. But we live to learn.

My own enlightenment came in Cleveland, Mississippi. I was leading the orchestra in a dance program when someone sent up an odd request. Would we play some of "our native music," the note asked. This baffled me. The men in this group could not "fake" and "sell it" like minstrel men. They were all musicians who bowed strictly to the authority of printed notes. So we played for our anonymous fan an old-time Southern melody, a melody more sophisticated than native. A few moments later a second request came up. Would we object if a local colored band played a few dances?

Object! That was funny. What hornblower would object to a time-out and a smoke—on pay? We eased out gracefully as the newcomers entered. They were led by a long-legged chocolate boy and their band consisted of just three pieces, a battered guitar, a mandolin and a worn-out bass.

The music they made was pretty well in keeping with their looks. They struck up one of those over-and-over strains that seem to have no very clear beginning and certainly no ending at all. The strumming attained a disturbing monotony, but on and on it went, a kind of stuff that has long been associated with cane rows and levee camps. Thump-thump-thump went their feet on the floor. Their eyes rolled. Their shoulders swayed. And through it all that little agonizing strain persisted. It was not really annoying or unpleasant. Perhaps "haunting" is a better word, but I commenced to wonder if anybody besides small town rounders and their running mates would go for it.

The answer was not long in coming. A rain of silver dollars began to fall around the outlandish, stomping feet. The dancers went wild. Dollars, quarters, halves—the shower grew heavier and continued so long I strained my neck to get a better look. There before the boys lay more money than my nine musicians were being paid for the entire engagement. Then I saw the beauty of primitive music. They had the stuff the people wanted. It touched the spot. Their music wanted polishing, but it contained the essence. Folks would pay money for it. The old conventional music was well and good and had its place, no denying that, but there was no virtue in being blind when you had good eyes.

That night a composer was born, an *American* composer. Those country black boys at Cleveland had taught me something that could not possibly have been gained from books, something that would, however, cause books to be written. Art, in the high-brow sense, was not in my mind. My idea of what constitutes music was changed by the sight of that silver money cascading around the splay feet of a Mississippi string band. Seven years prior to this, while playing a cornet solo, Hartman's *Mia*, on the stage in Oakland, California, I had come to the conclusion, because of what happened in this eleven minute solo, that the American people wanted movement and rhythm for their money. Then too, the Broadway hits, *Yankee Grit* and *Uncle Sammy*—two-steps in six-eight time that we featured in Mississippi—did not have this earthy flavor.

Once the purpose was fixed I let no grass grow under my feet. I returned to Clarksdale and began immediately to work on this type of music. Within a day or two I had orchestrated a number of local tunes, among them *The Last Shot Got Him, Your Clock Ain't Right,* and the distinctly Negroid *Make Me a Pallet on Your Floor.* My hunch was promptly justified, for the popularity of our orchestra increased by leaps and bounds. But there was also another consequence. Bids came to us to play in less respectable places. We took these in our stride on the grounds that music, like joy, should be unconfined. Moreover there was money to be made, and who were we to turn up our noses?

Across the tracks of the Y. & M. V. railroad in Clarksdale there was a section called the "New World." It was the local red-light district. To the New World came lush octoroons and quadroons from Louisiana, soft cream-colored fancy gals from Mississippi towns. Just beyond this section lived some of the oldest and most respectable Negro families. On their way to the Baptist or Methodist churches they were required to pass before the latticed houses of prostitution. Occasionally they caught glimpses of white men lounging with the pretty near-white "imports." By using their imaginations they could assume what went on in the dim rooms beyond.

As musicians we didn't have to guess. As musicians too, hired to play music rather than to discuss morals, we kept our mouths shut. We knew that big shot officials winked at the New World, but that was neither here nor there to the men with the horns and the fiddles. What was important was that these rouge-tinted girls, wearing silk stockings and short skirts, bobbing their soft hair and smoking cigarets in that prim era, long before these styles had gained respectability, were among the best patrons the orchestra had. They employed us for big nights, occasions when social or political figures of importance were expected to dine and dance with their favorite creole belles. Contacts made in these shady precincts often led to jobs in chaste great houses of the rich and well-to-do.

The shuttered houses of the New World called for appropriate music. This led us to arrange and play tunes that had never been written down and seldom sung outside the environment of the oldest profession. Boogie-house music, it was called. Much of it has since been fumigated and played in the best of society, but then Dopy McKnight thumped out the tunes on a rickety piano. We took them up, arranged orchestrations and played them to the wild approval of the richly scented yellow gals and their company. I have intimated that silver money had always been plentiful in the Delta; now at last we began to come in for our share of it.

The Delta had also its share of melodrama. Engagements in the New World plunged us into the tide. One evening a vivid octoroon, who had been winking at our violinist, shared a drink with him. Her ofay (white) company turned and put a pistol to the musician's temple. He promised to pull the trigger if he opened his mouth. He'd just as soon do it immediately, he said, if the boy felt like giving any back talk. When it was over, I recalled a saying that is almost an axiom among Negroes of the South. The thought of it is that more black men are killed by whites for merely conversing with colored girls of this type than for violating, as the orators like to put it, the sanctity of white womanhood. Ho-hum. The world is powerfully big, and a queer place.

As a side line in Clarksdale I did a kind of bootleg business in Northern Negro newspapers and magazines. Not only did I supply the colored folks of the town, but also got the trade of the farmers, the croppers and the hands from the outlying country. They would come to my house on their weekly visits to the city, give me the high sign, and I would slip them their copies of the *Chicago Defender*, the *Indianapolis Freeman* or the *Voice of the Negro*. This may sound like a tame

7

enough enterprise to those whose memories are short, but oldsters of those parts will not have to be told that I was venturing into risky business. Negro newspapers were not plentiful in those days, and their circulation in cities like Clarksdale was looked upon with strong disfavor by certain of the local powers. But because I was favorably known to most of the white folks as the leader of the band that gave the weekly concerts on the main street, they never suspected me of such dark business as distributing Northern literature to Negroes of the community. In fact, Clarksdale and I remained on such good terms that when there came a time to call upon the well-to-do townsfolk to help us foot the bill for new uniforms, instruments and other equipment for the men, the needed amount was oversubscribed before the bank closed on the day when the campaign was begun.

When we blossomed forth in the glad rags, the town stuck out its chest proudly. We were theirs, they had helped dress us up and everybody was pleased with the results, including ourselves. Senator John Sharp Williams, a great favorite of the people, came to town, giving us our first opportunity to show our appreciation by welcoming him with good music and gay uniforms. The occasion, as much as it pleased us all, was of no long-range consequence, so far as I recall, but it represents another line of the work that fell to our band during those days and in the years that followed. We were frequently hired, as on this occasion, to furnish music for political rallies.

This meant that we had to absorb a "passel" of oratory of the brand served by some Southern politicians just this side of the turn of the century. We appeared with one gubernatorial candidate who regularly treated his audiences to the following titbit:

Ladies and Gentlemen:

I come before you as a candidate for the governorship of the grand old state of Mississippi. And I pledge you my sacred word of honor that if you elect me your governor, I shall not spend one dollar for nigger education.

Now I want to tell you why I will not spend one dollar of the state's money for nigger education; education unfits the nigger. Let me prove it to you conclusively. I am right.

When this great country of ours was torn by strife, and we followed the fortunes of the Confederacy, we left behind our mothers, our daughters, our sweethearts and our wives; and we left them behind with our niggers, and they guarded them like so many faithful watch-dogs. Now what kind of nigger did we leave them with? It was the uneducated nigger.

Suppose we again had to go to war, would you trust them with the nigger of today? (A chorus of no's came in answer.) That's why I wouldn't spend one dollar for nigger education.

His voice quavered and a mist came to his eyes as he extended one arm while resting the other dramatically over his heart. Then as the concluding words trailed off, we struck up *Dixie*. Outside we exchanged amazed glances among ourselves and laughed. He was not elected.

Each time we played for him, I was reminded of the first time I had listened to oratory of this sort. As a schoolboy in Florence I had gone home, buried my head in a pillow and wept after listening to sentiments like these uttered from the courthouse steps by a politician of the same stripe. Later I had wandered off alone in the woods across the road from the cabin in which I was born. There, point by point, I had undertaken to answer the man of ill will. Slowly, deliberately, I had torn his arguments to bits. At the top of my voice I had hurled the lie into his teeth. The woodland took up my shouts. The words of my defiance echoed and reechoed. That pleased me. I went home and slept well, a great burden removed. In Clarksdale the members of my band nudged one another with their elbows when we were safely out of the crowd. Then we all laughed—laughed.

But playing for the political campaigns was not always the bitter pill this particular candidate made it. We were engaged for ex-Governor Earl Brewer when he made a delayed entrance into a red-hot, seven-cornered race for the governorship. Here the story was not the same. The ex-governor did not hesitate to touch on the Negro, but no tirade came from him. Instead he gave the finest tribute to Negro music that I had ever been permitted to hear. A tribute deeply felt and moving when he referred to our loyalty. He was not elected that year, but later when the time came for another campaign, he was not even opposed—elected unanimously.

Either way, however, we were undismayed. We could laugh and we could make rhythm. What better armor could you ask?

Negroes react rhythmically to everything. That's how the blues came to be. Sometimes I think that rhythm is our middle name. When the sweet good man packs his trunk and goes, that is occasion for some low moaning. When darktown puts on its new shoes and takes off the brakes, jazz steps in. If it's the New Jerusalem and the River Jordan we're studying, we make the spirituals. The rounders among us, those whose aim in life is just to become bigger rounders— well, they're the ones we can thank for the Frankie and Johnnie songs. In every case the songs come from down deep.

Speaking of rhythm recalls an experience told by J. Rosamond Johnson. Johnson was teaching in a Southern school when one day two of his boys squared off to battle. Alert and nimble-witted as ever, the teacher rushed between the fighters and thrust a menacing finger in the face of the guiltier-looking boy.

"Spell sugar, boy," he barked. "Spell sugar, I say."

Frightened out of his wits by the angry tone of the teacher's words and trembling visibly, the boy spelled rhythmically, "S-h-u-g—he-l-l."

Between playing for dances in magnificent plantation mansions from one end of the Delta country to the other, striking up the band for an occasional political candidate and conducting jam sessions in the New World, I made more money in Clarksdale than I had ever earned. This was not strange. Everybody prospered in that Green Eden. Cotton stalks here were as tall as Alabama corn. Delta land yielded three or four bales to one produced on the same amount of hill land. The cotton rows that I had seen around Florence were downright scrawny by comparison.

A number of years later, remembering this abundance, I wrote the *Yellow Dog Blues*, the second verse of which runs like this:

> I know the Yellow Dog District like a book,
> Indeed I know the route that Rider took,
> Ev'ry cross-tie, bayou, burg and bog.
> Way down where the Southern cross' the Dog,
> Money don't zactly grow on trees
> On cotton stalks it grows with ease;
> No race horse, race track, no grand stand—
> Is like Old Beck an' Buckshot land,
> Down where the Southern cross' the Dog.
> Every kitchen there is a cabaret,
> Down there the boll weevil works while the darkies play
> This Yellow Dog Blues the livelong day.[2]

Even the bears of the Mississippi backwoods found the pickings good in the Delta. One night when we had played till dawn for a well-known planter, we were suddenly called to the back steps to see a bear gathering roasting ears in the corn field. When the crafty old creature had filled his arms, he went to the hog pen and commenced tossing the ears to the porkers. But the bear was not fattening hogs for the planter's table, not by a long sight. While the hogs ate, the big animal lumbered over the low fence, batted down the fattest and juiciest one he could lay his paws on, and calmly threw his kill over the fence. He had climbed back and started off with his meat on his shoulder when the planter plugged him.

[2] From *Yellow Dog Rag* (*Yellow Dog Blues*), copyright 1914 by W. C. Handy.

On our way home that day one of the musicians told us a story that was gaining currency in the Delta. Everyone knew that President Theodore Roosevelt had just recently come to Bobo, about ten miles south of Clarksdale, for the purpose of bagging some of these Mississippi bears himself. It was not so generally known, however, that a member of the President's party had sought to borrow the bear hounds of a man who lived down the bayou. The emissary was politeness itself, and he made a point of conveying to the owner of the hounds that it was President Roosevelt himself who wished to hunt with his dogs. The old Negro assured the young man that what he said was all well and good but added, "I don't give a damn if Booker T. Washington wants them, he can't get my dogs less'n I comes along. On'erstand?" The story went on to conclude that the President accepted the services of the old man in the hunt and that—P. S.—he got the hounds.

On the same hunt President Roosevelt was quoted by highly enthusiastic home town folks as saying, "I'm not here as the President, but as a bear hunter, and all hunters—black and white—will mess from the same pot."

Still another legend that followed that bear hunt had the President amazed at the number of bears rounded up by the hounds of the old man from down the bayou. The Negro thereupon assured his President that this was not exceptional. His hounds always gave as good an account of themselves. As the bears came into sight, he made another observation. He had never shot a bear in his life.

"You haven't? Well how do you kill them?" the President asked.

"Well suh, I'll tell you," the old fellow replied. "When the hounds corner the bear, I jes steps up quick and sticks the bear with a knife."

He was said to have made a successful demonstration later.

Of course, bear stories are often very much like fish stories, but tough Negroes are something else again. In Mississippi we played for a country dance where the baddest of the bad were in command. They danced the old square dances with one of their own calling the figures. This quaint individual crooned all his calls in the key of G. Any other key upset his sense of rhythm and aroused his fighting blood. I can still hear his unusual voice. "Swing yo' partners . . . swing corners all . . . first lady on de head lead off to de right."

The first lady on the head did lead off all right, and she laughed out gaily as she did so. But her key was wrong. The crooner's eyes narrowed angrily, and his next call shocked us. "Swing on de corners . . . swing, you bitch!"

A big husky black glowered down. Instantly all of us got a feeling of approaching menace.

"Look out there, nigger. That's my sister."

Rhythmically—and still in the key of G—the answer came, "Too late now. The bitch done swung . . . All promenade."

My son Bill was born in Clarksdale. We lived in a frame cottage between others of its kind. The third house away, however, was a shack and a fire-trap. Instead of a chimney it had only an elongated stove pipe that poured smoke and sometimes sparks onto the very gable of the house next door. I noticed this danger and cautioned my wife to be ready for a fire. She promptly began holding fire drills with a baby carriage and the three children.

Then one cold night in January a salvo of gun and pistol shots awakened us from our sleep. This was the way of announcing a fire in Clarksdale in those days. I ran to a window and saw the shack disappearing like a matchbox. The flames reached out in our direction time and again. I began considering what was most worth saving among our household effects. There was a collection of books that had a value. There was an upright piano and a guitar that I had bought in Mexico. Mrs. Handy ran for the baby buggy and gathered up the brood. I commenced to struggle with the piano. A few moments later neighbors rushed in and began tossing furniture and bedclothes and glassware through the windows.

In the excitement my wife called me to come and help her with the babies, but I assured her that was not necessary. They could be easily rolled to safety. The big problem was to get the piano out of danger. I managed to save it, by dint of more muscle than I thought I had, but the next day I had occasion to wonder whether or not the instrument was worth the ridicule that fell upon me.

An old woman yelled to me from across the street, cackling in a high-pitched voice about the news that was going around town.

"Oh, I heard all 'bout you, Fess Handy," she twittered. "I heard what you done said at the fire."

"What'd I say at the fire?"

"Aw, you knows, Fess Handy. You said, 'Chillun is easy. Never mind de chillun, but it's hard to git another piano.'"

After the fire I missed my Mexican guitar. Someone told me that it had been saved by a spry one-legged man. I hurried to his home and asked about the instrument.

"Oh, you mean that box?" he replied oddly. "Hell, I cut that damn thing up for kindling."

More than once during my travels in the North and South I had passed through towns with signs saying, "Nigger don't let the sun go down on you here." And once, at least, we played in a town where the boot was on the other foot. Though Mound Bayou had no such words addressed to "peckerwoods" or "rednecks," the sentiment among its all Negro population was perhaps in some ways similar. Yet salesmen and other white visitors who found it necessary to spend the night there received all possible hospitality.

This town, thirty miles south of Clarksdale on the Y. & M. V. railroad, was founded by Isaiah T. Montgomery, former bodyguard and slave of Jeff Davis, President of the Con-

federacy. The occasion for our band's visit was the dedication
of the Bank of Mound Bayou, and we came largely through
the instigation of Charles Banks the cashier. A Clarksdale boy
himself, Banks had gained his training in the same Planters
Bank that now employed our Stack. We carried the band to
Mound Bayou to pay our respects to this home town boy, but
we stayed on to admire the new Carnegie Library and blink
in amazement at colored railroad ticket agents, colored tele-
graph operators and pretty brownskins at telephone switch-
boards.

My personal admiration for the enterprise of the Negroes
of Mound Bayou was so great that later, when they held the
grand opening of their oil mill, I brought a band from Memphis at my own expense just to help them do the thing up
brown. Booker T. Washington was the speaker for this occasion. After the address I dined with him in the home of Mr.
and Mrs. Charles Banks and began to feel that the privilege
of knowing the educator was ample recompense for my small
contribution to the event. Later, however, Banks and his associates insisted on sending us a check in token of their gratitude for our contribution.

A picture of Clarksdale during the years I spent there
would be incomplete without the blind singers and footloose
bards that were forever coming and going. Usually the fellows were destitute. Some came sauntering down the railroad
tracks, others dropped from freight cars, while still others
caught rides on the big road and entered town on the top of
cotton bales. A favorite hangout with them was the railroad
station. There, surrounded by crowds of country folks, they
would pour out their hearts in song while the audience ate
fish and bread, chewed sugar cane, dipped snuff while waiting
for trains to carry them down the line.

They earned their living by selling their own songs—"bal-
lets," as they called them—and I'm ready to say in their behalf
that seldom did their creations lack imagination. Many a less

gifted songsmith has plied his trade with passing success in Tin Pan Alley. Some of these country boys hustled on trains. Others visited churches. I remember buying such a ballet (ballad) entitled *I've Heard of a City Called Heaven*. It was printed on a slip of paper about the size of a postcard. Fifty years later, after I had published a choral arrangement of that piece, I heard the number sung with great success by the Hall Johnson Singers in *The Green Pastures*.

Mature years and a busy life have not enabled me to shake off a certain susceptibility to these dusky bards. Every time I put by enough money for a trip to Europe, I end up by purchasing a ticket to one of the more remote sections of the deep South, knowing fully in my mind that Europe and all its environs carry no such rich traditions and inspirational fertility as are embodied in this section of our America.

CHAPTER SEVEN

"Pee Wee's," Pimps and Politics

THE SAGA of Beale Street, as I knew it, goes back to a bright summer morning in the eighteen-eighties. A freight train slowed down and came to a stop in North Memphis. Presently a ragged immigrant boy, a dark-browed Italian youngster called Pee Wee, crept out from under one of the box cars. He had come all the way from New York on the rods.

For a moment Pee Wee stood blinking in the sun. A vision of far away Naples swam before his eyes. When the train pulled off again, the young hobo took his bearings and headed directly for the nearest water. On the banks of Wolf River he slipped off his miserable shirt and pants, plunged into the stream, and set about to remove the dust and soot and grime he had collected during the weeks spent in gutters, in ditches and on the rods of box cars. Wanting soap, he smeared himself with a handful of soft mud. When this was removed, he felt refreshed and clean. It was a glorious feeling, even though he had no satisfactory way to dry himself and had to get back into his rags with water clinging to his skin. Pee Wee didn't mind too much. He was in a mood to be grateful for little things.

An hour or two later, wandering from street to street in the strange new city, Pee Wee hitched up his suspenders and began to think about food. Holding a thin dime between his teeth, he turned his pockets inside out to make sure that no other coin hid down there between the seams. Nope, that dime was all. Enough for rolls and coffee perhaps. After that —well, after that the great adventure. Pee Wee walked and walked, passing dozens of grocery stores and beaneries at which he might have spent his money. But something seemed to hold his feet outside. Spending his last dime was not a thing he wished to be in a hurry about. Pee Wee shrank from the idea of being broke in a strange city. Even walking about hungry was not so terribly bad when you could flip a bright coin into the air. Like this.

Pee Wee flipped his dime high and caught it on the back of his left hand, covering it with his right.

"Heads," he guessed aloud.

Yep, heads is what it was.

"Heck, I ain't so unlucky," he told himself. He flipped again, and again he called it plunk on the nose. Then he began to turn things over in his head. Wouldn't he be a chump to spend this last, sweet dime on coffee and rolls? Why, if he kept his hands on the coin long enough the patient little thing might hatch chicks. Who could tell? No use getting shed of it too soon. Anyhow, there was no danger of starving for at least a day or two.

By that time Pee Wee had reached Beale Street. Before he knew it he was standing over a crap game where colored boys were down on their knees begging the bones to roll them the moon and the stars. Pee Wee watched, fascinated as much by the music and rhythm of the performance as by the game itself. Then suddenly he got down with the others, took out his dime and offered to fade the kid with the dice.

Beale Street has always known a good fellow when it sees one, and Beale Street has always been hospitable and big-hearted. From the moment he got down and put his money in sight, Pee Wee was in. It was just as simple as that. Moreover, his luck was right that day. He came out of the game with change enough to pay for a meal and a bed for the night. The next day he blew himself to a haircut. By the end of the month, he was a well-dressed, smart-looking young Italian whose only peculiarities were a heavy accent, a fondness for dice and an understandable tendency to prefer Beale Street to other parts of Memphis.

When I first visited the city as a boy, Pee Wee was running a saloon on the corner of Hernando and Beale. Jim Turner introduced me to the place in which L. Pacini and Angelo (his relatives) by now were part owners. Later, Pee Wee moved to 317 Beale, and his place became almost a landmark and a legend. Moreover, it was a headquarters for musicians. Each member of the family took a daily turn behind the bar during the four shifts, since the place never closed.

Just inside Pee Wee's entrance door there was a cigar stand. A side room was given to billiards and pool, another to crap games and cards. In a back room there was space where violins, horns and other musical instruments were checked by free lance musicians who got their calls there over phone number 2893. Sometimes you couldn't step for the bull fiddles. I've seen a dozen or more of them in there at one time. Upstairs a policy game was operated.

Through Pee Wee's swinging doors passed the heroic darktown figures of an age that is now becoming fabulous. They ranged from cooks and waiters to professional gamblers, jockeys and race track men of the period. Glittering young devils in silk toppers and Prince Alberts drifted in and out with insolent self-assurance. Chocolate dandies with red roses embroidered on cream waistcoats loitered at the bar. Now and again a fancy gal with shadowed eyes and a wedding-ring waist glanced through the doorway or ventured inside to ask if anybody had set eyes on the sweet good man who had temporarily strayed away. Her eyes couldn't miss seeing the large oil painting of a scene from *Othello* that has hung on the wall for more than half a century. Hack drivers and waiters were familiar in those days with Shakespearean plays and after a few drinks would imitate Joe Jefferson, Frederick Ward, Lewis James, Booth and Barrett, in their favorite rôles.

A wistful gaiety filled the place in the old days. Mack Harris was often there, one of the great poker players of his time. Gamblers of all complexions came from St. Louis, Chicago, Philadelphia and New York to take a hand with him and find out for themselves whether or not he was as good as his reputation. Mack entertained them all, even when the bets went into the thousands.

Hammitt Ashford was a familiar figure. The son of a Reconstruction sheriff at Cortland, Alabama, Hammitt was a quadroon of striking appearance. He was known, as were his father and brother, for fierce daring and an uncommon sense of honor about obligations. Hammitt carried a thousand-dollar stop watch, and he liked to come into Pee Wee's saloon, reach for the dice horn and offer to bet the proprietor a grand on a single turn of the bones.

"You're faded," Pee Wee would answer without a moment's hesitation.

Something hard to describe entered into these occasional meetings between Hammitt Ashford and the proprietors of Pee Wee's place. Hammitt was a saloon keeper. All were big shot gamblers. To backwater under such a challenge would have been fatal to either reputation.

With no money in sight the winnings or losings between them often soared outlandishly high at a single set-to. When it was over and the familiar, trick-proof horn put back in place, Pee Wee would go to his safe and calmly count out his debt. If Hammitt lost, he would return to his saloon and bring back payment. No trace of emotion or distrust would come to either face. Each respected the other enormously.

Dangerous Jim Ray from St. Louis and Fatty Grimes, who carried the biggest diamond in Memphis, swung Pee Wee's doors open occasionally. When Jim Ray, great good friend of

Hammitt, was killed in Fatty Grimes' place in St. Louis, the repercussions shook the panes in Pee Wee's saloon on Beale Street. When Fatty came to Memphis again and was lured by a two-timing girl into the pay-back trap, piano thumpers made songs about it in the red-light dives of that wide open city.

It was perfectly natural that Pee Wee's should become the headquarters for our band for a time at least, and in the fall of 1909 I often used to use his cigar stand to write out copies of the following lyric for visiting bands:

> Mr. Crump won't 'low no easy riders here
> Mr. Crump won't 'low no easy riders here
> We don't care what Mr. Crump don't 'low
> We gon' to bar'l-house anyhow—
> Mr. Crump can go and catch hisself some air!

The city was in the midst of a three-cornered campaign to elect a mayor, and our band was beating the drum for Mr. E. H. Crump, who was running on a strict reform platform. I had composed a special campaign tune for this purpose, but without words. We had played it, with success. Meanwhile I had heard various comments from the crowds around us, and even from my own men, which seemed to express their own feelings about reform. Most of these comments had been sung, impromptu, to my music. My lyric was based upon some of these spontaneous comments, with my own development and additions. Luckily for us, Mr. Crump himself didn't hear us singing these words. But we were hired * to help put over his campaign, and since I knew that reform was about as palatable to Beale Street voters as castor oil, I was sure those reassuring words would do him more good than harm.

I don't say that my campaign tune contributed to this result, but at any rate it has another claim. Its musical setting, which I afterwards published under the new title *Memphis Blues*, was the first of all the many published "blues," and it set a new

---

* Not by him personally—see my acknowledgments, p. xiv.

fashion in American popular music and contributed to the rise of jazz, or, if you prefer, swing, and even boogie-woogie. The 1909 campaign is only part of the story of this piece, which began in the back room of Thornton's barber shop near the Poplar Street Station.

While still doing the Dog and the Peavine out of Clarksdale, I was engaged to instruct Thornton's K. of P. band in Memphis. Twice a week, bent like a Santa Claus under cornet, saxophone, violin, typewriter and suitcase, I made the seventy-six mile trip to hold rehearsals at Thornton's. With this added work I soon found myself as busy as a hen with her brood, bounding back and forth between the cities, plunking out letters on the train and trying by every possible means to put the twenty-man Memphis outfit on its feet.

Thornton's was not a dance band. This was a pity and a shame, because Memphis has always been a grand dance town, one of the hottest of the hot. But ours was a military band, and besides, you don't get dances by talking about them. A build-up is required, and prospects for such a build-up in Memphis seemed slight, to say the least. They already had three established dance bands—Turner and Bynum's, Bryant and Smiley's, and Higgins and Eckford's. Failing to get the dances, however, we went to the opposite pole and took on the funerals. For these engagements, which were not to be sneezed at—paying, as they did, two or three dollars per man— we were indebted to T. H. Hayes, successful Negro undertaker who became my good friend and always spoke up for our aggregation when the occasion called for a sad, slow-marching band.

Funeral dirges were all right in their place but I immediately set about to improve things by organizing an orchestra from the band. That was a little more promising. You could stomp your feet when you felt like it. Still my orchestra was far from a finished product. In order to compete with the other dance organizations of the city they had to be taught

up-to-the-minute music and all the little tricks of the trade.
This was a challenge to me, but perhaps not so great a one as
the fact that I was a stranger on Beale Street and up against
the disadvantages that always confront the stranger in competition with local bands.

Our dance orchestra stepped out on Beale Street only
fourth best, and I wasn't satisfied. I had to swallow my pride
and watch the other three bands pass by at the head of the
parade while we brought up the rear. But good luck was not
long in overtaking us. Jim Turner, remembering my stout
words in his behalf when the minstrel bully threatened him,
quit Bynum and cast his lot with me and persuaded George
Williams, one of the best trombonists that ever pressed a
mouthpiece to his lips, to leave Bynum and join us. Then
James T. Osborne dropped from the sky, a tenor saxophone
player from out of this world. What Osborne couldn't do
with a sax just wasn't. He joined us, and our orchestra became
the first in the land to boast of a saxophone.

Saxophones, still a novel attraction with brass bands—more
for the appearance of the instrument than for the music perhaps—were untried as orchestral instruments. With the brilliant Osborne performing for us, we not only led the way but
cut quite a figure while doing it. This attracted Will Means,
another Bynum man. He brought us his bass fiddle and trombone. Then Henry Graves from Reuben Brooks' Vicksburg
orchestra and James Pratt added their cello and flute. My luck
was running again. Engagements started pouring in.

Then one evening when we were getting off the excursion
steamer *Pattona*, a shy stranger approached me and said he
had heard that I needed another good clarinetist. It was easy
to see that he had been having his downs. He reminded me of
myself back on the levee at St. Louis. He told me his name
was J. Paul Wyer.

That was a familiar name. A noted army bandsman by that
name had led an orchestra in Pensacola.

8

"Not any relation by any chance?"

"Yes," he nodded. "My father."

"What kind of music do you play?"

"Anything. Anything that's written." It was not spoken boastfully, but with a quiet assurance that I well understood. "I played in my father's theatre orchestra. We had to play for musical comedy shows from New York—had to read the scores off at sight."

I took him on for the night and gave him a chance to play with our large group at Buchignani's under rather trying circumstances. He was asked to play second clarinet without a prepared part. But the young musician improvised a part better than if one had been written. I was deeply impressed and genuinely sorry when I had to tell him that I couldn't see my way clear to hire a second clarinetist at the moment.

"But I can play the violin too," he suggested.

He gave us a demonstration. To my surprise, he could play any standard opera and many violin solos from memory. He left us all aghast.

"You must have been tops in your daddy's band," I said.

"Oh, no," he answered promptly. "Not quite tops. My brother Ed has me beat."

Naturally, I kept young Paul and lost no time sending for his brother Ed. From that time forward the boom was on where the Handy dance orchestra was concerned. Calls came from the towns and great houses down on the roads that crossed the Dog. Jim knew every pig path in Mississippi and Alabama. He had also played the river and was favorably known in Louisiana and Arkansas. All this territory we took under control and made it our stamping ground.

In those days they had a way of opening every new store in the Delta with a big free dance. And it was our fortune to come along at a time when country stores were popping open like cotton blossoms. We were engaged by the proprietors before the merchandise was shipped in.

We played for the colored folks too and opened up Dixie Park in Memphis, a sort of sun-tanned Coney Island. This engagement carried solid weight, stamping us as *the* dance band of those parts. We hit the park in high gear. Our band of twenty men and our orchestra of twelve held forth nightly and were received with loud approval.

The dance floor at Dixie Park was a spectacle. It accommodated a thousand dancers at a time. On Monday nights and on week-ends the park was jammed. Everybody and his brother were there. The dances brought out a great mass of color and rhythm. Sometimes they looked like a drill corps in review before a grandstand. More often I saw it as a monstrous pin wheel, blazing with color and spinning magically. One or the other of the two gaudy floor managers—Slick Henderson and Edgar Hodges—would signal with a whistle. My band would then play four bars of the next dance and pause while the dancers took their places. A moment later it would be under way. We played one-steps, polkas, schottisches and waltzes. Many times I remember wishing that the white folks for whom we played most of the time could have witnessed that Dixie Park scene. It was an extravaganza, a pageant, a sea of gliding figures. I remember the hands in particular—ebony hands, brown hands, yellow hands, ivory hands, all moving in coordination with nimble dancing feet. Then there were the teeth, the pearly teeth and the gay smiling faces that had forgotten yesterday and never heard of tomorrow.

During these nights at the Dixie Park I noticed something that struck me as a racial trait, and I immediately tucked it away for future use. It was the odd response of the dancers to Will H. Tyer's *Maori*. When we played this number and came to the Habanera rhythm, containing the beat of the tango, I observed that there was a sudden, proud and graceful reaction to the rhythm. Was it an accident, or could the response be traced to a real but hidden cause? I wondered. White dancers, as I had observed them, took the number in stride. I began to suspect that perhaps there was something Negroid in that beat, something that quickened the blood of the Dixie Park dançers. Well, there was a way to test it. If my suspicions were grounded, the same reaction should be manifest during the playing of *La Paloma*. We used that piece, and sure enough, there it was, that same calm yet ecstatic movement. I felt convinced. Later, because of this conviction, I introduced the rhythm into my own compositions. It may be noted in the introduction to the *St. Louis Blues*, the instrumental piano copy of *Memphis Blues*, the chorus of *Beale Street Blues* and other compositions.

The Dixie Park engagement, as I have indicated, stamped us as first string in the Memphis line-up of dance bands. Now in Memphis as in Clarksdale it was known to politicians that the best notes made the most votes, and there came a time when we were called upon to do our bit for the cause of good government. The occasion was the election campaign which I have already mentioned. The three leading Negro bands were sent out by the managers of each candidate to whoop it up and bring home the bacon. Bynum's with their flashy cornetist, Frank McDonald, hoped to win Beale Street for one candidate. Eckford's tried to blow another man into office with the help of Teddy Adams, the speed demon clarinetist. The third candidate, running on a platform that condemned easy riders, barrel houses and even dance halls, was Mr. Crump. And for some ironic reason one of Mr. Crump's committees hired our band.

Beale Street was expected to cast a lot of votes, and it was squarely up to us to get them. I began to rack my brain. A song like Moody and Sankey's *Pull For The Shore*, while it might have expressed the mood and temper of Mr. Crump's platform, would certainly not have pulled any votes for him in my opinion. Hot-cha music was the stuff we needed, and it had to be mellow. Where was it to be found? Certainly not in any existing files. I closed my eyes and tried to dream it. Let me see now—yes, that's it. I could hear what I wanted. It was a weird melody in much the same mood as the one that had been strummed on the guitar at Tutwiler.

It did the business, too. Folks went wild about it. No doubt Mr. Crump would have gone wild too, in quite a different way, had he been permitted to hear the words. But he didn't go with the band, so he never heard the song that many like to think whisked him into office on a reform ticket. That, of course, was neither here nor there. We were hired to beat the drum and blow the horn for Mr. Crump, and that we did—in our own way.

Since *Mr. Crump* was the first of the published blues compositions, the lyric that I have quoted demands an explanation. It was a five-line stanza, but the preceding strain and the strain that followed the refrain both called for three-line stanzas in the proper blues fashion (actually no words were written for these at this time). The three-line stanza had twelve instead of sixteen measures to the strain, another blues characteristic. The final strain in this piece had a spot for Osborne's tenor sax to do a haunting break just before the finish.

The melody of *Mr. Crump* was mine throughout. On the other hand, the twelve-bar, three-line form of the first and last strains, with its three-chord basic harmonic structure (tonic, subdominant, dominant seventh) was that already used by Negro roustabouts, honky-tonk piano players, wanderers and others of their underprivileged but undaunted class from Missouri to the Gulf, and had become a common medium through which any such individual might express his personal feelings in a sort of musical soliloquy. My part in their history was to introduce this, the "blues" form to the general public, as the medium for my own feelings and my own musical ideas. And the transitional flat thirds and sevenths in my melody, by which I was attempting to suggest the typical slurs of the Negro voice, were what have since become known as "blue notes."

Thoroughly rehearsed and intoxicated by the new melody, my musicians arrived at Main and Madison riding in a band wagon and got set to play the blues to the general public for the first time in America. It certainly did not occur to us that we were aiding or abetting any trend whatever, but subsequent events make it interesting to recall that the group that struck it up that afternoon consisted of Ed. Wyer, first violin; George Higgins, guitar; Archie Walls, string bass; Robert H. Young, clarinet; James Osborne, tenor saxophone; George Williams, trombone; and myself on the trumpet. We were all seated in chairs. I flashed the sign and the boys gave. Feet commenced to pat. A moment later there was dancing on the sidewalks below. Hands went into the air, bodies swayed like the reeds on the banks of the Congo. Now and again one got happy and shouted, "Aw, do it, Mister Man." In the office buildings about, the white folks pricked up their ears. Stenographers danced with their bosses. Everybody shouted for more. We heard them on all sides demanding that we play the song again. One bystander came directly in front of us and insisted on knowing the name of the tune.

"That's *Mr. Crump*," Higgins told them, missing a beat on his guitar. Then he sang the words again.

And that was how it all began. From that day our band was swamped with calls. We had to divide ourselves into three groups, each carrying violin, clarinet, cornet, trombone, guitar and bass, while the lone saxophone remained with the main division. Each combination was kept busy. Still there were more demands than we could supply. I sent to Jacksonville, Florida, for William King Phillips, composer of the *Florida Blues*, a remarkable clarinetist who doubled saxophone. Then I added William Singleton, saxophone, to the third division. The saxophonists taught other clarinetists the saxophone. We went into the high school and found boys and girls capable of playing the piano and coached them for jobs. These, and all others we could rake and scrape up, we sent out to fill such engagements as would be content with minor combinations of two or three musicians, in many cases just a piano and drums.

We were engaged to play the swanky Alaskan Roof Garden on top of the Falls Building (leading uptown dance spot of white Memphis), giving white society an opportunity to hear our wonderful xylophonist and drummer Jasper Taylor, who carried a whole rack of pots, pans and other kitchen utensils as Kinder Symphonie. We cornered the music on two excursion boats. All the parks and dance halls employed us. When the demand reached its height, we were using sixty-seven musicians.

My piece was through as a campaign tune when Edward H. Crump was elected, but it did not die. In spite of its honky-tonk words, *Mr. Crump* gained such popularity in those parts that I began to think it would have to be published.

But the idea of perpetuating the song in any form raised problems. To begin with, I was now embarrassed by the words. With Mr. Crump holding forth as mayor, I couldn't get the consent of my mind to keep on telling his honor to catch hisself some air. Of course, the title could be changed. So, in a mood of warm sentiment for the city that had been so good to me, and in memory of the nameless folk singers who had brought forth blues, I decided on a new title. *Mr. Crump*, still unpublished, became the *Memphis Blues*.

Of the many reactions to my tune, one still amuses me. We were playing the number at a colored dance in the old K. of P. Hall. During the playing I noticed periodic shouting from the floor, and a great roar of voices broke out when we came to a certain point in the piece. I didn't know what to make of it.

If you know the original *Memphis Blues*, you may recall that in the third and fourth measures of the instrumental score there is a sort of Italian climax with a tricky rhythm. Well, it was at this point that the shouting broke.

"Set in it," I heard them say. "Set *in* it!"

George Williams, our trombone player, who happened to be a creole from Donaldsonville and New Orleans, Louisiana, saw me looking sheepish.

"Didn' ya heah 'em?" he shouted. "Didn' ya heah 'em?"

"Sure," I said. "I heard. But what do they mean? Set in *what?*"

"Mon, wat do de jigwalk do wen de preacher make 'em happy, eh? Don' dey say 'hallelu' or 'glory be'? Well, dot piece make dem happy, too."

"They like it then?" I asked.

"Hell, yes, mon. Dey's crazy 'bout it."

Others told me of hearing little happy squeals among the Negro dancers for whom they had played the piece. Salem Tutt Whitney [1] told how he had heard the folks yell in delight after the first four bars and the "break." Yet this entire strain was dropped out bodily in the vocal edition put out after I sold my tune, and it became almost forgotten until, nearly thirty years after, I regained my rights and republished my work.

Judging from Memphis' reactions, it certainly seemed that I had a hit on my hands. But it also became a headache and a heartache.

[1] Salem Tutt Whitney, late of "Green Pastures," noted this reaction while touring with "Smart Set."

The Memphis Blues
or
(Mister Crump)

The sequence of this composition introduced something new, for there is no finality in the endings of the separate strains until the last two measures of the final strain.

By W. C. HANDY

The Memphis Blues . 3

The Memphis Blues . 3

CHAPTER EIGHT

Memphis Blues—*A Bungled Bargain*

I NEEDED a commercial outlet for my tune. That's where the misery began. Every reputable American publisher of popular music gave the *Memphis Blues* the go-by. The twelve-bar strains, where there should be sixteen, to them, lacked completeness. It's amusing to think about that now, but in those days when I was featuring their hits and comparing them with my own work, I felt that someone was overlooking a good bet. At any rate, in the late summer of 1912 I decided that I wanted to publish the *Memphis Blues*.

I had published nothing before, so I shopped around for some advice. I obtained it from a white man, whom I shall call X——— who was then employed by Bry's department store. Bry's music department was separately organized as the Southern Music Company. X——— (acting as an individual and not for his employers) offered to arrange for the printing and copyrighting, and to put the piece on sale at Bry's. I accepted. It was agreed between us that the engraving and printing was to be done by Otto Zimmerman & Son of Cincinnati, at my expense, and that the first printing should be of just one thousand copies (that figure is important as will be seen). I accordingly prepared and furnished X——— with my manuscript of the piece in early September, and a little later I went there and corrected the proof.

Another white man, whom I am calling Z———, had a music publishing company and also a store of his own in a Western city. He traveled extensively for his business, visiting retailers such as Bry's with whom he made local headquarters and spending weeks at a time with them busily demonstrating his music to their customers by both piano and voice. I also had been a frequent caller at Bry's since October 1909, when my band (playing on the steamer *Pattona*, as it escorted President Taft's vessel into Memphis on a river trip to encourage a deep Chicago-Gulf waterway), had plugged a tune of X———'s written for the same occasion along with my own blues. Through X———, I myself had occasionally met Z———, and he knew something about my work. And now while I was dealing with X——— about the *Memphis Blues*, Z——— appeared on one of his visits. On hearing of our plans and coming with X——— to rehear my tune at a Second Street dance hall, he persuaded me that with his out-of-town connections he could give the piece a wider circulation than I could, and without surrendering my ownership rights I consented to make him my sales representative.

On Friday afternoon, September 27th, word came to me from X——— that the shipment of *Memphis Blues* had arrived and that if I would come over next morning I could see it opened up and put on sale. I was early at Bry's, where I met both X——— and Z——— and was shown, in the music stockroom, a fascinating package which we opened, revealing the thousand copies in their blue jackets. I took out a hundred to try to place in other stores, X——— took more, and we proceeded to the music counter where I watched them put on sale. I paid out about $32.50 to X——— to cover the engraving and printing cost as reported by him, and an extra dollar for the copyright fee, and I left with the promise of an advertisement in Bry's newspaper space for Sunday.

My first hopes did not survive long. I found no such reception at the other Memphis stores as I had at Bry's. Even my friends, the O. K. Houck Piano Company on Main Street, shied away at first. Mr. Houck's attitude puzzled me, for at the time I approached him his windows were displaying *At the Ball* by J. Lubrie Hill, a colored composer, who had gone to New York from Memphis some time earlier. Around it were grouped copies of recent successes by such Negro composers as Cole and Johnson, Scott Joplin and the Williams and Walker musical comedies. So when he suggested that his trade wouldn't stand for his selling my work, I pointed out as tactfully as I could that the majority of his musical hits of the moment had come from the Gotham-Attucks Company, a firm of Negro publishers in New York.

I'll never forget his smile.

"Yes," he said pleasantly. "I know that—but my customers don't."

He turned me down, and I fared no better in other stores. Considerably later, I hasten to add, he more than made up for it; but meanwhile I had to take my copies back to Bry's.

The blows continued to fall. From day to day I asked X—— or Z—— what was happening, but their answer remained the same: the customers said the piece was too hard to play, and there were practically no sales. It was hard to believe that Memphis, which had loved its blues in the dance halls these two years, would now have none of it. But there lay the unsold copies as proof that my publishing venture was a failure. I was thoroughly discouraged, and when Z—— made me a proposal that would give me back my costs, with perhaps a tiny profit, I gave up and accepted.

I gave him a bill of sale of my music plates and my tune itself—saving authorship credit—free of royalties. For this I received fifty dollars cash, and also the nearly one thousand unsold copies left from my own original edition, as Z—— planned to republish under his own imprint and to try the tune out in New York and elsewhere. Z—— called it that I was selling for a hundred dollars rather than only fifty, since

the copies on hand had been carried at five cents apiece whole-
sale; and for years I accepted this theory myself because a
hundred dollars sounded better. Of course the flaw in this
comforting theory was that I had paid for the whole edition
in the first place. At any rate, I was through. Z—— left for
New York, and my prospect of ever making any more from
the *Memphis Blues* depended upon my surviving the next
twenty-eight years till I became entitled to the author's copy-
right-renewal privilege under the law.

Back in New York, Z—— started talking up an "unusual
band" he had heard in Memphis and an "unusual tune" he had
bought there. He himself met with difficulty for a little while,
for my strains were still unorthodox, but he made some headway. I now know that he ordered ten thousand copies from
Zimmerman's in October 1912, of which forty-eight hundred
went to Memphis and the rest to Denver, Omaha and New
York. He ordered another ten thousand the following March,
after which he took the plates out of their hands. Then the
white fiddler Waiman played the piece, and his full-length
picture went on the cover. On September 20, 1913, Z——
wrote me (on a letterhead which named X—— as his whole-
sale manager) that he had sold fifty thousand copies, that
George Evans' "Honey Boy" Minstrels had taken it up and
that he was about to publish a new vocal edition, with words
all about my band. I quote from other parts of the same letter:

"I am convinced that this number will sell several hundred
thousand copies, as a result of the advertising I am giving it. I have
confidence in the number or I would not spend the large amount
of money I am putting in it. I also believe in your ability as being
the greatest ragtime writer of the day. . . . You will realize that
you are about to land on the Honor Roll of hit writers.

"Once I get you landed there, you will have a demand from all
other big publishers for numbers. You will have to retire to the
field of composition and work some more wonderful melodies
like *Memphis Blues.* You may write some numbers just as good;

but you will have to work to write some any better. Even at that I believe that you have the ability to do it. . . ."

The new vocal version omitted my entire first strain, but at least its lyric was a useful compliment. It was written by George A. Norton (who with Ernie Burnett and Maybelle Watson wrote *Come to Me, My Melancholy Baby*) and Norton's words were all about that band of ours that Z——— had heard playing the blues in Memphis, words about the slick-haired fiddler and the trombone that moaned like a sinner on revival day. Never having heard of a saxophone in a dance orchestra, Norton's lyric had us using a "big bassoon" to "second to the trombone's croon." That was left uncorrected but I liked the words. Whenever I hear them now, "smoke gets in my eyes." An inner voice begins to scold: "Why did you leave the town where everybody grinned at Handy and every kid knew him? Why didn't you keep that band together, regardless of time and people and money?" Then mist comes in my eyes again and tells me that hairs are white and heads are "blossoming for the grave," and that while some of my best players have gone to the Celestial Band, their sons and grandsons have taken what I got from Juba and translated it into Jive for their Jitterbugs. Ah, well . . .

Z——— wrote me twenty years later that "a brown-skin gal," who had sung at Persica's in Memphis, finally put the new song over by her renditions at a 105th Street, New York, cabaret. He did not name her, but she must have been either Osceola Blanks or her sister Berliana, both of whom thereafter sang the piece all over the country. From then on it was easy and big money for Z———, till finally he became involved in some manner, lost control of his catalogue and at last died in reduced circumstances.

We met and corresponded from time to time from the Memphis days to his death. In 1933, inspired by a magazine article about me, he wrote me that he had composed a story for the same publication about "the daring man who bought *Memphis Blues* from you for $100," and he sent me a copy of his script, which was not accepted for publication. In this story, after referring to my bad luck with the New York publishers and crediting himself with the suggestion of publishing a thousand copies in Memphis to get the public's reaction, he made a statement which would have surprised me greatly at the time, save that I supposed I knew the facts, and passed it over as a bit of romancing. I quote his statement, and the italics are mine:

"*The thousand copies lasted three days.* Handy, *still* affected by his fruitless efforts, was glad to sell for $100 cash as a sure thing."

As I have said, my arrangement with Z——'s associate had been that he should order only one thousand copies. I had paid him for the engraving and printing, supposedly of one thousand copies only, and I had parted with my copyright on the statement that the piece did not sell, and had then received back nearly a thousand unsold copies.

It was only in the winter of 1939–40 that an investigation through the original printer's successors disclosed that the first *Memphis Blues* printing, ordered by X—— and for which I had ignorantly paid, had consisted of not one thousand but two thousand copies, of which half were shipped by express; the rest, separately by freight. The shipment took place September 25, 1912, and it was on October 7th, only nine days after first publication, that Z—— ordered the second edition of ten thousand copies, with change of imprint.

I do not know just how many copies of my piece had actually been sold when I parted with it. I understand that a fire long since destroyed the records of Bry's, which firm, of course, was in no way responsible for what may have happened to me. But I now know that Z—— and X—— were in a position to sell over a thousand copies of the *Memphis Blues* to the public and still have nearly a thousand left, the

9

sight of which would mean to me that there had been "practically no sales" at all and that my creation was a failure. And I received none of the proceeds of the missing thousand.

I have felt that this story should now be told, because these men constitute a part of the long list of exploiters of the works of composers and inventors. Such men must necessarily ease their conscience when withholding financial returns, by telling the creator of a work what a great name they have made for him. This was probably the case with Stephen Foster's *Old Folks at Home* (*Swanee River*), dear to the hearts of all Americans, though for years it was the minstrel E. P. Christy's name that went on the copies as composer, and from Howard's account [3] Christy apparently paid just five dollars for this amazing privilege. Although Foster received small remuneration for his works, it is my belief that *Old Kentucky Home* and *Old Black Joe* touched the heart of Lincoln, and thus helped to make this book possible.

The framers of our copyright law, knowing that such practices had long existed, divided the 56 years of copyright protection into two terms of 28 years each, and gave the second term to the author or his heirs regardless of his previous mistakes. The wisdom of this law I can attest to, since everybody connected with the *Memphis Blues* has made more money from it than I, yet the second 28 years will help to afford me protection in my old age when I may need it most.

However, things are better for a composer nowadays. Since with all the protection of copyright it is still a matter of impossibility for a composer to trace infringements wherever they may occur, powerful and reputable organizations have been formed to assist in the protection of musical creations. Such is the Song Writers' Protective Association, which protects the composer's interests against unscrupulous publishers if there be such. The Music Publishers' Protective Association looks after the interests of both composer and publisher in

[3] *Stephen Foster, America's Troubadour*, by John Tasker Howard.

mechanical reproductions such as phonograph records, electrical transcriptions and synchronized motion picture music, even licensing the latter for use throughout the world. Last but not least, the American Society of Composers, Authors and Publishers acts as an agent for authors, composers and publishers when copyrighted music is used by radio, theatres, cabarets and dance halls, and this great agency cares for the composer whose work has shown worth, regardless of whether or not he has disposed of his copyrights. More will be told about these organizations in another chapter.

In the year or two that followed my meeting with Z——in Bry's music department, I saw the song that I had sold for fifty dollars become a tremendous hit and a gold mine for the new owner. The Victor Company released a recording by the Jim Europe band. That sent that ball rolling. Meanwhile, as others pocketed the royalties, I reaped some of the glory. Arrangements were made for me to appear before the white women's music clubs of Memphis. The O. K. Houck Piano Company, which had refused to display the song, not only displayed it now but also displayed me in a life-size picture standing beside a Victor talking machine with ear bent to hear the new Jim Europe recording of my song. And when a big traveling band was announced at the East End Gardens by a great banner, the Alaskan Roof, at which my band was already playing, flung a tremendous streamer high across Madison and Main with these words: *Handy's Band*—ALASKAN ROOF GARDEN—*The Best Band in The South*. It dwarfed the East End Gardens banner.

But the musicians' union did not approve of these proceedings. First, they sent a committee to demand the removal from Houck's window of the Victor talking machine and Mr. Handy's attentive expression. The demand was complied with. They had just attended to this business when the Alaskan Roof unfurled its bold exasperating streamer. The committee visited the Alaskan Roof and demanded the removal of the banner, which the management refused. Finally, however, they succeeded in securing its removal through the fire and police commissioners.

It was now possible to heave a sigh of relief. All concerned seemed completely satisfied with the accomplishment. That same year, however, this same group of objectors became the greatest boosters of the *Memphis Blues*, regarding it with a certain home town pride. So while I was deprived of the banner over Madison Avenue, nightly I was able to hear E. K. White's Municipal Band playing the *Memphis Blues* in Court Square.

How the *Memphis Blues* had been received in other parts of the country I did not learn till I persuaded Mr. Tuohey, secretary of the Memphis Chamber of Commerce, to engage my men to play for a national convention of the Real Estate Men's Association. The secretary had other ideas about entertainment for the occasion. He had planned an old-time Southern banquet with possum and 'taters, shortnin' or cracklin' bread and persimmon beer, and he had asked me to round up a batch of country banjo players that could sing backwoods songs. It took fast talking to change his mind. I argued that our character artist, Sidney Easton, could handle that sort of darky business even more effectively than could the country boys. Eventually the secretary saw the point and gave us the job.

A great crowd filled the banquet hall on the big night. The secretary requested an opening song, and Sidney gave it to them, his pleasing dark face bright with a pearly smile. An encore was demanded, and then another. Finally Mr. Tuohey suggested that we play a piece with the band. We opened with the *Memphis Blues*, since we did not have to have music for that. The real estate men cut loose with one of those rare, spontaneous outbursts that all but shatter your eardrums. I was not only delighted but genuinely amazed. This was the first direct inkling I had gained of the success of my song in other parts of the country. Presently, however, I was to learn more.

After a number of preliminary speeches, Judge Greer, speaker of the evening, stunned us with this astonishing remark: "Gentlemen, I came here with a prepared speech on the old South, but after hearing that boy sing and that band play, I am going to throw away my speech and talk about the Negro, the most wonderful race on the face of God's green earth." That not only baffled us but left me, for one, apprehensive. When a man begins that way, you are inclined to wonder. But Judge Greer went on to say that Easton resembled a playmate of his boyhood days. Then he told the men how he used to slip away from the white church to go to the colored church with his playmate because, as he said, the Negroes seemed to have more religion, and he demonstrated by singing a strain of *Swing Low Sweet Chariot.*

A moment later, when the speaker returned to a portion of his prepared speech to relate his experiences as a drummer boy of fourteen, following the fortunes of the Confederacy, I began to think that he had said his say and was through with us. But I guessed wrong. He only wanted the real estate men from all over the country to know that when the cause was lost, he had pinned the Stars and Stripes on the lapel of his coat above the Southern Cross. His views, he wished to show, were not based on sectional feeling. He had only commenced to say what was on his mind concerning Negroes.

About that time he turned to C. P. J. Mooney, editor of the *Commercial Appeal,* and said, "We have made a serious mistake in inviting men from all parts of America to make investments in a city where one-third of its population is painted as vicious. No race that can sing and play as these men have done can be vicious. Why, the *Memphis Blues,*" he shouted, "has done more to advertise Memphis than all the publicity emanating from the Businessmen's Association." The businessmen gathered there seemed to approve. They applauded heartily. I wanted to join them, but I refrained from using my hands. Only my heart applauded. Curiously, however, it was less because of what he said about my song than because of his kindly generalizations about Negroes as a whole that I felt enraptured.

Judge Greer was followed by Editor Mooney. His theme was the same, but he added statistics to show the Negro's contribution to the wealth of that section of the Mississippi Valley. Nothing like this had ever been spoken in my presence before. A Kentuckian, speaking next, felt impressed to make a related point. Once, he explained, the best horses came from Arabia. In his home state they educated their Negroes, and now it could be said that the world's greatest horses were raised in Kentucky.

Another man, while adding his amen to the judge's observations, suggested that the *Memphis Blues* was all the more remarkable when one remembered that Tennessee had probably never spent a dollar on the musical education of a Negro.

My own reactions were confused. I took occasion to thank my stars that I had settled upon music as a career, despite opposition. Nothing made me glow so much as seeing the softening effect of music on racial antagonisms. On the other hand, there was a seed of bitterness in my heart. While I was getting the praise, another man owned the copyright to *Memphis Blues* and was getting the money. As a result of this evening's encouragement, however, I determined to swallow that resentment like a true philosopher, set my head to new things, and see if I couldn't do better next time. In fact, a bee was already buzzing in my bonnet.

Up and down Beale Street, in Pee Wee's saloon, at home—everywhere I went I heard it. A new tune was taking shape, a new hit that I hoped would compensate for the royalties that I was not getting from my first successful song. The inspiration for the new composition was a humorous Negro custom that could be traced to the Gullahs and from them all the way back to Africa. I had first noticed it among the troupers of the minstrel company. Whenever these fellows wanted to say something to one another—something not intended for outside ears—they used words invented by themselves for this purpose. Sometimes they simply attached new means to familiar words. For example, a white person was always "ofay," a Negro "jigwawk." The terms, as pliable as silk, were also extended to cover fine distinctions. Thus if the girl you were sparking at the moment was light colored, you might describe her as ofay jigwawk. If she was the stove-pipe variety, you might have to hear her called a jig-wawk-jigwawk. I recalled that back in the nineties Ben Harney wrote a ragtime song entitled *The Cake Walk in the Sky*. But when the jigs sang it, the audience heard something like this: *The Kigingy Kikake Wygingwawk Higin The Skigy*.

Of course, in the theatrical profession one meets alert ears and sharp wits, and the public early became familiar with words like "ousylay" and "umbay." To meet this cleverness, we used throw-offs to confuse them. "Siging Sigwatney" was such a throw-off—it meant nothing whatever. "Jogo" did have meaning, however. It meant colored and was a synonym for jigwawk. I decided to call my new composition the *Jogo Blues*.

Well, the *Jogo Blues* got a play. Michael Markels of New York was one Broadway band leader who featured it successfully. A St. Louis millionaire, Russell Gardner, "The Banner Buggy Man," liked it so well he sent me a twenty-dollar note every time we played it—which was every night when he was present. But *Jogo Blues* never became a hit and never fulfilled the hope I had entertained for a success to compensate for the earlier song.

The trouble may have been partly because *Jogo* was an instrumental number. Then another disadvantage was that only Negro musicians understood the title and the music. On the other hand, while my men liked it a great deal, many bands couldn't play it well because it was considered over the head of the ordinary pianist and too difficult for the average orchestra. I had made an orchestral arrangement too difficult for the average player, and profits in musical compositions come from widely repeated sales, not from an occasional yellowback from a single rich enthusiast. In short, I was still looking for that second hit.

It occurred to me that I could perhaps make more headway in this direction without the questionable help of my four lively and robust youngsters at home, all bent on using my legs for teeterboards. The noisy rumpus warmed the heart but it put a crimp in my work. I could feel the blues coming on, and I didn't want to be distracted, so I packed my grip and made my getaway.

I rented a room in the Beale Street section and went to work. Outside, the lights flickered. Chitterling joints were as crowded as the more fashionable resorts like the Iroquois. Piano thumpers tickled the ivories in the saloons to attract customers, furnishing a theme for the prayers at Beale Street Baptist Church and Avery Chapel (Methodist). Scores of powerfully built roustabouts from river boats sauntered along the pavement, elbowing fashionable browns in beautiful gowns. Pimps in boxback coats and undented Stetsons came out to get a breath of early evening air and to welcome the young night. The poolhall crowd grew livelier than they had been during the day. All that contributed to the color and spell of Beale Street mingled outside, but I neither saw nor heard it that night. I had a song to write.

My first decision was that my new song would be another blues, true to the soil and in the tradition of *Memphis Blues*. Ragtime, I had decided, was passing out. But this number would go beyond its predecessor and break new ground. I would begin with a down-home ditty fit to go with twanging banjos and yellow shoes. Songs of this sort could become tremendous hits sometimes. On the levee at St. Louis I had heard *Looking for the Bully* sung by the roustabouts, which later

was adopted and nationally popularized by May Irwin. I had
watched the joy-spreaders rarin' to go when it was played by
the bands on the *Gray Eagle*, or the *Spread Eagle*. I wanted
such a success, but I was determined that my song would have
an important difference. The emotions that it expressed were
going to be real. Moreover, it was going to be cut to the native blues pattern.

A flood of memories filled my mind. First, there was the
picture I had of myself, broke, unshaven, wanting even a decent meal, and standing before the lighted saloon in St. Louis
without a shirt under my frayed coat. There was also from
that same period a curious and dramatic little fragment that
till now had seemed to have little or no importance. While
occupied with my own miseries during that sojourn, I had
seen a woman whose pain seemed even greater. She had tried
to take the edge off her grief by heavy drinking, but it hadn't
worked. Stumbling along the poorly lighted street, she muttered as she walked, "Ma man's got a heart like a rock cast in
de sea."

The expression interested me, and I stopped another woman
to inquire what she meant. She replied, "Lawd, man, it's hard
and gone so far from her she can't reach it." Her language was
the same down-home medium that conveyed the laughable
woe of lamp-blacked lovers in hundreds of frothy songs, but
her plight was much too real to provoke much laughter. My
song was taking shape. I had now settled upon the mood.

Another recollection pressed in upon me. It was the memory of that odd gent who called figures for the Kentucky
breakdown—the one who everlastingly pitched his tones in the
key of G and moaned the calls like a presiding elder preaching
at a revival meeting. Ah, there was my key—I'd do the song
in G.

Well, that was the beginning. I was definitely on my way.
But when I got started, I found that many other considera-
tions also went into the composition. Ragtime had usually sac-

rificed melody for an exhilarating syncopation. My aim would
be to combine ragtime syncopation with a real melody in the
spiritual tradition. There was something from the tango that
I wanted too. The dancers at Dixie Park had convinced me
that there was something racial in their response to this
rhythm, and I had used it in a disguised form in the *Memphis
Blues*. Indeed, the very word "tango," as I now know, was
derived from the African "tangana," and signified this same
tom-tom beat. This would figure in my introduction, as well
as in the middle strain.

In the lyric I decided to use Negro phraseology and dialect.
I felt then, as I feel now, that this often implies more than
well-chosen English can briefly express. My plot centered
around the wail of a lovesick woman for her lost man, but in
the telling of it I resorted to the humorous spirit of the bygone
coon songs. I used the folk blues' three-line stanza that created the twelve-measure strain.

The primitive Southern Negro as he sang was sure to bear
down on the third and seventh tones of the scale, slurring between major and minor. Whether in the cotton fields of the
Delta or on the levee up St. Louis way, it was always the
same. Till then, however, I had never heard this slur used by
a more sophisticated Negro, or by any white man. I had tried
to convey this effect in *Memphis Blues* by introducing flat
thirds and sevenths (now called "blue notes") into my song,
although its prevailing key was the major; and I carried this
device into my new melody as well. I also struck upon the
idea of using the dominant seventh as the opening chord of
the verse. This was a distinct departure, but as it turned out,
it touched the spot.

In the folk blues the singer fills up occasional gaps with
words like "Oh, lawdy" or "Oh, baby" and the like. This
meant that in writing a melody to be sung in the blues manner one would have to provide gaps or waits. In my composition I decided to embellish the piano and orchestra score at

these points. This kind of business is called a "break"; entire books of different "breaks" for a single song can be found on the music counters today, and the breaks become a fertile source of the orchestral improvisation which became the essence of jazz. In the chorus I used plagal chords to give spiritual effects in the harmony. Altogether, I aimed to use all that is characteristic of the Negro from Africa to Alabama. By the time I had done all this heavy thinking and remembering, I figured it was time to get something down on paper, so I wrote, "I hate to see de evenin' sun go down." And if you ever had to sleep on the cobbles down by the river in St. Louis, you'll understand that complaint.

St. Louis had come into the composition in more ways than one before the sun peeped through my window. So when the song was completed, I dedicated the new piece to Mr. Russell Gardner, the St. Louis man who had liked *Jogo Blues*, and I proudly christened it the *St. Louis Blues*. The same day on Pee Wee's cigar stand I orchestrated the number and jotted down scores for the men of my band.

The song was off my chest, and secretly I was pleased with it, but I could scarcely wait for the public verdict. Blurry-eyed from loss of sleep, I went with the band to the evening's engagement on the Alaskan Roof.

CHAPTER NINE

St. Louis Blues *and Solvent Bank*

THE ONE-STEP, maxixe and other dances had been done to the
tempo of *Memphis Blues*, which the Vernon Castles slowed
up to introduce their original dance, the fox-trot. When *St.
Louis Blues* was written the tango was the vogue. I tricked
the dancers by arranging a tango introduction, breaking
abruptly then into a low-down blues. My eyes swept the floor
anxiously, then suddenly I saw the lightning strike. The dancers seemed electrified. Something within them came suddenly
to life. An instinct that wanted so much to live, to fling its
arms and to spread joy, took them by the heels. By this I was
convinced that my new song was accepted.

When the evening was over, the band piled into cabs and
followed me home to celebrate the birth of the new blues.
But Maggie, arms akimbo and rolling pin poised, was waiting
for Jiggs at the door. I had been away from home twenty-
four hours, burning up worlds of energy to produce a song,
but maybe I should have stated where I was going and what
I intended to do. Failing to make that clear, I presume, the
fault was mine. But it's an awkward thing to announce in advance your intention of composing a song hit between midnight and dawn. The talk more naturally follows the act, and
that is what ultimately happened in my case.

The men of the band got a big kick out of my domestic

drama. But after all, heads are made to be lumped in this funny-paper world—aren't they?

A criticism leveled at the *St. Louis Blues* by the trombonist of our band was that it needed a vamp, a vamp in the prevailing manner, to allow more time for the singer.

"Never. Never!" I exploded.

But the next day a pause mark was placed over the final note in the introduction in order to favor the singer with the required delay, and with that *St. Louis Blues* was completed, born in an age of vamps, September, 1914, without a vamp. Two years had elapsed since I first published *Memphis Blues*, five years since I played this first jazz composition using Osborne and the tenor sax that moaned like "a sinner on revival day." Well, they say that life begins at forty—I wouldn't know—but I was forty the year *St. Louis Blues* was composed, and ever since then my life has, in one sense at least, revolved around that composition.

Things began to happen immediately, big things and little things, pleasant and unpleasant. Through them all, as I see it now, Time and Chance were conspiring to snatch me away from Memphis, away from the wistful glamour of a swiftly changing Beale Street. The increasing success of my songs, the ups and downs of business, and the dread shadows in the sun—each played a part.

The *St. Louis Blues* was followed by *Yellow Dog Rag* (*Yellow Dog Blues*), a song in which I undertook to answer the question raised by Shelton Brooks in his remarkable hit, *I Wonder Where My Easy Rider's Gone.* The country had gone stark, raving mad over the sweet-loving jockey with the easy ways and the roving disposition. I proposed to pick up Susan Johnson and Jockey Lee, Brooks' characters, in a parody of the original lyric, locating the lost rider "down where the Southern cross' the Dog." Thus my song was made around the line (but not the music) I had heard the guitar player improvise that night at Tutwiler. Before *Yellow Dog* I had written *Joe Turner Blues*, which was followed by *Hesitating Blues, Shoeboot's Serenade* and finally *Beale Street* (*Beale Street Blues*), a hail and farewell to the old Beale, the street that was.

At our home at 659 Janette Street manuscripts were thrown on the floor for the ink to dry. Hour after hour I sat at the piano, elaborating new tunes, patting my foot and thumping the keys energetically. Meanwhile the wolves that had been yapping at Beale Street ever since I could remember finally caught up with their victim. Backed by excursion boat operators who wanted to draw the liquor trade, and shady characters who hoped to enjoy bigger profits from illicit business, the reformers eventually prevailed, passing a local option law for Memphis.

That was a calamity. Imagine Pee Wee's closing at twelve o'clock at night! Imagine Beale Street without liquor. The anticipation was almost too unpleasant to bear. I wrote:

> Goin' to the river, maybe bye and bye—
> Goin' to the river, and there's a reason why—
> Because the river's wet, and Beale Street's done gone dry.

Actually, I hollered before I was hit. Pee Wee's closed at twelve on the appointed night, but five minutes later the door swung open again. The lights came up. It was another day. By this time all the whisky and gin were out of sight, and the shelves were ornamented with coca-cola and ginger ale bottles. Since that one frightful scare the wolf of Beale Street has never returned, so far as I know. Pee Wee's has never again been closed for even five minutes. Still there's no denying that Beale Street changed. Even at that moment it was losing something essential to its former character. So my lamentation was not entirely without point. Beale Street finally lost L. Pacini, to whom my song was dedicated because of a long standing friendship.

My recollections of the Beale Street era are not solely con-

A Quartet of First Editions
(Covers)

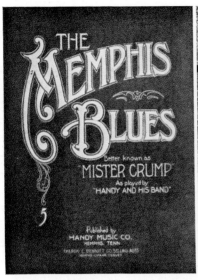

1912

1915

1915

1913

A belated correction. On the cover of *The Jogo Blues*, authorship of *The Girl You Never Have Met* was inadvertently credited to me instead of Pace. I was its composer.

cerned with the writing of blues. There are other threads to
the story. One of them goes back to 1907, the year that I first
became a tenant of the Solvent Savings Bank. The cashier of
this Negro enterprise was Harry H. Pace, a handsome young
man of striking personality and definite musical leanings. Pace
had written some first rate song lyrics and was in demand as a
vocal soloist at church programs and Sunday night concerts.
In 1907 we wrote *In the Cotton Fields of Dixie* which was
published by a Cincinnati firm. It was natural, if not inevitable, that he and I should gravitate together. We spoke the
same language. We collaborated on songs. Finally we became
partners in the "Pace & Handy Music Company—Publishers."

The first songs published by our firm included my *Jogo
Blues* and Pace's *The Girl You Never Have Met.* Just before
these numbers appeared, Pace left Memphis to become secretary-treasurer of the Standard Life Insurance Company of Atlanta, but he left with the bank his check to cover shipment
of the forthcoming songs. So later, when *St. Louis Blues* was
ready, I took my turn and decided to pay out of my pocket
for the printing of ten thousand copies.

By this time Pace was too busy and much too involved in
his new duties to give much thought to our fledgling enterprise. I went ahead on my own initiative, however, and before
the copies arrived from the Otto Zimmerman Company, the
Cincinnati printers (still doing business today at the old
stand), I had secured enough orders from the Kress and
Woolworth Music Departments to pay the entire printing
bill. Soon a profit of four hundred dollars accumulated. This
was immediately put back into the business. When Pace returned to Memphis on business for the insurance company, he
heard the song for the first time. It had not only been printed
but was on piano rolls before he knew about it.

Our publishing efforts were to remain tentative and tenu-
ous for long, however. My blues were fast gathering momen-
tum. George Evans of the old Honey Boy Minstrels featured

the *Memphis Blues* with Ed. V. Cupero's band on stage and street. The Victor catalogue listed the name of Handy between Handel and Haydn. Irving C. Miller, having fallen for *Memphis Blues* when he heard it sung by the Blanks sisters, came to Barasso's Palace Theatre with a new road show and presently became a *St. Louis Blues* fan. He bought a thousand copies to dispose of along the road. Later he reordered many times. Then when *Yellow Dog* was ready, he introduced the number through the jazzy singer Estelle Harris and became an outlet for the number in the East.

With all this going on the little firm of Pace & Handy put a carnation in its buttonhole and began to hold up its head. What's more, the originator of the blues threatened to become respectable. Negroes who once called our aggregation a barrel-house band began to prick up their ears. They seldom heard us play those days because we were engaged by the "quality" on the Alaskan Roof and Country Club, but when there was no longer any doubt that our new brand of music was cutting a figure, they made every effort to secure our services, offering as much as twice the fee we received from the white folks. But it was too late. We were under contract. Small-time white shopkeepers along Beale Street underwent a change too. Instead of trying to get my trade by calling me "Parson," they began to know me by my family name. I didn't tumble. They were likewise too late. Morris Lippman's loan office had known my name for years. He would often let me have the use of my musical instruments while they were still in pawn, to play engagements.

Once more it began to look like Easy Street for the blues. But this was just half the story. Aside from the publishing business and the business of composing new hits I continued to carry the staggering responsibility of keeping busy a dozen bands, employing over sixty people, playing for dances, touring on the road and through the sticks and giving concerts. The fortunes of our bands and particularly of the main unit rose with the success of the blues.

In the midst of this boom my partner arranged a concert for us in the colored auditorium in Atlanta, billing the thing like a circus. White folks of that city persuaded Pace to cancel this booking, however, and to place us instead in the auditorium where the Metropolitan Opera gave its Atlanta performances. Pace agreed promptly, and the auditoriums were switched. But when the *Atlanta Constitution* learned that we were to appear at the white auditorium, it began to stomp and fume. This did not discourage Pace. In fact, he took advantage of the newspaper's hostility and increased his publicity through *The Georgian* and *Journal*.

Back in Memphis I sweated blood to whip the show into shape. We needed a powerful attraction to conquer Atlanta, and we felt that we had it in our band, but just to make assurance doubly sure, we added Clarence Williams and Armand J. Piron to the program. This team did not belong in Memphis. They were New Orleans musicians and music publishers and had come to Memphis in the interest of their catalogue, plugging in particular *Brown Skin* and *I Can Beat You Doing What You're Doing Me*. Williams cut capers with the piano stool and played and sang superbly. Piron contributed his fancy fiddling. I had been instrumental in helping them get a listing with the five-and-ten-cent stores, a difficult assignment at that time. They had also made trips with our band through the Delta, winning many friends by their clever work. To help their business along as well as ours they agreed to make the trip with us.

An awe fell upon us as we took our places on the stage where Caruso had sung with the Metropolitan Opera Company in Atlanta. We faced the curtain like a flock of dusky Daniels come to judgment before an audience of seven thousand. Then the barrier went up. Before us a sea of faces rose

10

and a silence that was oppressive. A moment later the band struck up *Hail to the Spirit of Freedom*, a march which I wrote for the Lincoln Jubilee Exposition held at the Coliseum in Chicago. No one objected to that, so we followed it up with *Semiramis*, a classical overture which the boys played in conventional style. The audience gave us a good hand. Then the storm broke when we played the *Memphis Blues* and had to repeat it nine times. After that it was goodby to the printed program. We played only requests, and these called for blues, blues and more blues. Nothing but the blues. People seemed to be starving for blues. My daughter Katherine, then only twelve, sang the *St. Louis Blues* and, for encores, *Joe Turner* and again *Memphis Blues*. They wouldn't let us stop, so we rushed in Clarence Williams and Armand Piron. Well, they stopped the show, and I began to think that our boat had been torpedoed. We just couldn't let the final curtain down now. We'd be lost. Suddenly the words of George M. Cohan's song, *Always Leave 'Em Laughing When You Say Goodby*, occurred to me, and I commenced to dig down in the old bag of tricks.

We had a drummer named Jasper Taylor. Jasper had long slapsticks. The finale was his spot, I decided. The band took up *Memphis Blues* again and while Jasper went through his side-splitting antics, hands clapped, saxophones crooned and voices sang the tune to George Norton's lyrics:

> They had a fiddler there who always slickened his hair . . .

They were getting "jazz," though the word was little known at the time, and they liked it. The curtain came down amid a tumult of applause.

Next morning the paper that had opposed our appearance in the Auditorium gave us two front-page columns with a headline which said, "At last we see the democracy of rag-time." *The Georgian* and *Journal* carried a large front-page cartoon showing a white man in the Auditorium wearing a ball and chain on his leg to prevent him from dancing. Pace and the men who had been associated with him in the undertaking were elated. They guarded my every moment, watched over me like bodyguards and whisked me here and there in closed cars. It was not because I was a mortal too good for human eyes. I detected, or fancied I detected, a box-office twinkle in my partner's eye. We were kept over, and played Atlanta for a week.

Was it Easy Street I had reached, or was I riding for a fall? For some unaccountable reason my mind went back to my McGuffey's Fifth Reader. "Mediocrity is the best state of fortune," one of the axioms said. Another declared that there was "No Excellence without Great Labor." I had no mind to be dour while the cheers were still ringing. Yet I returned to Memphis to find a foreclosure about to be made on one of two cottages I had purchased there.

As odd as this may sound when you recall that my songs were going well and that the bands were in constant demand, it was a fact. Maybe I put my money in a sock with a hole in it. Anyhow, Pace arranged to pay off the indebtedness through the Standard Life Insurance Company, thinking that thereby he might relieve my mind. Of course, handling a dozen bands and carrying on the publishing business and working on new songs didn't count with Memphians. I wasn't supposed to be a businessman. After a dance engagement the colored bankers used to ask me if I'd had a good time last night. As if playing from 8 P.M. until 3 A.M. for other people's enjoyment was easier than counting and handling other people's money from 10 A.M. to 3 P.M.

They had a strange way of rating artistic work and worth. If any one owned a dozen cans and piled them on a couple of shelves behind a printed sign, he was a grocer and a businessman, if you please, but one who contracted for musicians and played for parties over a dozen states was a good-timer and a rounder, if not worse. But these men were no more intolerant than others I had known. In earlier days I had gone into church choirs with my violin or cornet under my arm only to hear elderly sisters whisper, "Yonder goes de devil." In traveling around with the minstrel company we bumped into society folks too dicty to buy tickets for our show. We were invited to their functions only when we brought our instruments along. Parents who would mortgage farm or home to educate their sons for medicine, law and the ministry would frown upon a child who wanted to study music and kick him out as a loafer.

One day I was elaborating some new tunes, thumping the piano energetically, when the doorbell rang. At the door stood an elderly white man wearing a broad grin and a big celluloid collar. He was an insurance collector for the National Life and Casualty Company, he explained. Then he apologized for the interruption.

He had been listening outside to my melodies. He had formerly been a vocal teacher and was familiar with old forms of music and wanted to talk about my new style of work. I had my own troubles and wanted to air them. My lack of capital, New York's remote opportunities—these were the things that burdened me. I wanted to upbraid my own people for being, as I thought, so slow to bestow their racial okays. He tried to flag me down, but I continued to cry woe.

"Listen. You're on the high road," he said eventually.

I looked at him strangely.

"How can you say that?"

Then he told me his story.

At one time he had been a well-to-do farmer. With his wife he had been contented and happy until one night he read that real money could be made in poultry. They had a little money between them, money enough to start raising chickens on a small scale, but he decided that that wasn't enough. He persuaded his wife to sign a mortgage on their farm in order to provide capital required to earn the wheelbarrow loads of money awaiting their efforts. He outfitted a modern poultry farm. Then came the chickens and the eggs. They came so fast the man and his wife had to stay up nights to count the profits. But there was a little difference in their calculations.

"My wife," he said, "figured the value of the eggs. I valued each egg as a chicken."

Then the world turned. Cholera came. The enterprising young man wheeled loads of dead profits away to be burned. Unable to pay the mortgage, he lost the poultry farm and their home as well. Then followed long hard years in which he and his wife worked, having bought a dozen hens and one rooster. Slowly they mastered the secrets of diseases common to poultry. Fortune showed her face. In time they bought back the old home and opened a bank account.

"But why the insurance business?"

"That is just a sideline to keep me busy," he said. "My chickens know how to lay eggs."

His story did me a lot of good. I decided that conditions had nothing to do with my own problems, that race and color did not enter, as I had suspected, and that possibly my blues would learn to lay eggs too. Why not let well enough alone?

That, however, was not possible in my case. I had not reached an age when I was content to let well enough alone. Moreover, Time and Chance were still conspiring. At that very moment Pace was in New York on business for his insurance company and making connections that eventually resulted in a contract for our band to make twelve records. The fee seemed to me a fabulous sum to pay twelve men traveling to and from New York for three days' work. But the offer was sound, and the records were made. The prosperity was short-lived, however. Soon the sock was empty again. And to make matters much worse, Pace gathered from one of my letters that I wanted him out of the business. I wanted him actively in. As a result, he demanded that I buy out his interest at a time when this was impossible.

I tried to interest Lawrence Rosenfield in making an investment with us. He was a Jewish friend for whom I had arranged music since first the publishing bug bit him. But his father refused to buy out the Pace interest unless I consented that Lawrence should become president and that I should work for seventy-five dollars a month the first year with no withdrawals. We didn't get together. Even going to New York and making records for Columbia, it now developed, didn't necessarily mean Easy Street.

The outlook grew dismal. Then one Saturday night when I was playing with the band at the Colonial Country Club, eagerly hoping that our time would be extended so that we could earn an extra dollar apiece, a telephone call came for me. My brother Charles E. was at the other end of the wire. Supervising the publishing affairs, particularly when the orchestra took me away, he had formed the habit of dropping by the post office at night to see what the midnight mail from New York and Chicago had brought.

Tonight there had been news that took his breath. He was so excited he could scarcely speak. He made me understand, however, that the Victor people had sent a check for royalties on Earl Fuller's recording of *Beale Street*.

"Guess how much!"

From his tone I judged that we had done better than the usual two hundred.

"Three hundred," I suggested.

"Up."

"Four hundred."

"Higher."

"Five hundred."

Here I commenced to gulp.

"Aw, come on up. Way up," he urged.

"A thousand."

"Up again."

"Fifteen hundred."

"Up. Up."

"I *give* up."

"One thousand, eight hundred and fifty-seven," he told me.

And I had just been hoping the white folks would hire us for one more hour so that we might earn an extra dollar apiece. Well, I had just replaced the receiver when the manager came and informed me that the Club wanted us not for an extra hour but an extra three hours. Lordy! With all that money waiting, with my heart pounding for joy, I had to stay on the job and blow for another three hours. These were the longest, hardest and most miserable three hours I have ever played.

I don't think I could have stood up under the pressure had it not been for the bubbling good humor and the kidding of my musicians.

"Ole Handy! Hot dog, he's out of the barrel!"

Then during the intermissions, of course, we had to celebrate this new-found wealth. Hip flasks came out, and I was toasted royally. After the dance Beale Street seemed a thousand miles away, but eventually we reached Pee Wee's and found Charlie waiting with the check we were all dying to see.

We spent all day Sunday writing checks to cover bills payable.

"You won't be satisfied," Charlie said with a grin, "till our account is overdrawn again."

This reminded me that on the previous Saturday the bank had refused to cash a Woolworth check for me for forty dollars and I had had to go across the street to Joe Rafonti's saloon to cash it. I couldn't help trying to imagine how they would feel when they saw this big check.

The band had to keep rolling, of course, and on Monday

and Tuesday nights we were currently booked to play for a dance in a hick town in Arkansas. The hall was a hillbilly barn, and our meals while there were served in a local fish place where soap boxes doubled for chairs. But dollars were bucks, and every one counted. So Monday morning found me standing on the platform of the Union Station as usual, perfunctorily counting my men as they reported for the train. The conductor looked at his watch and raised his hand to call "all aboard." But the words caught in his throat and his mouth sprang open as he saw an automobile arriving in a cloud of dust.

My mouth sprang open too, wider than the conductor's, when I saw Charlie leap from the car waving a piece of paper and shouting:

"Give the driver a dollar and look what came from Columbia Records in the morning's mail—three thousand eight hundred and twenty-seven dollars!"

"Whew! Give him five," I said.

The liveried chauffeur pocketed the fin and drove away, smiling from ear to ear. Then my brother and I made a race for the train the conductor had been holding.

Later Charlie told me how he had managed to head us off. He knew as soon as he looked at the clock that a street car was out of the question. It couldn't get him to the station before train time. There were no cabs in sight when he reached the curb. Even if there had been one, however, he would still have been standing there. The taxicabs in Memphis didn't haul any coal, as they used to say, referring to colored fares. But Charlie was determined to bring me the news at any cost. Reckless with excitement, he watched a chauffeur drive a limousine up to a curb, step out and open the door for a white lady who went directly into the Union and Planters Bank. When she had stepped out Charlie stepped in and excitedly told the fellow: "Take me to the Union Station—drive and drive like hell." The man objected at first, but Charlie convinced him promptly that he was not dealing with a crazy Negro or a bank robber, so the chauffeur not only agreed but brought him to the station in record time.

And here I was again, trotting off to a six-dollar engagement in a particularly backward part of Arkansas after a week-end which had brought nearly six thousand dollars. It wouldn't be easy to take all the little digs that one suffered in that sort of element. It would be hard to be tactful when commanded to play two extra hours or to do this or that monkey business for the delight of our audience, but even engagements like this had been welcome when the sock was empty, and perhaps it wasn't right to scorn them now. I made up my mind to endure it cheerfully. Every dime added to what you had made the going easier and lessened the headaches.

We lived through this engagement, and Wednesday morning I returned home to find another surprise waiting. The Emerson Company had sent a check for an additional thousand dollars. What I did with this check, together with the larger ones, can best be described as wish fulfillment.

Every man who has had his downs knows only too well the petty indignities the struggler suffers daily. The underdog catches it on all sides. So often he meets those who delight to add insult to injury. That is perhaps the reason why the secret dream of telling the one who has done you dirt to go somewheres is so universal. And that, subconsciously, may have been part of the reason why I had been careful to tell Charlie to hold all remittances until my return.

Less than two weeks had passed since both of Memphis' colored banks had refused to cash my forty-dollar check, and I could still remember with embarrassment a lecture that one of their cashiers had read me about a four dollar and fifty cent check that I had presented at his window. Now I was loaded for them. I went to the window of the first bank and showed the cashier the biggest check.

"Can you cash this?" I asked.

The cashier was so elated he ran through the bank showing it to all the officers. When he returned from this jaunt, he was grinning all over himself.

"How do you want it?" he asked, putting on his Sunday manners.

"I don't want it cashed," I told him coldly. "You couldn't cash my Saturday's check for forty dollars. Why are you so willing to handle this one? Huh?"

Then I flashed before his amazed eyes the rest of the deposit, explaining that I was on my way uptown to deposit all of it in a white bank. With this I left him and went to the other colored bank. I gave them a taste of the same medicine. It did me a peck of good.

Both of the banks remonstrated with me daily for the next two weeks. Both wanted to know—in more elegant words—just how come I did them like I did. Hadn't we always been friends and hadn't they befriended me in the past? This was all true to some extent, but it was also true that they suffered from the old conception of the musician. They had no respect for him except while he was entertaining them, if then. This experience was a lasting lesson to them. From that time onward my relationship with all of the men in these organizations has been most satisfactory. After I had driven the point home, I returned and opened accounts with each bank.

That done, I sent for Pace in Atlanta, relieved him of all obligations bearing his endorsement, cleared off pressing obligations, put the business on a surer foundation and handed him a substantial sum. This, I hoped, would make it clear to him that I wanted him in, not out. But through all these operations, while the money came and went, while we struggled and regained our feet, things were working out to a change. My days in Memphis were numbered.

CHAPTER TEN

Blue Diamonds in the Rough
Polished and Mounted

THE PRIMITIVE tone or a correlated note of the blues was born in my brain when a boy. In the valley of the Tennessee River was McFarland's Bottoms, which our school overlooked. In the spring, when doors and windows were thrown open, the song of a Negro plowman half a mile away fell on my ears. This is what he sang:

All through the years this snatch of song had been ringing in my ears. Many times I wondered what was in the singer's mind. What was wrong with Cairo? Was Cairo too far south in Illinois to be "up North," or too far north to be considered "down South"?

In any event, such bits of music or snatches of song generated the motif for my blues and with an imagination stimulated by such lines as "I wouldn't live in Cairo," I wrote my lyrics.

137

If I had published at that time a composition called *The Cairo Blues*, and this simple four-bar theme had been developed into a four-page musical classic, every grown-up who had then heard that four-bar wail would now claim that Handy didn't write this number. And you would hear them say, "I heard it when I was knee-high to a grasshopper." Politely put, this would be a misstatement of fact; bluntly written, it would be a falsehood. That two-line snatch couldn't form a four-page composition any more than the two letters *i-n* could spell the word *information*. Some of the hot jazz I've heard on the radio in recent years, jazz played by sophisticated bands, is simply expanded treatment of little four-bar rhythms similar to that played by Uncle Whit Walker on his fiddle back in the days when I stood behind him, leaned over his shoulder and went to town with a pair of knitting needles. Today the cats have ten or twelve instruments to replace the single fiddle of those old sundown days, but the rhythmic themes remain much the same. Play Uncle Whit's *Little Lady Goin' to the Country* on your piano and you can imagine what the saxes and brasses would do to it today, yet it was a stomp popular in the days of the five-string banjo.

Uncle Whit's Song

Arr. by W. C. HANDY

Uncle Whit had a tune called *Sail Away, Ladies*. To the same tune my wife and her school chums patted, danced and sang *Oh, di-di-de-O*. Likewise, Cab Calloway's *Hi-de-ho* is an evolution from music that Negroes made with their mouths, hands and feet in the days when no instruments were available, naked rhythm replacing musical strains.

As a water boy at the rock quarry near Muscle Shoals, I heard steel drivers singing:

> Oh, baby, 'member las' winter?
> Wasn't it cold-hunh?
> Wasn't it cold-hunh?

There the *hunh* was just a sort of musical grunt the workers made when striking with a hammer, tugging on a line or lifting a dead weight that required concerted action, but the seeds of modern, down-to-earth "jive" were in that grunt.

Colored laborers sing about *John Henry* all over this nation —John Henry the steel-driving man who died with a hammer in his hand. There are many legends about this mythical giant and many tunes for the words. My *John Henry* is a song of three distinct strains, two of which are pure composition, the third the simple melody I heard in the rock quarry when I was a kid. Even that folk passage, however, is embellished by my harmonization and rhythm.

In the McNabb furnace at Florence I belonged to the "shovel brigade." We worked twelve hours a day and eighteen hours to change shifts. When, after trotting for hours with the heavy coke or iron buggies, we were lucky enough to catch a "daddy," and had to wait till the overfilled furnace digested its ore, we would pass the time by making music. That is to say, we beat the shovels against the iron buggies, withdrawing or thrusting forward the metal part at the point of contact to alter the tone. The technique by which this shovel music was produced was similar to that used in playing musical saws. With a dozen men participating, the effect was sometimes remarkable. We would have stopped almost any Broadway show had there been a way to bring our brigade before the footlights. Even then, however, we got a monstrous kick out of such carrying on. It was better to us than the music of a martial drum corps, and our rhythms were far more complicated.

The evolution of blues lyrics is no less quaint. Give a Negro any incident, and he will make you a song about it—if he feels bad enough. At the pipe works at Bessemer, for example, back in '92 and '93, the husky duskies had one that went like this:

> Here comes Alius Brown, baby,
> Ridin' after me,
> Ridin' after me, baby
> Ridin' after me.
> Here comes Alius Brown
> Ridin' after me;
> I'm goin' back to 'Birn-in-ham.' *

In other parts of the country I found other words being sung to the same simple melody.

> Done laid aroun' an' fooled aroun'
> Till summer's almos' gone.
> Summer's almos' gone, baby,
> Summer's almos' gone.
>
> Done laid aroun' an' fooled aroun'
> Till summer's almos' gone
> Done laid aroun' dis town too long.

Alius Brown was, of course, the high sheriff of Jefferson County, but his claim to distinction was that he rode a remarkable white horse. The beast was so well trained, as the story went around Birmingham, that its owner never had to

* Meaning: Birmingham.

shoot at a fleeing Negro. Instead, he simply got down and let
the horse at the fugitive. The marvelous animal would set out
after the luckless individual like a hound dog after a rabbit.
Overtaking his victim, he would catch the Negro's arm in his
teeth and thus return the offender to Alius Brown. Naturally
that was worth a song in any pipe works. Years later I resur-
rected the melody and used it as a refrain in the *Harlem Blues*.
This piece, like my *John Henry Blues*, contained three strains
in all, and the other two were pure composition.

I got part of the basic material for another blues from a
levee song I picked up at Henderson, Kentucky:

> Got my dungeon loaded
> Bound to blow you down
> Got my dungeon loaded
> Bound to blow you down.
>
> Got my dungeon loaded
> Bound to blow you down;
> I just got back
> From Wheeling today.

> Oh partner, see can't you make it in the wind,
> Oh partner, see can't you make it in the wind,
> Oh partner, see can't you make it in the wind—
> I just got back from Wheeling today.

The "dungeon" referred to is a pistol. Wheeling was the location of the prison in West Virginia. Released prisoners were
in the habit of drifting down the river to levee towns like
Henderson. And the "Can't you make it in the wind" was
just a friendly tip to the sweet papa who happened to
be shining around the absentee prisoner's gal at the moment.

This song had dozens of verses. I used the melody in one of
the three strains in *Sundown Blues*. Instead of the original
words, I wrote:

I put ashes in my sweet papa's bed
So that he can't slip out.
Hoodoo in his bread,
Goofer dust all about—
I'll fix him!
Conjuration is in his socks and shoes
Tomorrow he'll have those mean Sundown Blues.[5]

While sleeping on the cobblestones in St. Louis ('92), I heard shabby guitarists picking out a tune called *East St. Louis*. It had numerous one-line verses and they would sing it all night.

> I walked all the way from old East St. Louis,
> And I didn't have but one po' measly dime.

That one line was an entire stanza. The impression made upon me by hearing this phrase and by the tonality of these men's singing may well have contributed to my writing the *St. Louis Blues*, but it should be clear by now that my blues are built around or suggested by, rather than constructed of, the snatches, phrases, cries and idioms such as I have illustrated.

The three-line structure I employed in my lyric was suggested by a song I heard Phil Jones sing in Evansville during my sojourn there.

> Gwine take morphine and die, Lawd,
> Gwine take morphine and die, Lawd,
> Gwine take morphine and die.
>
> Ain't got no friend nowhere, Lawd,
> Ain't got no friend nowhere, Lawd,
> Ain't got no friend nowhere.
>
> Got no more home than a dog, Lawd,
> Got no more home than a dog, Lawd,
> Got no more home than a dog.

[5] From *Sundown Blues*, copyright, 1926, by W. C. Handy. Published by Handy Brothers Music Co., Inc., New York.

Phil Jones called the song *Got No More Home Than a Dog*.
It was a blues, but the word formed no part of its title. What
we now call blues, to the folk musicians meant a *kind* of song;
individually they bore no such designation. They were known
by simple titles like *Stack O'Lee, Brady, Frankie and Johnnie,
John Henry, Stavin' Chain, Lost John, Joe Turner*, and the
like.

While I took the three-line stanza as a model for my lyric,
I found its repetition too monotonous. I figured it would have
taken too long to tell my story if I had repeated every thought
three times. Consequently I adopted the style of making a
statement, repeating the statement in the second line, and then
telling in the third line why the statement was made. Thus I
said in *St. Louis Blues*:

> I hate to see de eve'-nin sun go down,
> Hate to see de eve'-nin' sun go down,
> 'Cause my baby, he done lef' dis town.

> Feelin' tomorrow lak Ah feel today,
> Feel tomorrow lak Ah feel today,
> I'll pack my trunk and make ma get-away.

To vary the pattern still further, and to avoid monotony in
the music, I used a four-line unit in the next part of the lyric.

> Saint Louis woman wid her diamon' rings
> Pulls dat man roun' by her apron strings.
> 'Twant for powder an' for store-bought hair
> De man I love would not gone nowhere.[6]

Here, as in most of my other blues, three distinct musical
strains are carried as a means of avoiding the monotony that
always resulted in the three-line folk blues.

The question of language was a very real problem at the
time I wrote *St. Louis Blues*. Negro intellectuals were turning

[6] From *St. Louis Blues*, copyright, 1914, by W. C. Handy. Published by
Handy Brothers Music Co., Inc., New York.

from dialect in poetry as employed by Paul Lawrence Dunbar. I couldn't follow them, for I felt then, as I feel now, that certain words of Negro dialect are more musical and more expressive than pure English. Take the expression "Gonna walk all over God's Heaven." When Negro singers say "Heab'm" with their large nasal cavities serving as resonators and top it off by prolonging the *m*, they produce an effect that it is impossible for any other singers to match. Imagine sacrificing this pure magic for the sake of a properly enunciated "Heaven"!

Once I borrowed another composer's tune, but I did it openly. I had been commissioned down in Memphis to write the score to Arthur Zellner's musical comedy *Beloocher of Beloochistan*. The uproarious part of the business was that I was not allowed in the theatre to hear it. A white musician expressed doubt of my ability to write or even read music. I coldly, but politely, suggested to him that if he would name a classical melody, I would promptly give it a Negro setting, both words and music. He said: "See what you can do with Schubert's *Serenade*."

My answer was a song called *Shoeboot's Serenade* in which I used two bars of Schubert's *Serenade* as a motif. The words went like this.

SHOEBOOT'S SERENADE [7]

Shoeboot Reader was the leader
Of a colored band.
Music sweet and grand
How he sang and played!
One summer night, in southern moonlight
'Neath a vine-clad window
He to his Malinda
Sang this Serenade.

I woke up this morning with the Blues all 'round my bed
Thinking about what you, my baby, said.

[7] Copyright, 1915, by W. C. Handy. Published by Handy Brothers Music Co., Inc., New York.

Do say the word and give my poor heart ease,
The Blues ain't nothing but a fatal heart disease;
I'm going to leave this town just to wear you off my mind;
Can't sleep for dreaming, can't laugh for crying.
So in the moonlight, Shoeboot played
This little Serenade.

Under the window, Shoeboot took 'Linda
For his wedded wife,
Tied the knot for life,
Claimed her for his own.
Just a few pennies, twin pickaninnies,
Work scarce, just eats one meal a day,
Sad at heart, he tries to play on his old trombone:
"I woke up this morning with the Blues all 'round my bed."

Goin' to See My Sarah is a song that I did simply pick up and put down, but nevertheless introduced and preserved. What I did was to make a voice and piano arrangement and include the number—*as* a folk song—in my anthology *Blues*. In my memory the song goes back to the Henderson days when it was a favorite with roustabouts and miners from the coal-mining towns of Sebree and Earlington. No place else have I heard the song, but I felt that it was worth preserving. From my score Hall Johnson has made a choral arrangement for use in his concerts. The Southernaires have also used my printed arrangement in their broadcasts. The point is that the song is not an original composition of mine and does not belong in a category with *St. Louis Blues*.

Still another story is *Joe Turner Blues*. Here you get folklore with a bang. It goes back to Joe Turney (also called Turner), brother of Pete Turney, one-time governor of Tennessee. Joe had the responsibility of taking Negro prisoners from Memphis to the penitentiary at Nashville. Sometimes he took them to the "farms" along the Mississippi. Their crimes, when indeed there were any crimes, were usually very minor, the object of the arrests being to provide needed labor for spots along the river. As usual, the method was to set a stoolpigeon where he could start a game of craps. The bones would roll blissfully till the required number of laborers had been drawn into the circle. At that point the law would fall upon the poor devils, arrest as many as were needed for work, try them for gambling in a kangaroo court and then turn the culprits over to Joe Turney. That night, perhaps, there would be weeping and wailing among the dusky belles. If one of them chanced to ask a neighbor what had become of the sweet good man, she was likely to receive the pat reply, "They tell me Joe Turner's come and gone."

Repeat this line three times and you get what I've called folk blues. Living in a world of such amazing cruelty, bewildered by the doings of such men as Joe Turney, this simple people either sang or played whatever came into their minds.

> He come wid forty links of chain,
>   Oh Lawdy!
> Come wid forty links of chain,
>   Oh Lawdy!
> Got my man and gone.

Joe Turney had a way of handcuffing eighty prisoners to the forty links of chain, and from this situation grew many kinds of verses, all fitting the same musical mold. In Kentucky they called it *Goin' Down The River 'Fore Long*. There it was a steamboat song, but for tune it was *Joe Turner* right on. In Georgia you heard the same melody when they sang *Goin' Down That Long Lonesome Road*. You heard it all over the South, for that matter, but wherever it was sung the words dealt with a local situation.

Following my frequent custom of using a snatch of folk melody in one out of two or three strains of an otherwise original song, I wrote the *Joe Turner Blues* and adapted the twelve bars of old *Joe Turner* as one of its themes. Here Joe Turner himself was no longer the long-chain man; he was the masculine victim of unrequited love just as the singer in *St. Louis Blues* was the feminine, and he sang sadly and yet jauntily such thoughts as:

> You'll never miss the water
> Till your well runs dry;
> Till your well runs dry.
> You'll never miss Joe Turner
> Till he says goodbye.
> Sweet babe, I'm goin' to leave you
> An' the time ain't long.
> If you don't believe I'm leaving,
> Count the days I'm gone.[8]

It was difficult to get *Joe Turner* recorded. I came to New York for that purpose and while walking down Broadway I met my old friend Wilbur Sweatman—a killer-diller and jazz pioneer. He invited me home with him, and his wife Nettie prepared a lovely dinner. While dining she turned on the phonograph and lo and behold it played *Joe Turner Blues* which Sweatman had recorded not only on the Pathe but the Emerson records also.

Loveless Love is another of my songs of which one part has an easily traceable folk ancestry. It was based on the *Careless Love* melody that I had played first in Bessemer in 1892 and that had since become popular all over the South. In Henderson I was told that the words of *Careless Love* were based on a tragedy in a local family, and one night a gentleman of that city's tobacco-planter aristocracy requested our band to play and sing this folk melody, using the following words:

> You see what Careless Love has done,
> You see what Careless Love has done
> You see what Careless Love has done,
> It killed the Governor's only son.

[8] From *Joe Turner Blues*, copyright 1915 by Pace & Handy Music Co., copyright assigned to Richmond-Robbins, Inc., Robbins Music Corporation, successors. Used by permission of the copyright owners.

We did our best with these lines and then went into the second stanza:

> Poor Archie didn't mean no harm,
> Poor Archie didn't mean no harm,
> Poor Archie didn't mean no harm—

But there the song ended. The police stepped in and stopped us. The song, they said, was a reflection on two prominent families. *Careless Love* had too beautiful a melody to be lost or neglected, however, and I was determined to preserve it.

For years I had groped for an idea for a modern setting. It came on the corner of 45th Street and Broadway at noon when businessmen had stopped to listen to a minister sent by the Federation of Churches. He was bemoaning substitution and advising them to give value received. He said that he had attended a banquet given by the New England Clothing Manufacturers, wearing a twenty-five-year-old broadcloth full dress suit. The president admired the quality. He told the president he was going to buy a new one just like it since it was an old one. "My friend," said the president, "the King of England could not find an honest yard of broadcloth in his whole Empire." The Minister thundered, "You are adulterating everything." I said to myself, "Even love."

Having created a vogue for *Careless Love*, which John Niles calls *Kelly's Love* in his book of folk songs, I proposed to incorporate it in a new song with the verse in the three-line blues form.

That week I went to Chicago, and while there I sat in Brownlee's barber shop and wrote *Loveless Love*, beginning with "Love is like a gold brick in a bunko game." There I wrote the music and made an orchestration which I took next door to Erskin Tate in the Vendome Theatre. His orchestra played it over, and it sounded all right. A copy was immediately sent to the printers.

Without waiting to receive a printed copy, however, I

taught *Loveless Love* to Alberta Hunter, and she sang it at the Dreamland cabaret. It made a bull's-eye. Before Alberta reached my table on the night she introduced the song, her tips amounted to sixty-seven dollars. A moment later I saw another lady give her twelve dollars for "just one more chorus." I knew then and there that we had something on our hands and the later history of the song bore this out.

Bracketed with *Loveless Love* should be the story of another blues, completed on that same Chicago trip. This one went back to my childhood for its title. My mother had often told me that because of the Bible story of Abraham, Sarah, and Sarah's handmaiden Hagar, Negroes often spoke of themselves as Aunt Hagar's Children. With this in mind I christened my new composition *Aunt Hagar's Children.*

I had heard a washerwoman singing one cold night as she was taking her husband's frozen garments from the clothesline. In a moanful voice and unusual tonality she sang these words: "Yo' clothes looks lonesome hangin' on de line." That night I tried to reproduce this tonality on my violin and finally made a piano score with three distinct melodies. Therefore, that one line was the inspiration for one of my most popular works. Originally it was published to be played in the slow tempo of *Träumerei*. A song without words.

The well of sorrow from which Negro music is drawn is also a well of mystery. It's strange how the blues creep over you. I suspect that Stephen Foster owed something to this well, this mystery, this sorrow. *My Old Kentucky Home* makes you think so, at any rate. Something there suggests a close acquaintance with my people—Aunt Hagar's Children.

While I was experiencing the greatest difficulties in establishing my Memphis band, I complained to my Aunt Matt Jordan bitterly. I told her that the other bands made mistakes in playing and how perfect ours was. She said, "Honey, white folks like to hear colored folks make some mistakes." In this one remark can be hidden the source or secret of jazz.

I have taught beginners who taught themselves wrong on the clarinet and cornet. One on the clarinet had fingering that had never been written into diagrams. These notes he made by false fingering and incorrect lipping. He taught me something. This technique was made use of by musicians who liked to clown and finally a new technique was acquired by outstanding composers and instrumentalists. Theory once had it that no instruments other than the violin family and slide trombone family are capable of perfect legato or glissando. Had it not been for the mistakes of the ignorant and illiterate, Gershwin would not have been able to write a two-octave chromatic glissando clarinet passage for his *Rhapsody in Blue*. Edison made a mistake and discovered the electric light. Columbus made a mistake and discovered America. Theory made a mistake and had to be rewritten. Perfect glissandos now are made on clarinet, sax and trumpets.

In Memphis in the early summer evenings a blind woman would stand on the corner and sing in a weird voice, "Ah, Somebody's Wrong About Dis Bible." Something always compelled me to stop and listen to her while my band men would remind me that I would be late on the job. I remember one saying, "You are always standing around listening to people singing." At the time I didn't know why I was so drawn to this melody. The melody lingered with me. It was founded on two notes. Years later I set this to music. In New York I was one of a number of musicians who listened to Dr. Sigmund Spaeth in a discussion of the three-tone, four-tone and five-tone scale. This was illuminating. I sang for him the two-note melody that had lingered with me and it was a revelation to the "tune detective"—a two-tone scale.

There are those who wish me to approach the subject of blues as though this type of music should be shrouded in mystery. Thousands have heard the material which went into the making of the blues just as my band men heard the two-tone song, but they didn't write it down. I formed the habit of writing down ideas from watching my father. If he loaned someone a hoe or any other implement, he put it on the books as if it were money. When somebody was born and when somebody died he wrote it down.

Many articles and books have been written in an effort to change the locale of the blues from Memphis to New Orleans. Unfortunately, New Orleans musicians failed to write it down before my time.

In company with a poet and a sculptor in Greenwich Village, I heard footsteps behind us as we walked. They were rhythmical, so musical that I turned to see what the girl looked like. She was beautiful. As she turned the corner we all watched until she was lost in the crowd. The sculptor *saw something*, the poet *felt something*, and I *heard something*, but I could not write it down.

At the Monarch

The following style of piano playing, by Benny French and Sonny Butts at the Monarch on Beale Street, was my source of inspiration for the treatment given the printed piano copies of *Beale Street Blues, Yellow Dog Blues,* and a few others. The style is theirs; the tune is mine. (See, Foreword, p. xi.)

By W. C. HANDY

(picks up cigaret with right hand)

Excerpt from

Yellow Dog Blues

As it would have been notated before the advent of the Blues; when common simplicity was believed to make for larger copy sales.

By W. C. HANDY

Copyright, 1914, by W. C. Handy
(as "Yellow Dog Rag")
Published by Handy Brothers Music Co., Inc., New York

Yellow Dog Blues

"He's gone where the Southern cross' the Dog"

By W. C. HANDY

(Verse of the original edition)

etc.,

Beale Street Blues

The melody of the verse, carried by the left hand shows further influence of the Monarch's pianist. "Eight to the bar" ("boogie-woogie") pre-influence with jazz interpolations are shown in the right hand.

By W. C. HANDY

Excerpt from
Hesitating Blues

A natural clarinet break appears in measures seven and eight.

By W. C. HANDY

CHAPTER ELEVEN

Mother

HARRY T. BURLEIGH once said that "the blues and spirituals are first cousins." The spirituals are a peculiar product of the Negro. Their natural means of expression is the voice of the American Negro, and no reed, string or horn can do them justice. No other people can sing them with complete success, not even Negroes other than those born in the United States. To me these songs have always been irresistible. In our Florence Methodist church they were sung only moderately well —when they were used at all. The Methodists went in for hymns sung with dignity and when they installed an organ the church came near splitting. The Baptists went in for foot-patting and rhythmical spirituals, body-swaying long meters.

The Baptists had no organ in their church and no choir. They didn't need any. The lusty singers sat in the amen corner and raised the songs, raised them as they were intended to be raised, if I'm any judge. None of the dressed-up arrangements one sometimes hears on the concert stage or on the radio for them. They knew a better way. Theirs was pure rhythm. While critics like to describe their numbers as shouting songs, rhythm was their basic element. And rhythm was the thing that drew me and other members of our home town quartet to attend the Baptist services in much the same spirit, I imagine, as the young jitterbugs of today flock to hear their favorite swing bands.

Rhythm got into my blood early. My mother was a "shouting Methodist." But I'd say it was the way the Reverend Cordie White sang *Train's A-Comin'* that set the tom-toms beating in my blood. Then when Brother Tobe Rice chanted *Tell All the World, John,* and Uncle Job Kirkman raised *The Bridegroom Has Done Come,* my course was fixed. It may actually be that the blues owe as much to this source of inspiration as to any other. For me a reverence attaches to those old religious songs, and it would be as inappropriate for anyone to adapt them to the requirements of the ballroom and the cabaret as it would be to make the same use of *Eli Eli.*

While the blues were becoming a part of me, I saw myself as a child again, a child looking into the watery eyes of an old deacon.

"You's old enough to think 'bout yo' dyin' days, son," he had said.

The remark troubled me, and at the next revival meeting I took my place with the mourners on the bench to "get religion." The preacher preached and the singers sang. I listened solemnly, thinking all the while of dark dying days and trying my best to see visions of milk-white horses galloping down a cloudy highway.

One by one the other seekers found the pearl of great price. One by one they "came through" with a burst of uncontrollable happiness, came through leaping and whirling and shouting "Glory." Others remained "under conviction," as the preacher described it, quaking with sobs but failing to touch off the vital spark. To me nothing happened. I didn't get happy, and the thought of my dying days troubled me more than ever.

I took my trouble home, and my mother prayed for me. My father, preacher though he was, showed surprising sympathy. "It's not *getting* religion, sonny; it's *doing* religion that counts." These words, coming from him, helped a great deal. Maybe there was still hope for me in my dying days.

A few weeks later a quaint crowd of Negroes passed in front of our house bound for Africa. They had heard how Bishop H. McNeal Turner was advocating a return to Africa as a solution for the problems of the Negro. In their hope and zeal they had left their homes in the snow with little more for their journey than the clothes on their backs. One small boy among them was traveling barefoot. Altogether they were a sorrowful, lost-looking procession, and my father must have read the hurt expression on my face as he and I watched them from our doorway.

"Don't you want to give that boy your shoes and stockings?" he asked suddenly.

"Yes," I told him. "I'd like to."

My father immediately called to the group, asking them to wait for the gift. The change was made, and the young stranger seemed very happy about it. Then the weary travelers resumed their wintry journey. Presently it occurred to me that this was the sort of thing my father had in mind when he said that *doing* religion was more important than *getting* religion. The idea went home. No other religion seemed important after that. In spite of morning and evening prayers, scriptures and hymns, this was the part of my father's Christian teaching that stuck. I am impressed with the fact that as a preacher he had been many jumps ahead of his time. In his preaching he had expounded scriptures quietly and sensibly in a day when bellowing and stomping and frothing at the mouth were the rule among colored preachers. While many of his contemporaries had worn enormous and absurd gold watch chains around their necks, paced the platform like caged beasts and thundered louder than lions, he had remained calm, dressed simply. Maybe this had been the reason why he never landed one of the so-called "big" charges. However that may have been, he had been earnest and sincere. His

12

words had never failed to strike home. To this day it is impossible for me to forget his prayers.

And while my own attempt to get religion on the mourner's bench had failed, it now occurred to me that where I was concerned my preacher father had succeeded better than he had imagined. As evidence of the impression he had left on my mind I had only to recall a day in Michigan with the minstrel outfit. Certain showmen sometimes argued that when a man dies that is the end—that no more account is taken of such an event than of a swatted fly or mashed bug. They lived in a world of aggressive skepticism. They wore buttons bearing the slogan *Reason vs. Superstition.* Well, some of our boys, contrary to their pious upbringing, had become disciples and on that day in Michigan they had expressed their disillusionment with considerable heat. And without a second thought I had flung myself into the argument as defender of the faith that I had so often heard my father say needs no defense.

My companions had ridiculed me and I had left them in the train parked on a siding near Calumet and walked to the outskirts of the town to be alone. I could remember passing a white church and being inclined to enter, but I had changed my mind and turned away at the door. Instead, I had continued to walk till I came to a deep gash in the earth, a hole marking the entrance to a copper mine. I had ventured inside and found the place deserted. Climbing down one ladder and then another and another, I reached the bottom of the mine and walked until I was entirely shut out from God's sunlight. There amid the veins of copper, I had turned things over in my mind.

Snatches of remembered scripture had come to my lips. I had repeated the 23rd Psalm. Hymns and spirituals had welled in my throat. *Give me that old-time Religion. There are depths of love that I cannot know.* Tears had come to my eyes so that I could almost have cried "Glory." I had climbed out of the mine with a deep feeling of satisfaction. Yes, my father had his victory at last.

It was impossible to think of my father then without at the same time recalling my mother. The youngest of six Brewer children, she had been called Babe by the family. To no one else, however, had she answered to the nickname. And she had tolerated no name other than William for me. In that attitude I saw mirrored an essential part of her character. Though shy and gentle by nature, she could and did stand her ground when her pride was threatened.

There was the time, for example, when a well-known white lady of Florence stopped me on my way home from school and directed me to deliver a number of baskets of vegetables to her friends and customers. At her command I made several trips, but when the errands showed signs of drawing out all afternoon, I suddenly called a halt and refused to make more deliveries, explaining that I was hungry. Furthermore, my mother would be expecting me at home. The lady insisted on my making another delivery, however; and when I yielded, she rewarded me with a buttered biscuit.

There was anxiety on my mother's face when I reached home, and when I explained my delay, this expression changed to one of indignation. Without comment she reached for her bonnet, and tied it with a snap.

"William, you come with me."

Tired and puzzled, I followed her to the home of the lady who had commandeered my services. Without mincing words my mother spoke her mind. Never again was I to be sent on errands without her permission. "As for the biscuit," she added emphatically, "he has better at home."

That last remark, needless to say, could not be denied. My mother was an accomplished cook. Curiously, however, as so often is the case when things like this happen down home, the lady in question had meant no harm. While my mother spoke, tears appeared in the other's eyes, tears of astonishment and honest regret. It had never dawned on her that her action would be interpreted as an unkind deed. Perhaps it had never before occurred to her that a small colored boy could feel tired or hungry, or that his mother could be anxious about his return from school. And as to the aspersion upon her biscuit —well, she had given me a dime to augment it. Presently I saw the dawn of understanding. The two women parted without rancor. I could recall in my gloom that several years later I enjoyed a very good dinner at the home of that same prominent lady. At least once I waited on her table. And both with my mother's hearty consent.

To make the experience even more remarkable, the time came when this same member of Florence's first families entertained at dinner a group of Negro clergymen of the A. M. E. Church without making the slightest concession to the old Southern bugaboo of social equality.

My mother deserves credit for setting me straight one Sunday morning. My father had borrowed Captain Andrew Brown's horse and buggy and we were driving out to Hopewell Church. We had untold kin people out that way— the Wilsons, the Claybornes, the Brewers, all representing branches of my mother's family, and the church itself had been built by Grandpa Handy. We were going out to worship with our country cousins in their own church that Sunday morning, and I was richly dressed for the occasion.

My mother had made me a fluted waist, lace embroidered and carefully ironed. In addition to this garment I sported gleaming, red-topped, brass-toed boots and a sailor suit. Despite tender years, if I must say so, I was something of a killer. Naturally I laughed at the dusky country boys we saw perched like crows on a rail as we drove past. These kids wore long shirts made of flour sacks—and nothing more.

My father explained to me that as a slave boy he had dressed in similar manner—long shirt-tails, no pants. Astonished, but also amused, I continued to laugh till my mother waved with her hand and called to the youngsters. The horse stopped, and the boys drew near timidly.

"Who is your mother, boys?"

They gave an unfamiliar name. My mother promptly turned to me and said, "William, these are your third cousins." My feathers had fallen. My kinfolks! Wasn't there something about a chain being no stronger than its weakest link? Well, I think I caught the idea.

I recalled that my mother had never opposed my leaving home to work or venture into the world. It may have been that she found her time fully taken up by my baby brother. But it was more likely that she had simply seen a brighter future for me in the world beyond the horizon. The same had been true of her attitude toward my father. Frequently she had chided him for becoming rooted to one spot. The world is big. Why not transfer to another state? My father, as I recalled, hadn't been able to see the point. Grandma Thumuthis needed him. The poor church people of Alabama needed him. He couldn't leave.

When finally I did strike out on my own, I carried with me the strange feeling that my mother was with me. In far places I fancied that I saw her face before me. At every opportunity I hurried home for a holiday. I regularly sent gifts to her and to my brother. And now again I could see her vividly in my mind's eye. Almost as vividly, in fact, as during the summer of '94.

That summer I had been playing an engagement on the excursion steamer *W. F. Nesbitt*. The boat operated between Evansville and Shiloh battlefield at Pittsburg Landing on the Tennessee River. At one point this brought me within fifty miles of my home in Florence. Each week during the engagement I had therefore planned to take advantage of the proximity and run home for a visit with my mother. Always, however, I had postponed the trip. Maybe next week I'd have more money and be able to take her a finer present. But next week came and passed, again and again, and finally the *Nesbitt* made the last trip of the season. This time I would certainly visit home.

During this last excursion of the season the Ohio River had become too shallow in spots for this steamer. On the bow of the *Nesbitt* stood a black rouster holding a line at the end of which was a lead sinker. Periodically he threw this sinker into the river to determine the depth of the water. Having taken the measure, he would announce in a sonorous voice the number of feet. Another boatman, standing on the upper deck, would take up the mournful chant and announce it to another near the pilot's cabin so that it could be heard within. I could still hear the blue notes of that melancholy antiphony of Negro boatmen:

"Three feet, mark twain!"

"Quarter-less twain," the voice on the forward upper deck had repeated. "Quarter-less twain."

Then faintly from the pilot's cabin had come the final echo, "Quarter-less twain."

Then the pilot's bells had rung, bells signalling the engineer.

Thus the last excursion of the season had been made, but still I had not made the visit home. Back in Henderson, where I had been making my headquarters that year, I found a telegram which should have been relayed to Louisville. "Come at once if you want to see your mother alive." Already days had passed before the message arrived. The words blurred before me as I re-read the wire.

Reaching Florence, I met the crowd returning from the cemetery. I had arrived too late. I learned, however, that my mother had been buried from the small church my father pastored, a church which my own hands had helped build. The funeral had been a big one. The crowd had overflowed the meeting place. During the service the floor of the church had given way under the unusual strain. In much the same

manner something had given way in my heart. Church bells
were tolling when I reached the scene. Curiously I had not
thought of them as church bells. In fancy they had seemed
to be the pilot's bells ringing on board the *Nesbitt*. And my
heart had echoed the mournful voices of Negro boatmen
sounding shallow waters "quarter-less twain." The first cry
had died away. A moment later it had come again as it had
been repeated from the upper deck:

> Quarter-less twain,
> Three feet-six feet
> Mark twain . . . Quarter-less twain.

A dark tide of memories, once started, cannot easily be
stemmed. My own youth came before me like a reflection in
a well. Now again I had a sense of desolation and loss, just
as I had had after my mother's death. The warm memory of
rose-lipped girls did no more to dispel it now than their living presence had done back in the minstrel days. This was
hard to explain, for there had been such exciting girls in those
days.

The one in Charles City, Iowa, for example. She had grown
up in a white community, and I had discovered with amazed
surprise that the white gentlemen there tipped their hats to
her. This was thoroughly astonishing to a colored boy from
Alabama. Also surprising to me was the fact that she paid us
no mind, though we bowed and scraped and cut our eyes for
all we were worth. She was a lady, and we had not been introduced.

In the Far West many colored girls seemed to be "passing."
If they couldn't possibly be white, then they straightened
their hair, learned Spanish and posed as Mexicans. In some
towns we found colored fancy gals sitting exclusively for
white company. More often than not, there were no Negro
men in the whole town. In such places they had taken us in
surreptitiously, locked the doors, thrown lavish parties and

fairly smothered us in the pure joy of entertaining some of their own kind for a change.

The times had been colorful, the girls gay, the music exciting. But as I recalled the past now, there had been little color or gaiety or excitement for me after I met Elizabeth Price in Henderson. I'd been looking for such a girl, and we met in Held's Park during an Emancipation Day celebration. Then suddenly my world changed.

The courtship that followed was not a perfumed memory. After our meeting I had written letters. In due time I had popped the question and confirmed it by writing a simultaneous letter to her father. When arrangements were made for our wedding, I jumped the minstrel outfit at Fargo, North Dakota, and hurried down to Henderson. The understanding had been that I would be back in thirty days, but W. A. Mahara, fearing disorganization of the band during my absence, had shrewdly held out a bait for an earlier return. If I joined them before the thirty days were completed, he would pay my wife's transportation and hotel expenses.

Well, we were married on a lawn drenched with Kentucky moonlight on July 19, 1898. A local band and orchestra played, and there was additional music from Evansville. Gifts were heaped high, and presently there was another Elizabeth Handy. A two-week vacation followed. Then I broached the question of W. A. Mahara's offer. All expenses paid. A chance to see the country. Why, it would be a sort of extended honeymoon.

She shook her head gloomily. Show people being what they were reputed to be, she was not able to see herself traveling around with an outfit of them. Instead, she urged me to save my money and go into the grocery business in Henderson. But Henderson being what it was—a tobacco town definitely on the downgrade—I shook my head. I had seen an English firm buying up tobacco and shipping it abroad while the local factories retrenched. Naturally I wasn't impressed with pros-

pects for a new grocery store. I went back to Mahara and
sent my wife my salary.

There had come a time, of course, when she wavered somewhat in her hostility toward the show business and joined me
for brief periods. Once, I remembered, we met at Rhine-
lander, Wisconsin, and I watched with interest her reactions
to the unfamiliar customs of the North. It had surprised her,
for instance, when white women in the North solicited our
laundry, while in the South we couldn't even find colored
women who would launder the clothes of traveling Negroes.

Even the South had not been without its surprises for her,
once she ventured beyond her home town. I recalled bitterly
a time when we had gone to church in a small Dixie town.
Each of us had dropped a dollar in the collection as the plates
were passed. Our folding money had looked important surrounded by nickels and dimes and pennies, and when the
plates returned to the parson, that deft individual had pocketed the bills so fast it looked like sleight of hand. Then forthwith he had cleared his throat and made the following announcement: "There's a nigger minstrel in town, but if I hear
tell that any of you-all go, I'll bring you up on the carpet
and have you churched, 'cause show folks ain't nothin'. You
hear me? They ain't nothin'."

So the minstrel years had gone. Then there had been Memphis. We had settled down in time to celebrate the birth of
our fourth child, Florence. We had named her for the Alabama city in which I had been born, but death had written
Florence's name while she was still an infant. And again it
had been my misfortune to be away, this time, when the hour
came, playing for a military ball in Columbus, Mississippi.
Yet time had flown swiftly in Memphis. A fifth child, Elizabeth, had come to replace the absent Florence in my affec-
tions. We had moved to the cottage on Janette Street, and
there my youngest son had been born. We had named him
Wyer, after the first violinist of my orchestra. The children

had grown fast, played energetically and eaten well. In Turner's grocery store the clerk had said that whenever he saw one of them coming down the street he automatically reached for a package of grits, some beans, bacon and sugar-house molasses.

Well, anyhow, the *Memphis Blues* had been written at 246 Ayres Street, our former home, just a few doors from Turner's grocery in Greasy Plank. After buying the home on Janette Street, I published it. I had set out an orchard, planted flowers, cultivated a garden and the friendship of Harry Pace. I had set his lyrics to music, and I had felt then, as I still feel, that some of the songs that grew from this collaboration might have become hits in later years had not my name become so completely identified with blues. You can't get away from a trademark, once the goods has been stamped.

I liked very much the style of Pace's early lyrics. They were a departure from the levee songs I knew, and I was delighted to make musical settings for such verses as:

When the day begins to close and shadows flee
O'er the sunset's golden throes, I think of thee;
Lyra in the distance blinking, tries to lure me by her winking
But of thee alone I'm thinking, tenderly.
                    Mother.

CHAPTER TWELVE

From Beale Street to Broadway

THE DRAFT thinned the ranks of the old crowd at Pee Wee's. My own band was not exempted. Some of the best players were called to the colors. I hired the best musicians obtainable.

These men didn't have the spirit or pride of organization. While most of them played their instruments well enough, some lacked, for the most part, the character of the outfit they replaced. And with them the fortunes of the Handy band went from bad to worse.

One day at Pee Wee's I began singing the blues to a music professor of the old school. Handling so many men and struggling to control the local entertainment field had been no fun. Sometimes I could have wished for an easier lot. My aim had been to gain a certain measure of security for my men, and doing that had given me satisfaction. But now I began to wonder just how much they appreciated my efforts. The revamped outfit was acting strangely, whispering behind their hands.

Professor Todd, an old musician, gave me an understanding glance.

"That's just the trouble," he said suddenly. "If you're so powerful you can tell them where they are to work, they figure you may become powerful enough to tell them where they *can't* work."

The truth of the old professor's remark was not long in dawning, but where I was concerned, it was already too late to do anything about it. I was too deeply involved in the web of my own enterprises. It would be necessary to wait till the whole business choked itself in the mesh. Such a time, I felt, was not far distant.

The telephone rang and another of the musicians who received his calls at the saloon stepped from the bar to answer.

"No, we can't play for you on that date," I heard him say. There was a pause while he listened to the voice on the wire. Presently he added, "No, we can't recommend anybody but our own band."

There had been a time when I begged for a chance to fill these engagements that other musicians were forced to turn down, but they only laughed in my face. To overcome this attitude I arranged to have telephones, local and long-distance, placed in my home. There I could always be reached; and when I was not at home my wife could take the calls. In that way, I reasoned, I could build up our business on what the other fellow threw away.

The plan succeeded. I put a chattel mortgage on my household goods, got out letterheads, rented an office at 392 Beale, put in two phones there and, for a time, worked night and day booking bands—I from the office, my wife from our home. Business poured in, but the profits were not large. The commissions were only ten cents for a three-dollar job and two bits for a job up to six dollars. At that, some of the new men would quit, loaf or go hungry rather than pay the dime for bookings. Others worked steadily but never appeared to have the dime. The going was tough. Then presently it got tougher.

One day my own men got together, held a meeting, and then told me the telephones would have to come out of my

home and that my bookings must be supervised by a man
of their selection, one who would tell me what to do and
where to play. Imagine someone telling me where to play
in Memphis?

Well, I met them on their own terms and calmly invited
them to build their own organization, put in their own
phones, rent their own office, get their own advertising and
go fish for themselves. "When you do this, however," I
added, "I will get more musicians from out of town."

They backed water, every one of them. They wouldn't
take me up and they were afraid to call my hand. Instead
they continued to grumble and work.

About that time the Columbia Phonograph Company sent
me a contract to bring twelve musicians to New York to
make a dozen records as a result of Pace's previous build-up.
Quite naturally I had to leave a band of eight on the Alaskan
Roof Garden, which included G. I. Desverney, H. P. McGill
and Charlie Williamson. Other units were under the management of John W. Lewis, R. K. Eckford and M. Thornton.
Under these circumstances it was impossible for me to get
more than four who were able and willing to make the trip.
Some must have doubted my ability to advance their fares
to and from the big town, pay their expenses while there and
then pay them a large salary.

"Whew! Go way up to New York for three days work
and *dream* money? Uhn, Uh!" And that was that.

I didn't beg them. Instead, I took the next train for Chicago.

Like Memphians, Chicago musicians had never heard of a
colored band traveling to and from New York to make records. But the men who agreed to go, William King Phillips,
Ed. M. Wyer and others, belonged to my original Memphis
band. They had migrated to Chicago and now belonged to
the union (Local 208) and were threatened with from one-
hundred to five-hundred dollars fine if they left town with

me. We all joined the Chicago local to avail ourselves of the services of the men we wanted.

I had brought with me from Memphis, Edward Alexander, violin; Charles Hillman, piano; Sylvester V. Bevard, trombone; and Wilson Townes, saxophone and clarinet. To these I added four Chicago musicians: William Tyler and Darnell Howard, violinists; Charlie Harris and A. R. Poole, saxophonists. To complete the twelve I hired three from my original Memphis blues band located in Chicago, Henry Graves, cellist; Archie Walls, bass; and Jasper Taylor, xylophonist and drums. In New York, I contracted Nelson Kincaid, clarinet.

But there were hectic moments in Chicago before we got away.

Not being certain till the last minute that I could fill the New York engagement, I had kept the unsigned contracts in my briefcase. To complicate things further, a wire came from another man offering to double Columbia's offer. This meant a conference with Columbia's Chicago office. Ho-hum, did you ever get dizzy? In the midst of this whirl I neglected to secure transportation for my men. At the last minute I scrambled out of the conference, dashed to a phone and arranged for tickets. Then, hopping into an auto, I made a race to catch the New York Central express.

I arrived at the station ten minutes late. The train was still waiting. The men were bunched around the gate when I came storming up to join them. I could see that they were panicky, and there wasn't another minute to waste. We lit out together toward the Pullman. Passing the observation car, I noticed a crowd of people who had gathered there to see what was delaying this fast train. Among them was a portly dowager with several chins.

"My God," she exclaimed. "A gang of niggers!"

In the car I learned that the train had been in motion when a station master came running out, called to the conductor, and had it stopped. In the meantime it had taken tall talking and persuading by my brother Charlie to keep one of our high-strung Chicago fiddlers from selling out and going back to the South Side. But Charlie assured him that I was not above playing the *Hazards of Helen,* if need be, taking an automobile and beating the express to the crossing before I'd leave the men stranded. The musicians had waited to find out whether or not it was true, I suppose.

In New York our troubles continued. The new men had not been rehearsed. This would have been no problem with my old band, but with the new men we were compelled to ask a postponement for the purpose of rehearsing.

In the meantime I had occasion to recall my first experience with a talking machine. That had been back in Helena, Montana, in 1897. I had made a record with my minstrel band on an old cylinder machine. Funny contraption, that old affair. To hear the recording you had to place two rubber tubes in your ears. Each record began with a spoken announcement much like the radio announcer's lines today. Before we played, the announcer spoke into a horn and said, "You will now hear *Cotton Blossoms* as played by Mahara's Minstrel Band on Edison records." After playing our number, each one of us was permitted to put the rubber tubes in his ears and thus listen to ourselves. Other music lovers who wished to hear the record had to pay five cents for the privilege.

During the twenty years that had intervened since that experience the art and science of recording had passed through a remarkable evolution. Hardly greater, however, than the stages of change through which it has passed in the twenty odd years that have elapsed since Columbia brought us to New York to make records in their little airtight studios during my Beale Street days.

Our clarinetist sat in the corner on a six-foot stool and played into a megaphone near the ceiling. There were stools of varying heights for the other players. The three violinists stood directly in front of the recording apparatus and played into megaphones there. The saxophonists were seated on the side and played into their own megaphones. Cornet and trombone played into one in the rear. The cellist occupied another corner and another megaphone. But the poor drummer was a dead goose where the record was concerned. While they played as hard as ever in life, the drums and basses could not be recorded in those days. All megaphones emptied into one recording horn.

In these quaint positions we did *Old Miss, Snakey Blues, Hooking Cow Blues, Livery Stable Blues, Preparedness Blues, The Old Town Pump, Jazz Dance, Moonlight Blues* (waltz), *It's a Mean Job, Drafting Blues, Fuzzy Wuzzy Rag,* and *Sweet Child,* introducing *Pallet on the Floor.* Jasper Taylor recorded two of these on his xylophone.

To my way of thinking the records were not up to scratch. Our band was capable of better work, but the Columbia people seemed satisfied. They immediately paid us a good part of our money, not even waiting for test pressings to be made. To cap it off, they asked for a picture of our group. But, odd as it may seem, we had none.

Sitting for a picture had been one thing in which I'd never been able to interest the band back in Memphis. Only a few individual pictures of the members are now available. When the question of photographs arose, they always shrugged their shoulders and began to think of more immediately pressing problems. Thus a band that played the first published blues and thereby earned a little niche in the annals of American music never had its picture taken.

Columbia, however, made their own drawings of Handy's Band and launched an extensive campaign in all their shops throughout the United States, displaying posters that featured the drawings. A *Handy Week* was announced everywhere to stimulate the sale of these new records. At home my local stock soared on a bull market, but even this boom failed to down the discontent that had sprung up among the men of the band.

The Colored Fair Association contracted with me for a uniformed band and orchestra. Those men who favored the proposition stood for measurement. For those opposed I guessed their measurements, and some swelled heads settled for surprisingly small caps. When the uniforms were delivered, some of the men cut the name of Handy from their caps and inserted another name.

At that time our band was also playing eight trips a week on the *Pattona*. I had to be present on Sundays for whites and Mondays for colored. The number two band went to Captain Young and told him that they had deserted me and that I would therefore be unable to fill the engagements. They had, they said, refused to work under my direction. The captain listened, but said nothing on his own part. As soon as they were gone, he phoned me.

"Keep this under your hat," he confided. Then he explained what had happened and added, "Just bring your cornet and a good piano player. I'll let the men come aboard with their instruments. Then I'll call them before me in your presence and tell them that if they would quit you like that, they would quit me. Then I'll order them off the boat."

That sort of thing continued, but the end was not yet. We worried along together and weathered a surprising number of tempests. Pace planned and advertised a second concert in Atlanta. About the same time the University of North Carolina engaged us for three days at Chapel Hill. Each of these engagements came off well and proved to be financially successful. Other calls came, and while we were in North Carolina, Atlanta wired for us to play at the Piedmont Exposition for colored folks.

We accepted and returned to lead a gala parade of beautiful floats down streets bright with golden sunshine. The air

13

was perfumed with roses. Spectators leaned out of windows. Others lined the streets. But a bad spirit still prevailed in the band. It smoldered during the early stages of the parade, and by the time we reached the residential section the devil broke loose and got out of control.

Well, it had been a long time coming to a head, and I can't say that it was a surprise, but it does seem odd that the cork had to pop during the parade. Yet that is exactly what happened. As we rode on a float two of my men fought on the way to the Exposition grounds. The band divided into factions, attempting to keep one from cutting or shooting the other. This rowdy spectacle put me in a most embarrassing position. I endured it by the hardest, but when we reached the Exposition, I called a policeman and kept him with the band throughout the remainder of the engagement.

The presence of the policeman made it possible for us to discharge our obligation, but nothing was settled. The next day I walked up Auburn Avenue and visited the spacious offices of the Standard Life Insurance Company. Occupying several floors of a building, this was probably the biggest company of its kind operated for and by Negroes at the time. Its president was Heman Perry; its secretary-treasurer, my partner Harry H. Pace to whom I told what had transpired.

Later, we looked down on Auburn Avenue and saw the band boys still huffing and puffing.

"What's the trouble with them?" Pace asked.

"I signed for a return engagement at Chapel Hill. They want me to cancel it."

"Why are they so hot to get back to Memphis?"

"Beale Street. Good times. I don't know of anything else."

Pace became thoughtful.

"Not like the members of the original band, are they?"

I shook my head ruefully.

"They play the same instruments but they're not the same men."

There was another pause, then Pace said, "You know, W. C., I think I'd let them have it their way if I were you. I'd cancel the engagement."

His answer did not displease me, sick and tired as I was of the wrangling, but it called up a mood of deepest indigo.

"Cancel the engagement? I have never cancelled an engagement in my life."

"I'd cancel it."

"Then what?"

"Go to New York and open up our publishing business there."

"Yes, but I've moved the business to Chicago already. My family is even there."

"Then, move them to New York," Pace said.

On the curbstone below there was still no peace among the boys of the band. I stood at the window with bowed head, trying hard to reach a decision. Then suddenly I looked up and began to see shadows in the sun.

CHAPTER THIRTEEN

"Trouble, Trouble, I've Had It All My Days!"

CONCERNING one of these shadows I had written Pace a few months earlier. One morning, while passing the square on Beale Street that now bears my name, I noticed a crowd of Negroes gathered around a skull. The day before, that skull had belonged to a pleasant, easy-going young fellow named Tom Smith. Now it was severed from his body. The eyes had been burned out with red-hot irons. A rural mob, not satisfied with burning his body, had brought the skull back to town and tossed it into a crowd of Negroes to humiliate and intimidate them.

Stunned, deeply resentful, I had walked slowly to the office. All the savor had gone out of life. For the moment only a sense of ashes in the mouth remained. All the brutal, savage acts I had seen wreaked against unfortunate human beings came back to torment me—particularly those in which the luckless one came near being myself.

I thought of Grandpa Handy's rebellion against the conditions of his servitude, and suddenly I knew that the old Nick was alive in me as he had been in my old grandparent and that there were limits to endurance. Some day I would be gone. They'd look for me on Beale Street, up and down the river, along the Yellow Dog and the Peavine, but I would not be there. Somebody else would have to play the New York productions on the swanky Alaskan Roof and fill my place on church and school programs. Somebody else would have to play for our elite at Church's auditorium, which demanded the best in music and deportment. Who would play the blues on the excursion boats when I was gone? Yes, I would be gone, but I suspected that I'd cry like a baby when it came time to leave.

Now, however, I could think of nothing but outrages and grim hateful crimes. There was, for example, the occasion when we played for a dance in a Mississippi town. We finished the engagement and were about to catch a train for Memphis when a white man in a dangerous temper came to the platform and ordered us to accompany him to another town.

There was no refusing. He was not bargaining with us to fill an engagement. Neither was he making a request. He was *telling* us, and not one of the band needed to be told that this was one of those times when discretion is the better part of valor. Even when the man explained that he had just bought three barrels of whisky for the Negroes on his five-thousand acre plantation and that he aimed to kill a man in the town to which he was carrying us, we did not hedge.

Chairs were placed in a wagon, and in the bitter cold of a January day we rode out to the place of the victim.

"Keep perked up, you boys," the bad man instructed us. "Then when I raise my hand and give you the high sign, you strike up *The Last Shot Got Him*. Understand? When I kill him I want to hear you playing like sixty. That's the way I planned it. Hell, this is going to be the last word in killing. Classiest damn thing you ever heard tell of."

We reached the store, and the proprietor was called to the door. He was a white man. Our employer brought an equally disagreeable brother along. When the man spat in the other's face, kicked him and tried in every way he knew to make his victim show some fight, we commenced to wonder what it was all about. Then suddenly we heard him mutter, "Insulting one of my niggers, hunh?"

The situation was hard to accept. It seemed grotesque in the light of everything we knew about the Delta country, grotesque too in the light of our position on the wagon, playing as we were required to do all kinds of pieces as they were demanded by the bad man's brother, but holding in reserve *The Last Shot*. The torture continued for an hour. Through it all the brother of the aggressor stood with his hand on his pistol, watching every move. When our employer tried to thrust the butt of his own gun into the victim's hand, the brother stood ready to shoot as soon as the man's hand touched the gun. But the poor fellow was careful to avoid doing this, and though he took a frightful beating, he was not killed. We never got our cue to strike up *The Last Shot Got Him*.

As might be expected though, the blood lust was not so easily quenched. His first plans thwarted, the man who had commandeered our band ordered us to stay over and play a dance. That night we played till a late hour, but no ladies came to the dance, and that made the would-be killers more furious. When they finally let us go, we met one of the white men on the road. He had a rope around a Negro's neck. In the next few hours three Negroes were murdered. They had to kill somebody.

We were playing for a dance at Batesville, Mississippi, when a loafer stepped up and struck one of my men. I protested to my employer, but before he could intervene, the intruder struck me in the eye. A period of wild disorder followed. When this calmed down, we resumed the music, but the fellow waited outside for me. When the dance was over, he came upstairs with a bullwhip to be used on me.

"Run!" someone shouted.

Had I done so, I might have been shot. Instead, I made up my mind to die fighting. Meanwhile a crowd gathered, among them an upstanding man from Sardis named Maddox. I remember Mr. Maddox partly because of his bright red hair and partly because he was a godsend to me. He stepped up and low-rated the local boys for not protecting me after bringing me there to play for them. Then he turned on the fellow with the whip.

"Hit me, if you dare," he said. "I've done more to you than Handy has." Then he knocked him down and beat him.

Someone again told me to run. Somehow I didn't feel like running. Instead, I stood and watched the battle. Maddox had administered as sound a beating to his opponent as you would want to see, but the fight did not stop there. It spread out, and I could see that it was shaping itself into a battle royal between the local boys and the Sardis crowd. Eventually guns were whipped out, the gangs scattered temporarily and the boys of my band took to cover. During this lull the Sardis crowd prevailed upon the proprietor of the local hardware store to open up and provide them with guns. At the same time I appealed to the town marshal for protection. He scoffed at my plea and went to the aid of the man who had struck me. So at last, with no place else to turn, I took to my heels, and the hunt was on.

All night I hid in the fields. Then in the early morning, chilled from the cold, I went to the kitchen door of an elderly white man and explained to him the fix I was in. He was a Mason. After providing me with breakfast he armed himself with a double-barreled shotgun and drove me to the train in his buggy.

"If that fellow shows up this morning, I'll fill his hide with buckshot," he proudly promised as we drove along the road.

When I finally boarded the train, I met most of my boys. They had walked to the next station south. All of them now carried guns. The conductor, it seems, knowing our band, had armed them with pistols he had gathered from passengers and train men.

Then there was the time we played a dance for the post-master at M——. A lanky tobacco-chewer with a lobster-red neck walked up to the band. He was in his shirtsleeves and wore corduroy pants. Presently he whipped a knife from his pocket and cut the fiddle strings.

"Ain't gonna be no damned dance tonight. Get me?"

We did—and there wasn't. We went to our rooms.

At midnight we heard heavy footsteps in the hall. When the door opened, we lost our breath. There, as big as life and just as rough, stood the tall, menacing individual.

"Who's the leader of this here band?"

Nobody, *nobody* was the leader! He couldn't get to first base there.

"Well, tell me this, then. How much did they promise to pay you for playing?" he demanded.

That was a little different, so we answered him honestly. Then to our surprise he paid the entire bill, gave us an extra ten dollars, plus a quart of whisky. He then paid for the fiddle strings he had cut. Whisky in, wits out, the old folks used to say. Presently we began to think that he was not such a bad guy after all.

But that was not the end of the fiddle-string cutter. We ran into him again during the next Lenten season. As usual, business around Memphis slowed down for us then. We had consequently formed the habit of serenading some wealthy planters in Mississippi during that season, planters whose families had a taste for music. Captain Tom James who owned many miles of plantation out at Swan Lake was an old standby. Often we dropped in on Captain Tom and received more for a single day's work than we earned in a week of Memphis engagements. Well, one day during Lent, we were returning from Captain Tom's and peering out of the train window to see if we could accidentally spot the fiddle-string cutter when someone brought in the news that he was on the same train. With him, we learned, was a brother who had to travel on a stretcher. All of us became interested immediately. Presently we learned the brother's trouble; he had been shot full of holes. Then the string-cutter discovered us and ordered us off the train with him.

On the platform he pointed to his brother on the stretcher and explained proudly, "He got his man. They are having a trial today. All I want you all to do is when the judge finds my brother *not guilty*, play *Dixie*."

He advanced us hard money, ordered our meals and told us to be at the trial at 1 P.M.

We were on hand when the court was called to order. The first witness, a white man, pointed the guilty finger at the wounded brother. A second white man followed, corroborating the first testimony. Then a bewildered Negro with a watermelon head loaded with good hard sense was called to the stand and examined briefly.

Q. Did you see this shooting?
A. Naw-suh.
Q. Who pulled out his gun first?
A. I didn't wait to see.
Q. Well, what did you hear?
A. I heard Mr. A— say that Mr. B— wa'n't white 'n I knowed they was gwine be trouble, so I hauled it.

"That's all," said the judge.

All this time the fiddle-string cutter was pacing the court-room in his shirtsleeves with two guns exposed, ready to see that justice was done. His neck seemed redder than ever.

After a short pause the judge cleared his throat and summed up the case.

" 'Cordin' to my way o' thinkin', 'pears to me that this here nigger is the best witness. I'm satisfied that ever' white man did just what this nigger did. When they heard what was said, they all knew there was goin' to be trouble, and nobody waited to see who was goin' to fire the first shot.

"Now this we do know," he went on. "Mr. A—— is dead. Mr. B—— lies before you on the stretcher, shot in fo' places. If we turn him loose, he ain't goin' nowheres. If we put him in jail, his brothers'll get him out. If we find him guilty, well, that would be a sad and needless reflection on his old mother and his sisters. So I find Mr. B—— *not guilty*."

BOOM! Ta-ta-tum, ta-ta-tum—

"I Wish I Was In Dixie, Hooray, Hooray!"

In Pace's office, looking down on the quarreling members of my band, this grim, backwoods humor seemed as full of peril as the anger of the mob that had cut off Tom Smith's head and tossed it into the crowd of his Beale Street friends. Yes, the southern sun was full of shadows. I welcomed Pace's suggestion. New York! A publishing business on Broadway! Certainly I'd do it.

With Pace an idea called for action. We went downstairs immediately and opened a line of credit with the Atlanta State Bank. I then dictated a telegram to the University of North Carolina explaining that the war and draft had taken my best players (which was true in a roundabout way) and that consequently I would be unable to fill the engagement. I was, I added, sending them word in time to allow them to secure another band. Then I concluded with the hope that the war would soon be over and that we could again be of service.

When I rejoined the members of the band on the curb, I told them that after considering the matter I had concluded that I was wrong and they were right. This pleased them enormously. They couldn't praise me enough. They were in the best of humor as we went to the depot. Big times awaited them in Memphis, and they were anxious to be getting there.

We bought tickets, and almost every man in the group offered to carry my instruments and luggage.

"Never mind," I told them. "I'm going to leave it in the station. Thanks."

"What?"

"I'm not going back to Memphis. I'm heading for New York."

There was an awkward moment then. A trace of sadness came into many of the voices. No one seemed to know just what to say.

"Well, when are you comin' back?"

I outlined my plan briefly. Things had been moving toward a change for a long time. Life was like that. I hoped they would understand. For my part I didn't hold their fighting and contention against them. They had fought for what seemed right to them at the time. They didn't need to assure me that at heart every one of them was my friend.

By now night had fallen. As the train pulled out, I saw every head looking back from the coach windows. Every eye was moist. And in that mist I baptized each of them in my memory.

Since that time I have frequently had offers to lead bands of one kind or another, but the memory of these men has left me cold to all such proposals.

CHAPTER FOURTEEN

Pace & Handy—Setting a Pace

In 1918 the firm of Pace & Handy came into New York City flaunting a brand new hit, *A Good Man Is Hard to Find*. Alberta Hunter had introduced it at the Dreamland Cabaret in Chicago. Sophie Tucker heard her sing it, learned the number by rote, with the help of Ted Shapiro, her pianist, and brought it to Broadway audiences before we could get sales copies printed. Jack Norworth did likewise, singing it at the Palace Theatre with great success for two weeks. We rushed out special editions of the song with title pages that featured pictures of these artists. Miss Tucker went on to sing the song for twenty weeks at Reisenweber's. Grateful for these mighty plugs, we placed full-page advertisements in the *Dramatic Mirror* and *Billboard*, advertisements which included photographs of the two singers. We were off to a great start in the new venture, and we felt like telling the world.

Eddie Green had written the song. He had placed it with me for publication some time earlier, but I had neglected to bring out an edition immediately. When we turned our faces toward Broadway, however, we decided to fly the new item at our masthead. Our hopes of impressing New York with the value of our catalogue were largely pinned to *A Good Man*. The immediate results were most gratifying.

Of course, New York City wasn't an entirely new experi-

ence to me. The Pace & Handy Music Company of Memphis
had New York connections. I had once booked my band on a
tour that promised to include Broadway. We planned to go
by way of Washington, where we were scheduled to play an
engagement during the inauguration of President Wilson.
Then, as on so many other occasions, I had allowed the tail to
wag the dog with the result that I was talked out of the trip
on the grounds that "we'd go to New York some other time."

Later, deserted by the band, I had made the trip alone. I
spent two weeks in Chicago for business reasons, making various stops along the way, and found myself arriving in New
York over the Erie line with exactly seventy-five cents in my
pocket. This was enough to wire my wife for money, but not
enough to send the wire and also pay for an overdue breakfast.

But fate is funny. I got off the ferry at 23rd Street, walked
to West 20th Street and stood blinking before the sign of the
Plaza Music Company. Here was one of the local jobbers that
bought from our catalogue. I had never been there before, but
I decided to step inside. Jerry Vogel, the manager of the sheet
music department, greeted me cordially. The morning was
just beginning, and C. J. Kronberg, the boss, hadn't yet arrived, but Jerry persuaded me to wait for the man who ran
the business.

C. J., as they called him, was not long in coming. He
greeted me enthusiastically and asked me into his office. There
he displayed a check that was about to be mailed to our Memphis office, a check for $187. What a break! I pocketed the
precious paper and went outside with a bright idea shining in
my mind. I would visit other jobbers and dealers who handled our catalogue. No better time than the present! Before
nightfall I had collected almost a thousand dollars.

That accomplished, I headed for Harlem. And what a Harlem it was! Big old, good-looking, easy-going, proud-walking
Harlem. I strolled through the principal streets of Harlem and

on 135th Street, near the old Lincoln Theatre, I saw a sign on the door. It read: "Harlem Musicians' Association." I paused to listen to a saxophone sextette and walked in, wondering whom I would meet and if anyone would know me. I was instantly recognized and, instead of a group of mediocre musicians, met the cream of New York's leaders at that time. Will Vodery, arranger of numerous Ziegfeld musical scores, invited me as his guest to the Cocoanut Grove on the Century Roof. And on the following night I was the guest of Ford Dabney at the Ziegfeld Roof. Vodery introduced me to Mr. Ziegfeld as composer of the *Memphis Blues*. In acknowledging the introduction Mr. Ziegfeld said, "I'll forgive you!"

It was not until years after that I learned why the remark was made. It seems that the *Memphis Blues* was so much to Ziegfeld's liking that when he heard this number he usually threw a big party for his friends, including the band, where money flowed in the Ziegfeldian way.

J. Tim Brymn took me to the largest dance pavilion in Newark, where his band was playing an engagement. Everywhere I was richly entertained, and the treats were all on my hosts. They would not even let me put my hand in my pocket. Vodery declared that I was responsible for five Negro bands being on Broadway, thanks to the peculiarities of the *Memphis Blues*, which other musicians of the time found difficult to interpret. That seemed to be worth a blank check to me, where the local musicians were concerned.

Later my rounds with Vodery included stops at the New Amsterdam Musical Association and the Clef Club. These were well-housed Negro organizations with all the facilities of modern clubs. I was so pleased that I spent the night at the Clef Club. It was here I met for the first time James Reese Europe, its founder, and our talk turned to the possibility of America's entrance into the first World War. Jim Europe, Will Vodery and Tim Brymn, it seemed, were all playing with the idea of organizing bands for service overseas. Later their plans materialized, and the three band leaders were commissioned lieutenants in the United States Army, but at the time their optimistic talk gave me sad reflections.

I couldn't help remembering the preparedness parade in Memphis. There my band had not been invited to join in the parade, though I had desired earnestly to contribute my bit. In fact, the only Negro marchers in the whole procession were those who carried buckets of water or shuffled along in a handy position to assist some white gentleman should he fall from exhaustion along the line of march. An aftermath to this was just as bitter.

The Liberty Bell, on its way from California to Philadelphia, passed through Memphis, and all the white children of the Memphis schools passed down Main Street in review. But the colored children had to see their Liberty Bell as best they could from the sidewalks. Well, judging by the optimism of the Harlem band leaders, things were different in New York.

In this I was not disappointed. Before many years rolled by I was to see my daughter Katherine chosen to head the receiving line at her school on the occasion of a visit paid them by the King and Queen of Belgium. Again I was to see another daughter take a part in the classic dances performed by three hundred school girls, when Cardinal Mercier visited New York. But then I could only wonder and hope, and not too much of that. The down-to-earth business of picking a New York office could not be delayed. Almost immediately I commenced looking around.

The Gaiety Building on Broadway interested me, and I noticed that it had signs up announcing "space to let." For three weeks I tried to do business with the person in charge of renting, but each time I was given the run-around. Then I tried Harlem, but Harlem business locations were more expensive than some on Broadway, so back I came to the Gaiety Building. Failing to get an office, I finally managed to land desk space. Through Manny Eichner I secured a desk opposite Phil Sheridan, at a rental of fifteen dollars per month. Then things started happening.

To start the ball rolling, I placed an ad in the *N. Y. Clipper* and another in *The Billboard*, telling the world that W. C. Handy, composer of *Memphis Blues, St. Louis Blues* and other indigo products, had taken this location with a fresh piece of hit material, *A Good Man Is Hard to Find*. Across the bottom of the ads was splashed the name of our firm: Pace & Handy Music Co. Inc., 1547 Broadway. Eichner's office was presently overflowing with professional callers.

In tune with this flow of business he raised my rent to fifty dollars, ten dollars more than he was paying for the whole place. I had to grin and bear it—but not for long. Things have a way of getting around, and already some of them had reached the manager of the building. While Eichner might have raised my rent to the sky, the manager was doing some figuring on his own part. John, the Negro superintendent, had been whispering in his ear. The substance of his tip was that we received more mail than anyone in the building; that Woolworth, Kresge, Kress and McCrory, not to mention numerous other syndicate stores, were our customers; that Broadway celebrities were making frequent visits for our music. Mr. Stern, the rental agent, had John call me into his office. What was all this he had been hearing?

Well, in any case, Mr. Stern would have me know that my color had nothing whatever to do with my failure to get an office in the first place. I could see for myself that he used colored help. It was the same throughout his other buildings.

I restrained a yawn, saying to myself, "Yes, yes. Pour it on. I know that old line." I was thinking of all those people who were so quick to profess love for the Negroes as a group and to cover up their devilment by saying, "We have the sweetest old black mammy in our family! She's been with us for years and years." Generally this is the preamble to an act of discrimination. So I took Mr. Stern's words with more than one

grain of salt. But I was wrong in that judgment. I rented a
five-room office in the Gaiety Building and retained it for several years, during which time I had many opportunities to
find that he was sincere. When he died, he left five thousand
dollars to John, his West Indian superintendent. To Negro
education he made gifts totalling approximately a million dollars. He had been chairman of the Board of Education, City
of New York.

The headache of finding an office disposed of, I got down
to the bigger problem of publishing on the main stem. Here
too, I quickly discovered, headaches abounded. One of them
concerned *A Good Man*, our reigning hit. While Western
jobbers were ordering the song in thousand lots, New York
firms were placing orders for twenty-five, fifty and one hundred copies. We could not understand why they would not
order the song in larger quantities. Perhaps we were small
ducks in a big pond. Throughout the day my phone was ringing. Would I come in and have a talk with them? For a few
days I was puzzled. Then the light broke. They wanted to
buy the song outright knowing that I had sold *Memphis Blues*
for a paltry sum.

One jobber offered five hundred dollars for the copyright.
Three publishers bid the same amount. I laughed that off. We
had spent more than that advertising it.

His offer spurned, one man tried a new line. If we refused
to sell *A Good Man*, he would see to it that we didn't put it
over, pointing out that we had violated a rule of the Music
Publishers' Protective Association by giving publicity to theatrical artists in trade papers. Why, he would have Sophie
Tucker and the others who were using the number drop it
like a hot potato.

We protested that we were not members of the organization he mentioned. This did not silence the persistent individual, but a few days later we received application forms and
forthwith joined the Music Publishers' Protective Associa-
14

tion, paying the fifty dollars per month dues and enjoying all benefits. Membership in this organization was an education in itself and a great protecting influence. However, all this did not stop the offers for the outright sale of the song. The offer rose to ten thousand dollars. By then, however, *A Good Man* had been recorded on all phonograph records, and royalties from that source alone promised to bring us much more than the amount offered. Why sell? The prospective buyers were convinced that we intended to cash in on this natural hit. The local jobbers then settled down to the business of selling the number as they would sell any other successful song. Indeed, they tried to make up for lost time. A single jobber placed orders for thirty-six thousand copies in one day. *A Good Man Is Hard to Find* sold half a million copies, despite our limited Broadway experience and small staff. Many publishers could have run it to an easy two million. In the midst of these conversations and negotiations we received a visit from John J. Abbott of the firm of Francis, Day & Hunter, Ltd., London, England. We signed contracts for *A Good Man*, receiving a substantial check as a guarantee for regular accountings. We gave them world rights excluding the United States, Canada and Australia. Australian rights had been given to another firm. In less than two weeks we had received four cablegram offers from as many countries in Europe aggregating ten thousand dollars for rights in that one song. We could not accept. In the twenty-two years of pleasant and profitable business relations with this old conservative London firm, we have had no reason to regret the loss of Continental European contacts.

Almost ten years later in 1927, I sold *A Good Man Is Hard to Find* to Joe Davis Music Co. at a price several times larger than the first offers.

That experience was my baptism as a New York music publisher. It was also a fair specimen of the battles that lay ahead. But unique as my problems have sometimes been, I

have never been naive enough to think that they were all to
be blamed on the fact that I'm a Negro. In the business in
which I was engaged, it seemed that the sharp contest for
financial advantage was at the center of practically every
conflict.

In the fledgling Broadway firm of Pace & Handy, Harry
H. Pace was president, my brother Charles vice-president, and
I secretary-treasurer. Our office staff was under my general
managership. Charles was sales manager. J. Russel Robinson
was associated with us as professional manager and after twenty
years he is with us again. Carrie Collins was assigned to the
professional and shipping departments. H. Qualli Clark did
arrangements, and Daniel F. Haynes headed the bookkeeping
department. We employed as stenographers Mamie Wright,
Elvira and Alice Murray. With the cooperation of this force
business grew.

Little by little we lengthened our cords, extended our space.
By similar stages our rent increased. In time we were paying
more than three hundred dollars monthly and our quarters
were still too small, our help insufficient. Checks rolled in,
some of them fat ones from recording companies. The bank
downstairs, having hemmed and hawed when we first sought
to open an account for the corporation, treated us with def-
erence after learning that our president, Pace, was himself a
banker.

Meanwhile life was not entirely office routine. The Clef
Club invited me to conduct *Beale Street Blues* at a concert on
the Century Roof, a concert for the benefit of the boys "over
there." The aggregation of musicians set to play the number
consisted of forty banjos of every kind and about a hundred
instruments in all. The boys could really sing and play. I'd
never heard such music. The numbers were run off amid generous applause. Finally, following my program, I saw *Beale
Street* coming up. Before I could reach the stage, however,
the conductor touched me on the shoulder and called me

aside. "You're out," he said curtly. "The program's too long."
This seemed strange, especially when other New York com-
poser-conductors were introduced here and there and asked
to play unprogrammed numbers, but I swallowed the pill and
made a mental note. The next time the representative of the
Clef Club invited me to appear on one of their programs I was
ready for them. This time Deacon Johnson, on behalf of the
Club, again invited me to conduct the *Memphis Blues* for a
finale at the Selwyn Theatre. The invitation was accepted,
along with the protective demand for a payment of one hundred dollars for this service.

All the while I had been wondering why I had been "cut
out" of the previous concert. At the Selwyn Theatre, the reason appeared. The Clef Club played an all Negro program
with Fred M. Bryan, conductor. It was a splendid entertainment of Negro music. They sang Burleigh's *Deep River*,
Cook's *Exhortation*, music from Cole and Johnson's *Red
Moon* and Williams and Walker's shows; they played Joplin's
Maple Leaf Rag and Tyer's *Maori*, Jim Europe's *Clef Club
March*, and the conductor's own compositions, *The Dancing
Deacon* and *Mauvoleyne Waltz*—numbers that had marked
milestones along the road to the best in American music.

At the finale of this classical program I entered to introduce
the blues and received a tremendous ovation, which I did not
expect, being an unknown quantity in New York and forgetting that my music was not.

At the conclusion of *Memphis Blues* many bows were taken
and the audience demanded a repeat. How the band played it!
Beale Street and *St. Louis Blues* were demanded and again
played and repeated. I stepped from the stage to overhear theatrical managers telling the head of the Clef Club something
about engaging me. I could easily have fallen for the lure of
footlights in those days. My business associates had cautioned
me to put the business over and to leave bands alone, and I

resolved to follow their advice. This resolution sent me out to seek the friendship of band and orchestra leaders, men I hoped would introduce my new numbers. Having spent much time in Jim Crow towns, I was under the illusion that these Negro musicians would jump at the chance to patronize one of their own publishers. They didn't. It can be said, in justice to them, however, that they meant well.

The Negro musicians simply played the hits of the day, whether composed by me or someone else. They followed the parade. Many white bands and orchestra leaders, on the other hand, were on the alert for novelties. They were therefore the ones most ready to introduce our numbers.

With Negro vaudeville artists it was different. They wanted songs that would not conflict with the white acts on the bill. The result was that these performers became our most effective pluggers.

Of course we did not depend on these alone. Like all other publishers of the day we found it necessary to hire professional pluggers to go on the road with our songs, sing and play them, introduce the numbers to established artists and otherwise promote their use. I'll never forget two individuals we once employed for this work; believe it or not, one was a Greek, the other an Armenian.

At a salary of forty dollars a week, each of our ill-assorted pluggers took up his task with great energy. Three weeks of harmony followed. Then hell broke loose. The Greek refused to work with the Armenian, and the Armenian refused to work with the Greek. This situation led to words, and the air was presently filled with racial epithets, plus fitting adjectives. During the course of their war a strange bit of truth leaked out. Each one, judging by the reciprocal accusations, had been copying other pluggers' borrowed route-sheets and submitting them to me as evidence of work done by themselves. Meanwhile, as a matter of fact, my two song pluggers were spending their nights—their proper working hours—in the speakeasies. Thus began my education in the ways of Broadway parasites.

Through other similar experiences I learned to keep an eye open for grafters of many sorts. There were those who knew when we got our royalties from the phonograph companies—and how much. There were the ones who could always spot *other* parasites who sold our songs in unauthorized editions and through unknown trade channels. This kind demanded pay for divulging their secrets. I learned to give them all a long, sidewise glance.

After *A Good Man* had ridden the tide out, we came up with another success, *Oh Death, Where Is Thy Sting*, a Negro comic song by Clarence A. Stout of Vincennes, Indiana. Here again we proved that hits can come from sources other than Broadway. Bert Williams recorded the number on Columbia Records, and other companies promptly followed this lead. Earlier an Okeh record of the song had been made by Ernest Hare, a record which enjoyed a good sale, but the thundering success of the Bert Williams recording touched off an honest-to-goodness boom for *Oh Death*. We poked out our chest. It made us feel good to have ourselves linked in this way to the success of a man whom we have always considered an inimitable recording artist.

Another cause for pride came one morning later when a young white man visited us, a young man fresh from New Orleans. We were impressed by his good looks and his soft Southern accent as well as by the fact that he had been manager of stock companies in the South and that he could sing all my Blues. Before he left the office we wrote a letter introducing him to Thomas A. Edison, requesting a test recording of *St. Louis Blues*. The singer's name was Al Bernard; J. Russel Robinson was at the piano. Mr. Edison did not approve of blues. Moreover, he had a way of tossing out all recordings that did not come up to his own rigid standard of quality, regardless of how much money they would yield. But he liked Al Bernard's test and immediately contracted for this blue song as well as other numbers that might be sung by the young Southerner. This launched an impressive series of successes for the young artist, successes in which we proudly shared.

For instance, Bernard wrote *Shake, Rattle and Roll* and *Saxophone Blues* for us, and we published *Satan, I'm Here* by Marshall Walker, all of which Bernard recorded. He also recorded *St. Louis Blues* for nine different companies, including the sensational Victor recording in which he sang with the Dixieland Jazz Band.

Good luck came our way again one morning when I was about to take a trip. Two young white ladies from Selma, Alabama, came in and offered to show me some manuscripts. I rested my luggage on the floor and glanced at the songs. One was *Pickaninny Rose*, the other *O Saroo*. Without wasting more than a few moments, I contracted for the numbers, snatched my hat and bags and hurried to the railroad station. The young composers were Madelyn Sheppard and Annelu Burns. They succeeded in having their songs recorded on Brunswick, Edison and Victor records by such artists as Dorothy Jordan and Olive Cline, the latter doing a Victor Blue Seal record of *Pickaninny Rose*.

These numbers, plus our blues, gave us a reputation as publishers of Negro music. Character artists in search of such material were referred to us by many Broadway publishers. Business was humming. We employed three more pianists, Fletcher Henderson, Artemas Smith and Georgia Gorham; additional stenographers, among them my two daughters, Lucile and Katherine. William Grant Still took charge of the arranging department with J. Berni Barbour, Phil Worde and Frederick M. Bryan, copyists. We hired more accountants, arrangers, shippers and pluggers—about twenty-five persons in all. Trade papers carried special articles throwing flowers our way. Members of our own group, however, got a huge kick out of referring to the Gaiety Building as "Uncle Tom's Cabin" and avoided us as much as possible.

That did not stop the business from flowing our way, however. We dusted off the old number that I had written under the title of *Yellow Dog Rag* and republished it as *Yellow Dog Blues*.

Yellow Dog Rag had been recorded twice and brought small royalties. In this title we took out *Rag* and inserted *Blues*. Joe Smith, Victor artist, made a new recording of it, introducing for the first time the laughing trombone. Harry Raderman was the trombonist. Victor sent a man to our office with a contract for this recording. I signed, saying to myself, "Another hundred or so," and forgot all about it. A few weeks later a Texan wrote that he had sold more *Yellow Dog Blues* records than anything in the history of his business which he had conducted from the beginning of the phonograph industry. This letter made little impression. Other dealers wrote in to the same effect but we were so much concerned with trying to put over hits that we failed to grasp the significance of these letters. We didn't know then that *hits* are like *babies*. To some they come every year or so and to others they never come. Actually, we were crying with a loaf of bread under our arm.

One morning I came to the office needing fifty dollars very much since our funds were being drawn on heavily. There were at least two hundred letters before me in the morning's mail. I opened them searching for checks, all of which did not amount to fifty dollars. I was thoroughly disgusted and had to go out and borrow the fifty dollars not knowing that I had overlooked one letter. Upon my return I noticed it and found that it contained a check for about seven thousand dollars. This could not be ours, there must be some mistake. Then I saw it was for Pace & Handy Music Co. Still there was doubt until I read what my eyes could not make my mind believe.

Finally, I saw the number of *Yellow Dog* records that had been sold—unbelievable! These records created a demand for orchestrations and sheet music in thousands. Before our print- ers could deliver ten thousand copies we had orders for one hundred thousand. Money was pouring in from recording companies and other sources in amounts more unbelievable than the first check.

Harlem was overcrowded and an apartment for my family could not be found in the city. With all this money in hand I found it was easier to buy than to rent. In what was swanky Striver's Row (a string of houses built by Stanford White) were two available houses for which I contracted, having in mind that Pace might want one of them, and at the same time writing him. Things were rosy and the business needed him. He came and took over the house, giving up his work with the Standard Life.

With Pace installed in the president's office, a new day dawned for the Pace & Handy Company. A valuable and capable man, Pace installed a new system, enlarged our finan- cial contacts, opened up lines of credit with five leading col- ored banks in the South and otherwise demonstrated his worth. Presently we outgrew our clothes, so to speak, and moved to 232 West 46th Street, taking over the entire build- ing and patting ourselves on the back for the achievements this move connoted. We were bragging too soon.

One day Pace and I stood at our window and saw a group of men standing on 46th Street and pointing up at our offices. A moment or two later we recognized a department manager of a phonograph company which was prominent then, but is now out of business. What his odd gesture meant it did not take us long to learn. The beast of racial prejudice was rear- ing its head.

Marion Harris, celebrated white blues singer, left a record- ing company that objected to her making a record of *St. Louis Blues*. Miss Harris had used our numbers in vaudeville for a long time, and she sang blues so well that people hearing her records sometimes thought that the singer was colored. When she signed with another company that permitted her to select her own material—often from our catalogue—one of the managers of this company got hot under the collar.

That was why the department manager stood across the street and pointed to our window. Immediately he telephoned Pace to say that certain of these numbers recorded from our catalogue would not be released by them. The conversation became definitely unpleasant. That evening this same man waited on the street for me. When I left the building, he stepped up and spoke his mind. He said that we had made ten times too much money from their phonograph company. Nothing more came of the incident at that time, but already the air was charged.

I caught another glimpse of the same prejudice when I tried to introduce colored girls for recording our blues. In every case the managers quickly turned thumbs down. "Their voices were not suitable." "Their diction was different from white girls." "They couldn't possibly fill the bill." In my opinion this was the usual cock and bull story, and I often insisted strongly that they were making a mistake. Viola McCoy, who was under contract with me, made test records for seven companies, all of whom turned her down. They said her voice would not record. I released her and then the seven companies brought out records of Viola McCoy and praised her artistry in their catalogues. We were making too much money evidently.

Perry Bradford got a break for Mamie Smith who was the first colored girl to make a record. She recorded two songs written by Perry, *That Thing Called Love* and *You Can't Keep a Good Man Down*, published by us. The sales on these numbers had been very large, but still some recording managers were not convinced. Even when the same composer's *Crazy Blues* netted him fifty-three thousand dollars in phonograph royalties alone, they failed to take the tip. While they hesitated, however, Okeh Records[9] made hay with Mamie's records.

They had been paying our royalties in notes. When Mamie Smith commenced her low moanin' for them, they paid in cash. My brother happened to be in their office one day when he overheard Perry discussing his account with the company. An official tried to persuade Bradford to waive certain rights, whereupon the composer exploded, "No, no! I don't wave nothing but the American flag, and I don't wave that long."

I was convinced that our people were lovers of music and that they were great buyers, and I had seen things that strengthened this conviction. In Chicago large crowds of domestic servants and packing house workers waited outside Tate's Music Shop on South State Street to hear us demonstrate *You Can't Keep a Good Man Down*, as sung by Mamie. All over the country colored music dealers begged for Okeh agencies in vain. Spikes Brothers and Carter, a relatively small store on Central Avenue in Los Angeles, offered to buy five hundred dollars worth of the records when they failed to get an agency. We bought the records, shipped them and received a prompt check. This was followed by repeated orders of comparable size. Finally the Negro dealers got their agencies.

The market was definitely there, waiting to be tapped. In Clarence Williams' place and in Thomas' Music Store in Chicago I had seen cooks and Pullman porters buying a dozen or two dozen records at one time. Not sophisticated music, of course, but oddities that appealed to them, and blues—always blues. We undertook to publish for this market, but usually the material was turned down in the major recording departments. Others saw money in the blues now and competition was keen. Colored blues singers, being in great demand, were contracted forthwith.

[9] One of the smaller concerns of that time, not connected with the distributors of the Okeh records of today.

Add to such difficulties the bitterness of sharp competition, and you have the materials for a minor tragedy. Our business began to fall away as steadily as it had grown. Circumstances beyond our control played a part. Woolworth took out their music counters, leaving us with more than three hundred thousand copies of ten-cent store music on our hands, music that could not be sold now that the price had been raised to twenty-five cents.

Printing and advertising bills accumulated. Our large pay-roll was not cut. Income from records fell. Some recording companies went out of business owing us. Others sent us promissory notes instead of checks with our royalty statements. These notes we discounted through local banks and colored banks in the South. In some cases bankruptcies followed, leaving us to make good. One company gave us a five thousand dollar note which I locked in our safe. This was eventually paid, but later on they gave us an additional three thousand five hundred dollar note which we discounted at the bank. The company thereupon kicked the bucket, and we had to make their note good in twenty-four hours. But the water was low in the rain barrel with no more rain in sight. I'm sure there was a frantic gleam in my eye as I suddenly realized that we couldn't meet our obligations.

To add to my woes, my partner withdrew from the business. He had disagreed with some of my business methods, but no harsh words were involved. He simply chose this time to sever connections with our firm in order that he might organize the Pace Phonograph Company, issuing *Black Swan Records*, and making a serious bid for the Negro market in this field. With Pace went a large number of our employees, persons especially trained for the requirements of our business and therefore hard to replace.

Still more confusion and anguish grew out of the fact that people did not generally know that I had no stake in the Black Swan record company. Other recording companies must have felt that by doing business with me as a publisher they were helping a rival recording outfit, fattening frogs for snakes, as it were. Naturally our royalties from records continued to decline. Bad luck had certainly overtaken me.

In spite of everything I kept throwing punches. Beaten to the ropes and badly slugged, I felt sure I could fight it out. Always in the past my best work had been done when opposition was strongest. When I was deep in the dumps, I wrote my best songs. When it looked like curtains for sure, I had always managed to come through. I was sure I could do it again. With a terrific burst of energy I set myself for a life and death stand.

At night I did the work our arrangers had formerly done. Often the midnight oil burned till the gray dawn came into the room. On Sundays I worked on the accounts in an effort to keep the books straight, doing the work of bookkeepers. Between times I mapped my strategy for meeting situations I expected to arise. But every man has his limit, and I discovered with a pang that I was no exception. Darkness closed in upon me. The nervous strain was too great. Something gave way. I found myself broke at the bank, broken in health and blind.

CHAPTER FIFTEEN

All In—Down and Out

As a traveling minstrel and man of the world, it had not been easy for me to make myself content in a small town and a few rooms. It had therefore been a great day when I met a kindred mind, a man who understood and could say, "I see."

Pace had understood. Our association had been harmonious, and our business had grown by leaps. After the World War, however, with the things we knew dislocated, Pace and I had been caught in the general maelstrom of humanity, and the time had come when I felt he didn't understand. And I—well, I couldn't see.

So here I was. I had lost my sight. I had sold my home on Striver's Row to safeguard wreckage of the business. Sitting in darkness, in a rented apartment amid successes of a sort, I was constantly reminded of my affliction, my kinship with Job. As a child I had often been called upon to read that Bible story to my blind grandfather. Now, at my request, my children read the old story of tribulation to me.

Essentially, I thought, life was black, sinister, foreboding. I resented it. Job had been a just man—I tried to be. He wished for death—so did I. Old hates came back to rage in my heart. Thoughts blacker than my destroyed sight burned in my mind. Suddenly terrified, I commenced grasping for straws.

> But for us He gives the keeping
> Of the lights along the shore.

Lights for me, huh? What a laugh!

In my tumult and confusion I suddenly recalled a remark made by an old half-illiterate barber in Atlanta.

"Don't sour, W. C.—Lincoln didn't sour, Booker T. didn't sour," he said, detecting something unhealthy in my mood.

Recalling his words, I paused to listen to the beating of my own heart.

> God will not cast away a perfect man,
> Neither will He help evil doers.
>
> Till He fills thy mouth with laughter
> And thy lips with rejoicing.

Mine, as I now saw it, was leading me back to even older themes, back to the spirituals. In them was to be found a message for a world sitting in darkness. And I felt that my own tribulations had fitted me to set that message forth with a certain clearness.

Throughout my life I had been blessed with good health. I can't recall if I ever had a chill. Hard work, long parades, deep respiration that the trumpet demands, all contributed to keeping the doctor away. I know now that I should have consulted one periodically. When I was a boy, school children laughed at my squint eyes and teasingly called me "squinch-eyed monkey." Sunlight hurt my eyes but I didn't mind. I was a catcher behind the powerful pitching of Jim McClure who threw a ball after the school bell had rung. This caught me off guard and inadvertently I was struck in the right eye. While at the Furnace and Pipe Works I had to work over blinding hot molten iron. We did not use eye shields as they do nowadays. Many nights while with the minstrels we read our music by coal-oil lamps and poor gas lighting. Some of my music was written by the light of coal-oil lamps. While with Mahara

I had a front tooth crowned. It must have completed the impairment of my eyesight. But the thing that put me in bed was fear. Fear of what might happen to my business, my family and me. Fear of what people would think and say. Fear of what Pace might do. Worry and fear. Fear and worry. Nerves —jangling nerves!

My eyes pained me when I read letters, and letters were numerous. Every afternoon around four o'clock my eyes pained like a toothache. I went to get glasses from an optician. The optician said, "You don't need glasses, you need a specialist." I saw the specialist and took to my bed for the first time in my life. After many nights of suffering I made an important discovery while trying to ease the pain by covering my eyes with my fingers. Accidentally, my little finger rested on the upper lip. The throbbing ceased. It was that capped tooth. I had it and others removed. The real pain in my eyes ceased, but my nerves—shattered! People had always spoken of my eyes—my smile. I tried to look at them in the mirror but I couldn't see the mirror. Oh my eyes! They pained again— imaginary. My wife would wring out hot towels and apply them. That helped some. But when I heard Bert Williams' record, *Elder Eatmore's Sermon* by Alex Rogers, "We Shall Reap Our Joys in the Harvest Time by What We Sow Today," the pains left and I got up and out of that bed for good. They did, however, have to lead me around for a considerable time. I found something to do to keep myself busy, in this way forgetting my condition. R. S. Peer and Fred Hagar of the Okeh Company engaged me to make records with a band under my name. Although I couldn't see the notes I did have definite ideas of how the arrangements should be made and interpreted.

Advised by three doctors and as many lawyers, I sat in darkness and tried to piece together the broken fragments of things. The lawyers advised me to go into bankruptcy, but hiding behind the corporation in that fashion struck me as an act of dishonesty. I couldn't do it. However, since I was the owner of a greater part of the stock of the corporation and with no financial interest in the Pace records, it seemed advisable to amend our name to read "Handy Brothers Music Co., Inc." Though Pace & Handy debts amounted to approximately twenty-five thousand dollars, I refused to admit that we were bankrupt.

Didn't Stevenson say that no man is useless while he has a friend? Well, I had a friend and more than one. During those days a flock of small bills plagued me more than the large debts since they were bound by collateral security. I was told that at the offices you could scarcely open the door without admitting a marshal who had come to close up the business. As many as five of them called in a single day. The furies were on us for fair, and they seemed determined not to give us any peace. I kept my wife and brother busy guiding my hand while I signed notes, checks and contracts at home. It was fortunate that I had friends, many of whom would not want their names disclosed here.

There was Charley Thorpe, for example, bulky, good-looking and amiable. He was head of the Harlem Musical Association and had been among those I met on the occasion of my first call. Charley Thorpe was everybody's friend, and his readiness to come to my rescue is simply a sidelight on the character of this generous, easy-going man, an illustration of his vast capacity for good deeds. When the marshals seemed determined, to myself I would say, "Clap hands here comes Charley." Once he came to visit me and offered to send me to the Mayo Brothers' Clinic in Minnesota at his own expense. Again he brought the head of Knapp's Eye Hospital to my home and arrangements were made for my admittance. They spent the entire Sunday with me while my wife was in Woman's Hospital and my youngest son Wyer was isolated for scarlet fever.

Bill Robinson made offers of assistance, reminding me that

15

his wife, whom he jocularly refers to as "Little Bo" when not speaking of her as Mrs. Robinson, also came from Memphis.

Thorpe offered to stand behind my business while I was away. This seemed too much. It was too good to be true. I could not accept these generous proposals, yet when times grew desperate I sought Charley again and again. I can still hear his half-teasing remark, "Come tomorrow at ten o'clock, Bill." The next day the money was always there. Yes, I had a friend, more than one.

There was also Eva Taylor, the wife of Clarence Williams. Clarence had come from Chicago to establish his music business in New York. I welcomed and encouraged wholesome competition from one of my own race and felt sure there was room for us both on Broadway. Clarence prospered and accumulated a small fortune. I was able to pass along some of the benefits of my experience and often we talked over conditions.

One day Clarence and his wife dropped in, when he took the occasion to pay a long overdue account. During the conversation that followed, Eva Taylor discovered that a thousand dollars would do me a world of good and perhaps enable me to keep my head above water. She prevailed upon her husband and the loan was made. A printer whom I had previously befriended, upon hearing of my plight, brought me two one-thousand-dollar bills and asked for no security.

There was Lester Walton, now Minister to Liberia, a Negro feature writer on the staff of the old *New York World*. There was Robert Clairmont, and there was Dr. Paul A. Collins, the eye specialist. Thanks to the skill of Dr. Collins, the time came when I was able to return to my desk again. What I found when I got there was another question.

We were back in the Gaiety Building, doing business at the old stand, but sales had fallen to the new low of thirty-seven dollars and fifty cents for the preceding month. My brother Charles was so concerned he suggested that I make the rounds of the trade and recording companies to see what I could stir

up. But I had another hunch. Instead I wrote a letter to Lester
Walton. The result of my letter was a two-column article in
the Sunday edition of the *World*, an article which sang out
the news that I had regained my sight and was back on the
job. With me, helping to salvage the wreckage of the business,
was my entire family and H. Qualli Clark, who hadn't gone
with Pace, all working unselfishly in the office.

Then came an equally long and forceful article in the
Brooklyn Eagle. It was written by Nunnally Johnson, and it
carried the same punch as the piece by my colored friend. I
reprinted both of the articles in thousands and mailed them to
the trade, trade journals and newspapers all over the country.
Something told me that this publicity would bring far more
business than direct visits such as Charlie suggested, and I was
right.

I discovered to my great satisfaction that there was still life
in our blues. Following the vogue of my numbers, other blues
had fallen upon the land like autumn leaves. Many of them
were downright infringements of my copyrights, and as the
result, I was awarded enough monies from various violations
to furnish living expenses for a year or more. A flock of low-
down dirty blues appeared on records, not witty double en-
tendre but just plain smut. These got a play in college frater-
nities, speakeasies and rowdy spots. Their appeal was largely
to whites, though they were labelled "race records." All this
blues competition we rode out successfully. Perhaps it was a
case of the survival of the fittest.

Another break came when my *Aunt Hagar's Blues* suddenly perked up. I had written this number some time earlier,
but we had never been able to persuade the principal record
companies to wax it. During my absence from the office, however, several smaller companies made remarkable use of the
song. On my return I turned *Aunt Hagar* over to the Robbins-Engel Corporation. Within ninety days of that transac-
tion I was again getting out of the barrel. Though I was now

receiving only royalties from this number, they were sufficient
to pay almost all the colored bank loans. Later I polished them
off in full. On the strength of this success, the Robbins-Engel
Corporation published a folio containing nine of my blues
in which a foreword told of my contribution to American
music.

In 1925 I was asked for a series of interviews on the why
and how of the blues by Edward Abbe Niles, a Wall Street
lawyer who makes his hobby the study of American folk
and popular music and who shortly became my friend
and counsel. We worked up so much material that I concluded to assemble and edit an anthology embracing not only
my work but examples of the folk songs that preceded and
influenced it and the later compositions of both Negroes and
whites representing the blues influence. Albert and Charles
Boni, Inc., of New York published this collection in the following year in book form, under the title *Blues—An Anthology*, with illustrations by Miguel Covarrubias done in his best
manner and with notes and an historical and critical introduction by Niles. This was one of the first books on American
Negro secular songs published and I believe the first devoted
to the influence of Negro secular music upon American popular, jazz and serious music generally. Numerous other publishers cooperated by allowing characteristic work to be included. George Gershwin let us use excerpts from his *Rhapsody in Blue* as well as from the *Concerto in F*, no part of
which had been published elsewhere at that time. This book,
now long out of print, was reviewed in all classes of periodi-
cals and helped to widen my public.

Another step toward recovery was taken when I got things
finally straightened out with my partner. In the Black Swan
Company, Pace had scored heavily with a recording of Ethel
Waters singing *The Down Home Blues*. In fact, he had
started a stampede. All the remaining big recording companies
issued "race catalogues," as they called them. Hundreds of

Negroes became recording "artists" overnight. Negro bands couldn't supply the demand for this new variety of music. Some companies sent their recording apparatus to the backwoods of the South and the wilds of the West to record unsophisticated Negro talent. The Black Swan Company had a big moment in the sun. Then the competition became too swift. The Paramount Record Company and others pressed millions of records of this type through their enormous laboratory facilities, and while they were on the toboggan slide the Black Swan was doomed. The vogue passed and others folded as radio became a reality. During 1930 Pace wrote me a letter proposing to sell his stock in our firm. He accompanied the proposal with some personal remarks that sounded much indeed like the Pace of earlier days. He wished, he said, to see me come into all the benefits that my struggles deserved. Well, the deal was made and was closed in a Harlem undertaker's parlor late one spring night after Pace, Abbe Niles and I had spent an hour hunting for a notary public in working order. With this, all the eggs had come back to the same basket. Presently our heavy indebtedness vanished. One of the lawyers who had advised me to go into bankruptcy took a dive off a tall building. A banker friend went suicide, using a pistol. He left a note saying that if after fifty a man was not a success, there was no chance for him. That was not and is not my philosophy of life. I decided thereafter to "wear the world as a loose garment" and went out with a "rainbow 'round my shoulder."

In this one particular I determined to follow in my father's footsteps: he "wore the world as a loose garment." And so, with a "rainbow 'round my shoulder," I scattered sunshine as best I could whenever and wherever possible. If work for the time interfered with play, I cut out work. If play interfered with work, I cut out play. If I visited other cities I loafed and laughed, wrote new songs, visited old friends and lived again the "good old days." I danced and sang advisedly in order to reclaim ten or fifteen years of youth. I found pleasure in the company of children, old folks, women, men, rich or poor; became interested in the humble, desolate and destitute. People of all races came with their troubles and for advice. Never so busy that I could not listen, I always tried to send them away comforted and with a better spirit. This is what is meant when I say that "I was wearing the world as a loose garment."

On one of those rounds I was introduced to a hatless bohemian from the "Village." He wore a black shirt without a tie, and his name was Abraham Brown. He was eager to do Harlem and to meet Hubert Harrison, the Negro editor of *The Voice of the Negro*, one of the magazines I had bootlegged back in Clarksdale, Mississippi. Brown was a good conversationalist and we did Harlem down to the bricks, but we didn't meet Hubert Harrison. We must have gotten sidetracked in one of the Harlem night clubs. The bills were on me.

A few days later Brown came to my Broadway office bringing with him a friend named Robert Clairmont. It seems that Brown had, with his gift for talk, painted a rich picture of our Harlem visit. Now Clairmont wanted to make the tour. He too was a hatless Villager, but instead of a black shirt, he wore brown, without a tie. This time the three of us did Harlem, and again the festivities were on me. But a week later Clairmont returned and said that I had given him such a good time he wanted to take me out at his expense. I agreed, and he spent money like a Wall Street broker before '29. We got along well together and became good friends.

Then one night Clairmont said suddenly, "Say, why don't you give a concert at Carnegie Hall—a concert showing the evolution of Negro music?"

"I don't know," I said. "Maybe because I never thought of it, but if I had my May royalties, I might take a chance."

"How much do you think such a concert would cost?"

"Oh, three thousand dollars, perhaps—to do it up brown."

"I'll be in to see you Monday," he said. "I'll bring you the money."

I laughed. "No kidding?"

Monday morning Clairmont appeared, begged pardon for cutting in on the dictation of my morning's mail, and laid a certified check on the table. It was for five thousand dollars.

"Try to arrange the concert for an early date," he stated.

There was no turning back now. I went to work on the program. First I rounded up a chorus of sixty voices and an orchestra of thirty musicians. Then I got busy and lined up J. Rosamond Johnson, Taylor Gordon, Josephine Hall and Thomas (Fats) Waller, among many others, and the show was on with a howling storm outside but plenty of company within.

In addition to his piano numbers Fats played *Beale Street Blues* on the big pipe organ and with the thirty-piece orchestra. Minnie Brown, formerly a Williams and Walker prima donna and credited with introducing Roland Hayes to his first New York audience, was our principal soloist. Seventy-year-old Madame Robinson, white-haired and agile, led a cakewalk and brought back memories of Ada Overton Walker and Dora Dean. Tom Fletcher sang Joe Jordan's *Wouldn't It Be a Dream*, à la Ernest Hogan of blessed memory. I directed the orchestra in the playing of James P. Johnson's *Yamekraw*, a Negro rhapsody, an arrangement by William Grant Still. This was its first presentation, and Still's pencil score was so fine that I had to stoop over, bending my knees to see it. What did I do that for! A caricaturist caught me in that position. When Johnson and Gordon sang *Joshua Fit the Battle of Jericho*, the audience kept them on the stage twenty minutes more than they were allotted on the program. Altogether it was a big night, and the first time a program so studded with blues had been presented on that stage.

When it was over, Clairmont was happy. In spite of rain the concert grossed about three thousand dollars. It had cost eight

hundred more than that to stage the show, the orchestra rehearsals alone having set us back twelve hundred dollars, but
what was lost in money was more than regained in favorable
publicity. The metropolitan press was more than generous.

"Are you satisfied?" Clairmont asked.

I assured him that I was, and that seemed to be all he
wanted to know. I had entertained an angel unawares and the
five thousand dollars was a gift from him.

He and I remained good friends, though we ventured no
further together in things theatrical. He continued to play the
stock market while I kept busy trying to put over new song
hits. In 1929, when the crash came, my first thought was of
Robert Clairmont. Presently I began hearing rumors. Clairmont, according to one report, had lost nine hundred and
eighty-six thousand dollars in a single week. Later, New York
papers carried his picture, along with a story that told how a
reporter had discovered him in the breadline at the Municipal
Pier.

The next morning after reading the story I went with my
friend Jerry Vogel of the Plaza Music Company to visit the
Municipal Pier, since I was on the emergency relief committee. Vogel always devoted his spare time to charitable work,
and this trip was right in line with his custom. I had been with
him before on such visits to flop houses, asylums, hospitals and
churches. To the Municipal Pier we carried cigarets, candies,
fruits and Christmas cards from Vogel's charity fund, to nine
thousand eight hundred men, and I learned that these men
received well-cooked meals three times a day from the city's
emergency fund. Four thousand of them slept in fresh night-
ies, between clean sheets, thanks to the same humanitarian
sources. Ex-millionaires and bums, Negroes and hunkies,
scholars and crackpots, all mingled cheerfully in this breadline
fraternity. The only complaint I heard came from one of my
colored brethren. He held up a well-loaded plate to me,

pointed and shook his head gloomily: "Ain't this a damn shame? Only one piece of chicken."

Through Vogel I made the acquaintance of all the officers in charge, and eventually we found Clairmont, though he was not in the breadline. He joined us and went home with me that night. He was the same modest, smiling man he had been when he was worth a million. My family enjoyed entertaining him. Seemingly he didn't feel as sorry for himself as we felt. One thing, he didn't blame his losses on Hoover.

He and I took up where we had left off, and visited the old haunts where we had struck up our first friendly acquaintance. Later I was astonished to learn that he had given the newspapers a story of our existing friendship. It was widely syndicated. I didn't expect that. However, I never doubted that Clairmont would presently be on his way to the top again.

You can't keep a good man down, if you can believe what you sing. I had come out of my calamities in fine shape, thanks to some mighty fine friends, plus my own inability to know when I was licked, but this has delighted me no more than the brave comeback of Robert Clairmont.

CHAPTER SIXTEEN

The Blues Get Glorified

THE BLUES were all born humble but they were not content to stay in the shady districts beyond the railroad tracks. Time came when they put on top hat and tails, so to speak.

In one of his first books, the late James Weldon Johnson predicted that the blues would form a basis for symphonic structure. This I doubted, but having a true appreciation for Mr. Johnson's unusual mind, I keenly awaited for proof of this (to me) surprising prediction.

His prophecy was fulfilled when Paul Whiteman played a program at Carnegie Hall a few years later, where for the first time I heard and enjoyed Gershwin's *Rhapsody In Blue* with Gershwin at the piano. Whiteman has played and recorded many symphonic arrangements of *St. Louis Blues*, but to my mind his most outstanding arrangement was played at the Hippodrome, December 1, 1936, by his orchestra in combination with the Philadelphia Orchestra, with Casper Reardon, harpist. "Living Program Notes" were delivered by the eminent composer and critic, Deems Taylor. He kept the audience giggling and tittering by his witticisms. Coming to *St. Louis Blues* he said, "The next number on our program marks an epoch in musical history. There are two schools of thought regarding the invention of the blues. One regards it as an event equal in importance to Edison's invention of the incan-

Here Comes Alius Brown

("Done Laid Aroun'" Version)

Arr. by W. C. HANDY

descent light. The other is inclined to classify it rather with Lincoln's assassination."

Vincent Lopez was the first to give a jazz recital in the swanky Metropolitan Opera House. He was on the lookout for a symphonic number in blue and sent his arranger, Joseph Nussbaum, to me, whereupon I gave him the score of *Evolution of the Blues*. The *Alius Brown* melody in a sixty-five piece orchestra sounded somewhat like a Wagnerian brass choir or an *Andante Religioso* by Handel.

Noticing the success of concerts at Carnegie Hall and the Metropolitan Opera House, band leaders began to arrange extravagant symphonic orchestrations of the blues, and radio stations from coast to coast continued to announce So and So's Band in some glorified Handy number. Many of these arrangements sounded to me like a farmer plowing in evening dress. Nevertheless, these dolled-up symphonies had their followers who frequently told me of "marvelous" arrangements heard over station "X" by So and So's orchestra.

One of the first bands to record for the Columbia Phonograph Company was directed by Harry A. Yerkes, an early devotee of the blues. In his office in the Metropolitan Opera House, I met his associate, Albert Chiaffarelli, who showed me the score of a symphony by himself in four movements. At a concert at Aeolian Hall this symphony was first introduced to the public. Needless to say, I arrived early. The rendition of this pretentious number had been divided—Yerkes directing the first two movements and Chiaffarelli the final score. In the first movement the motif was a part of the *St. Louis Blues*. The second opened with five string basses developing the first four bars of *Beale Street*. This unfolded and blended with an additional movement from the first composition. Next came a scherzo, and again a portion of the *St. Louis Blues* was the motif. In the finale, *St. Louis Blues*, *Beale Street* and Philip Braham's *Limehouse Blues* were all used in a musical structure that managed at the same time to show the influence of Tchaikowsky.

Never before had I heard such a masterful blending of my themes. It caused those peculiar sensations that sometime race up and down one's spine or tug at one's heartstrings. The next day a recognized music critic wrote in his column: "The symphony was not as beautiful as the originals on which it was founded." Perhaps this critic had in mind that clever entrepreneur and band leader, Ted Lewis, with his delightful version of *St. Louis Blues*. Again, he may have heard the Old Maestro Ben Bernie, who was among the first to play it in a quasi-symphonic score.

Recording companies, noting this trend to the symphonic in blues, made them available on wax. Don Vorhees was one of the first to record such blues symphonically in parts one and two on Columbia Records. Then, Louis Katzman on the Brunswick, whose record was used in the first American Negro Ballet produced by Von Grona. Other surprises were to come in this most surprising of all places—Manhattan.

One day a visitor dropped in. "My name is Thomas Neely and I am from the Program Department of the National Broadcasting Company," he said.

"Have a seat, sir," I said.

He began, "Handy, I knew you down in Kentucky. Remember the dances that you played for in Danville?"

"I certainly do," I said.

"Well, I sat up all night outside, when a boy, listening to your music, and from that night on I decided on a musical career."

"What is your instrument?" I inquired.

"Trombone—I took that up against my father's wishes."

"I did almost the same thing."

"Well, Handy," he said, "I want to do something to repay you for the inspiration you have been to me. Will you come and be guest conductor on the program with Hugo Mariani if I arrange it?"

"Yes," I replied. It was arranged.

Sitting in the commodious studio I watched with admiration this remarkable conductor, Signor Mariani playing on the emotions of his seventy-five picked musicians and drawing from them indescribable music just as an organist gets effects by the blended use of certain stops. He played James P. Johnson's *Yamekraw* and Gershwin's *Rhapsody*. The announcer in his build-up for what was to follow gave a résumé of my life and work more eloquently than any I had ever heard before. His voice raised to a climax, "Signor Mariani hands W. C. Handy his baton which he is about to wave into the immortal strains—the *St. Louis Blues*."

In that exciting moment before me I saw musicians who had made names for themselves in the jazz world. Such men as Ross Gorman, who plays more than nine different reed mouth-pieces, Miff Mole, Phil Napoleon, Enric Madriguera. Never before had I felt such a response nor had I conducted such a large group of white musicians—and so distinguished.

In Chicago I had conducted a one-hour illustrated blues program over WLS, the guest of Dr. Charles L. Cooke's Orchestra. On the following morning the *Tribune* read: "Last night we were turning our dial and stumbled into a program of the blues which we consider one of the outstanding programs of the year."

During my six months stay in Chicago I had been introduced in about eighteen churches to speak, play or to render a program of spiritual music by a chorus with which I had become identified. Society matrons were presenting me here and there. Newspapermen had been running me down for interviews. University students and educators had me for their guest. I was associated with a Little Theatre movement that kept me on the go with things theatrical and out of which came Katherine Dunham. I was called on to address various organizations, one of which entertained the entire cast of *Porgy;* and after my talk, on the source of my material which came from the man furthest down, Miss Jane Addams of Hull-House said it was one of the most interesting talks on sociology that she had ever heard.

This may have puffed me up a little, swelled my head or pleased my vanity so much that the following incident may show that I must have been taking myself too seriously. All along I had fought for betterment of conditions, for higher idealism and for recognition of the worth to society of the members of the musical profession with whom I had cast my lot. Had the head of any but a musical organization acted as did the president of a Chicago local, the incident would have deserved no mention here.

Anyway, pride goeth before a fall! All over Chicago advertisements announced that the colored musicians' Local 208 would give a benefit dance. Fourteen bands would be heard at Savoy Hall and W. C. Handy would be guest conductor. Well, the fourteen bands were present. I had remained in Chicago two weeks to be present also. Nine of the bands featured *St. Louis Blues* with their individual arrangements. The manager of the Savoy observed that I had not been presented and suggested to the president of the Local that their guest conductor be introduced with all the bands assembled to play *St. Louis Blues* under his direction. He bluntly refused even to introduce me.

In the bands were musicians, many of whom had played with me on various occasions, some when I began on Beale Street. Many were anxious to sit under my baton. I hung around inactive until I heard the announcement, at five-thirty, "that a local favorite, Guy Lombardo, would play a few selections." He received a well-merited ovation and his numbers proved that colored people like their music sweet as well as hot. The disappointed guest conductor caught the first train for Washington to see Herbert C. Hoover inaugurated.

Meditating in the smoking compartment he puffed a cigar, studied the rings of smoke and wondered why Negro musicians in a big city like Chicago had such a man as president. In the curling smoke he saw his membership in New York's Local 802, to which also belonged thousands of musicians of all races, creeds and colors. Gradually the harmonious smoke rings curled into human beings and the "Jim Crow" president went up in smoke.

Returning home I surprised my family at the dinner hour, just as the radio was announcing my name. It was a strange reception for a traveler entering his own door to be announced by radio, and stranger still to hear my daughter Elizabeth excitedly exclaim, "I believe, my soul, that's Rudy Vallee!" He played the *St. Louis Blues* followed by *Beale Street* and the announcement customary on the Old Gold Hour boomed on the air. I asked, "Who is this Rudy Vallee?" Well, this was a good lesson. After that I made it my business to know what our youngsters were thinking about musically and to learn more about their radio heroes. Not long after this incident Rudy recorded *St. Louis Blues*, and the record backed by the *Stein Song* sold from here to Rio, from Rio to Bali.

When the Columbia Broadcasting System instituted a Negro Achievement Hour over WABC, we gave the first program of the series. My son Bill played the xylophone; my daughter played the piano and sang, and our staff pianist, Russell Smith, played his own compositions at the piano. I discussed the influence of blues on American music.

Dave Rubinoff invited me to hear his violin solo of *St. Louis Blues* with orchestral accompaniment on a nationwide hookup. On this occasion Willard Robison sang the *Memphis Blues* as I'd never heard it before, with an effective diminuendo and improvised words: "I'd love to hear Handy play that tune again—the *Memphis Blues*." The music got me. As it died away I exclaimed, "That's my heart." A newspaperman sitting near overheard, and next day wrote: "If *Memphis Blues* is Handy's heart, *St. Louis Blues* must be his soul."

Willard Robison with his Deep River Orchestra featured many of my blues that other artists neglected, doing them so well that I was kept busy telling inquiring friends he is not colored.

Even in sports the blues got glorified. When the St. Louis Cardinals won the pennant and world's championship the band played their Municipal Air. When they lost, the Athletics' band razzed with the *St. Louis Blues*. Colonel Joe Williams, sports writer and versatile man of the *New York World-Telegram*, has his own story of the blues which he ties in with famous boxers, remembering how our band down in Memphis saved the blues for Joe Mandot's entrance to the prize ring. He writes that the blues derived this title because of the blue uniforms our Memphis band wore.

On my way to the University of Iowa to give an illustrated lecture on blues, through the invitation of Dr. Frank Luther Mott, the conductor was telling me what a wonderful fighter Joe Louis is and that I shouldn't miss the chance to see him fight Tony Lazer in Chicago. There I saw him in action for the first time. Joe seemed to be a combination of Joe Gans and Jack Johnson. After the fight I visited Jack Johnson's cabaret to confirm my opinion. Jack dismissed my question with one complimentary remark about Joe's fighting ability and began to tell about the countries in which he had heard *St. Louis Blues* played. Even how he had played it himself in different parts of the world on the cello and bass. In my scrapbook there is a half-page photograph of Joe Louis that gave me the blues. He is playing a harmonica and under the picture are these words: "Ah hates to see the evenin' sun go down." Joe's left eye is discolored and his left jaw is still slightly swollen, and he doesn't feel so good. So he plays those *St. Louis Blues* while reminiscing about a fellow named Max Schmeling.

16

Lew Leslie's production, *Blackbirds of 1928*, will long be remembered for its musical hits, but not its least memorable scene was Russell Wooding's choral version of *St. Louis Blues*, sung by Cecil Mack's choir, augmented by Pike Davis' orchestra, which created a demand for choral arrangements.

In 1929, in collaboration with Kenneth W. Adams a scenario for a serious picture of Negro life entitled *St. Louis Blues* was written and offered to RCA Photophone, who agreed to produce it as a two-reel short under the direction of Dudley Murphy, starring Bessie Smith, backed by a chorus of forty-two voices and an excellent orchestra.

While shooting the scenes and listening to this wonderful chorus, one of the executives remarked to me, "It's too bad that we didn't make a feature picture out of this." When approached by Paramount Pictures in 1938 for the title "St. Louis Blues" for a feature production, I said to myself, "At last I am getting a break." Later, a feature picture entitled "St. Louis Blues" was produced, starring Dorothy Lamour. The story and *St. Louis Blues* were unrelated, however, and yet the excellent rendition of the song by Maxine Sullivan and Hall Johnson's choir, together with Matt Malneck's orchestra, compensated somewhat for what otherwise might have been a disappointment to me.

Those who keep a scrapbook are familiar with the unexpected kicks its pages reveal. The last number in the program, for instance, on President Harding's Flagship, on his return from Alaska to San Francisco, was *St. Louis Blues*.

When the English statesman Premier MacDonald visited America, Nathaniel Shilkret, then with Victor, carried his orchestra to Washington to entertain this distinguished visitor with four American numbers, one of which was *St. Louis Blues*.

In the days of Pace & Handy we received a letter from London, England. It came from Buckingham Palace and was from a musician who played for the King's functions. The letter expressed a complaint; it stated that the "nigger" musicians in London received our music before he did. He wanted to make some arrangement whereby he could get our music to play for the King ahead of the "nigger" bands.

Pace undertook to advise the gentleman that since we are members of that group to which he referred to as "niggers," they were therefore entitled to get our music even before the King's musicians.

We had many friends in Europe, and thanks to Aileen Stanley and Alberta Hunter, the Prince of Wales knew our best numbers. We had not anticipated the democratic ideals of the Prince who became King Edward VIII, nor had we listened to his farewell address when he became Duke of Windsor. But his fondness for our music is evidenced by clippings from the American press, one of which I quote:

> "King Edward VIII
> "Has Pipers Play St. Louis Blues.
>
> "Balmoral Castle, Scotland, Sept. 24.—King Edward VIII ordered the nine pipers at Balmoral Castle to play St. Louis Blues today to entertain Mrs. Ernest Simpson and his other guests on his vacation in Scotland who were forced to spend most of the day indoors because of rain and high winds.
> "The wind, adding to the wails of the Scottish bagpipes, made the St. Louis Blues really sound blue."

A most pleasant companion to this despatch appeared in an article on the present Queen Elizabeth in *Life* of March 17, 1941, where the writer says:

> "The Queen . . . often plays for the King during week ends at Windsor. The selections are usually Beethoven and Bach, with an occasional bit from Ravel and Debussy. Her favorite piece of dance music was once reported to be the *St. Louis Blues*. . . ."

At the wedding of Prince George and Princess Marina of Greece, they danced to the music of the *St. Louis Blues*.

But what about the band that played the *St. Louis Blues* in front of Haile Selassie's palace as a sort of Battle Hymn of the Lion of Judah?

When Noble Sissle (President of the Negro Actors Guild of America, Inc.) and I get together, we reminisce enthusiastically. One of his stories involves the *Memphis Blues* as the inspiration for the fox-trot created by the famous American dancing stars of yesteryears, Vernon and Irene Castle.

Jim Europe, head of the local Clef Club, was the Castles' musical director. The Castle Walk and One-step were fast numbers. During breath-catching intermissions, Jim would sit at the piano and play slowly the *Memphis Blues*. He did this so often that the Castles became intrigued by its rhythm, and Jim asked why they didn't originate a slow dance adaptable to it.

The Castles liked the idea and a new dance was introduced by them which in a magazine article they called the "Bunny hug." They went abroad and while in mid-ocean sent a wireless to the magazine to change the "Bunny hug" to the "Foxtrot."

Sissle also tells some unusual overseas stories. When the bands of the Allies played at the Tuileries Garden the players in the foreign bands numbered about a hundred men and each band played the classical music of its native land. When the time came for Jim Europe's band to play, wisely he said to his men that it was useless to attempt classical music. "Let's play *Dixie*, *Memphis Blues* and *St. Louis Blues*."

Jazz music was something new over there and at the end of Jim's program there was a stampede of all the other bands. They crowded around the American musicians and could not be held with their own detachments. The crowd was almost unmanageable. One leader asked for a copy of the *Memphis Blues* which Lieutenant Europe supplied. But during their rehearsals the foreign band leader couldn't "parlezvous" jazz. He said, "The piece don't *sound* like we heard it!" Bach,

Beethoven or Brahms could not have made it "sound" as those descendants of Africa did. It's in the blood.

Sissle tells another dramatic story and one of his best. There had been a prolonged engagement in the trenches and the morale of the American troops was breaking down from lack of entertainment. American soldiers, weary, shell-shocked and wounded, were coming out of the trenches. Jim Europe's band had been dispatched to play for the doughboys, together with a French band. In a gesture of respect the French band was to play the *Star-Spangled Banner* and Jim's band the *Marseillaise*. When the *Star-Spangled Banner* blared forth in slow tempo it didn't get a look from the tired American troops. When Jim's band played the *Marseillaise* in warmer style, some of the doughboys looked up and then decided that these black faces were Senegalese or French Colonials; but when the band struck up the blues the American doughboys tossed away their crutches, danced and hobbled, yelling, "They're from home! They're from home! They're from home!"

When our boys came back from over there and paraded up Fifth Avenue it was my good fortune to be one of millions to welcome the 369th Regiment of which Colonel William Hayward and Colonel Arthur W. Little were so justly proud. When Lieutenant James Europe led the band under the Triumphal Arch at Fifth Avenue and 23rd Street, erected for this homecoming, I confess that, in patriotic pride, I wished that the baton directing his men might for a moment have been held in my own hand. I envied every man who had returned so gloriously from overseas.

My feeling for Jim Europe was deep and warm. We were both from Alabama and he had done much to make my music known around the world. Seeing him in New York again, hearing him play the *St. Louis Blues* in Hammerstein's Manhattan Opera House just as he had played it in France, my gratitude and admiration reached new heights. I felt then, as I feel now, that the gifted president of New York's Clef Club was not only a loyal friend but a great musician and leader of men.

I was nursing feelings like these one night a short while later when, for some unknown reason, I suddenly became depressed and sleepless. Unable to shake the mood off, I got out of bed about one o'clock, dressed and stepped out into a misty rain. There was cool comfort in the low-hanging clouds and the fine spray. I was prompted to walk. Before I knew it, I was standing before the subway entrance at 135th Street. I entered and caught a Seventh Avenue Express. During the hours that followed, I rode from one end of the line to the other, back and forth, back and forth, time and again. Why I had come out of my house at that hour, why I had walked in the rain, why I continued to ride the subway from one end of the line to the other, I didn't know. A strange sleeplessness and depression had come over me. That was my only explanation.

The rumble of the subway was disturbing too. It was ghostly like the rumble of train wheels out of the past. What trains? What past? For me life had been filled with melancholy journeys, filled with trains rumbling through the night. There were the freight trains that took our quartet to Chicago back in '93. There were the trains that carried our minstrel show from ocean to ocean, over mountains and through tunnels. Always in the rumble of trains there had been the echoes of something sweetly sad, something lost perhaps. Sometimes they had inspired musical thoughts, as when I sat down and wrote the railroad song *Old Miss*.

But tonight no music came. I heard only the click-click of wheels and felt only numbness and foreboding.

When I finally emerged from the subway, it was broad day. At 135th Street newsboys were excited. I stopped dead still and heard one say, "Extra! Extra! All about the murder of Jim Europe! Extra!"

The man who had just come through the baptism of war's fire and steel without a mark had been stabbed by one of his own musicians during a band performance in Boston. No wonder I couldn't sleep. No wonder the rumble of the empty subway had been a ghostly sound without music. I felt that I could at last put my finger on the strange restlessness that had troubled me. More than once I had met that forerunner of bad news.

The sun was in the sky. The new day promised peace. But all suns had gone down for Jim Europe, and Harlem didn't seem the same.

In our daily activities what would we do without newspapers, magazines and books? The mouthpiece of the National Association for the Advancement of Colored People is a metropolitan magazine, *The Crisis*, and upon its staff were such eminent members of our race as Dr. W. E. Burghardt DuBois, Walter White and James Weldon Johnson, to each of whom I am indebted for kindly commendation. In the first mention of my work in the columns of *The Crisis* about 1915, a letter reached me from an African trader in Sierra Leone. He was on the subscriber's list of *The Crisis* and wrote:

"Seeing that you are bone of my bone and flesh of my flesh, I desire to enter into some relations whereby we [in Africa] may avail ourselves of your music."

Strange it is how the blues follow the maps of the world even to distant lands that welcome, perhaps, African ideas in a new American dress.

The blues found a faithful friend in the late Noah D. Thompson, formerly on the staff of the *Los Angeles Express*, and later connected in the East with a journal of Negro life, *Opportunity*, a mouthpiece of the National Urban League.

But more than any other, perhaps, the pen that set tongues

to wagging, ears listening and feet dancing to the blues was that of the celebrated author and writer, Carl Van Vechten, who said the folk blues "far transcend the spirituals in their poetic values, while as music they are frequently of at least equal importance."

The late Dr. Isaac Goldberg's descriptive book, *Tin Pan Alley*, a history of American composers, devotes considerable space to the blues. And as I write these lines, Adrian De Hass of the *Jazz Wereld*, Holland, calls pleasantly at our New York office for a photograph of the "old man" of the blues. My daughter Elizabeth told me that when she and a party visited a night club in Amsterdam, the orchestra leader sensed that they were Americans and accordingly struck up the *St. Louis Blues*.

Langston Hughes, the first Negro poet to recognize the potency of the three-line verse, wrote two volumes of poetry in folk verse, one entitled *Weary Blues*, the other *Fine Clothes to the Jew*.

Sterling Brown followed with poems entitled the *Memphis Blues* and *New St. Louis Blues*.

In his book, *New Negro*, Dr. Alain Locke introduces a chapter on jazz in which James A. Rogers goes into detail and establishes jazz with the coming of the *Memphis Blues*. He traces the term to a trombone player in Chicago called "Jasbo." When this fellow had finished playing, dancers on the floor used to shout, "More, Jazz, more!"

There have been many contradictory articles and books written about jazz and blues, but from the inception of this music I have tried to keep the record straight.

Terrell's band in Huntsville, Alabama, substituted an iron pipe for a string bass in the late eighties. "Lard Can Charlie" played a can with me in Bessemer in the early nineties. Jim Turner made jackass brays, rooster crows, all kinds of barnyard imitations on his violin all over the country in 1882. Billy Nichols made all kinds of imitations on a cracker box in vaudeville. All of this was what we now know as jazz.

In truth, *Memphis Blues* is not the first title to combine the name of a city with the word "blues." There was a *Richmond Blues* decades before the *Memphis Blues*. But it was not a *blues;* it was a six-eight tempo military march dedicated to a military company similar to the Washington Grays. However, as a matter of fact I have recently learned that an edition of the *Dallas Blues* for piano, composer anonymous, arranged by M. Annabel Robbins, and published by Wand Publishing Co. of Oklahoma City, was registered for copyright by Hart A. Wand just two days before the publication of the *Memphis Blues*. It appears in two different versions in my collection, *Blues—An Anthology*.

I shall refer to a work that is recognized throughout the English speaking world for a definition of jazz, with illustrations of the technique of jazz, by Abbe Niles, found in the fourteenth edition of the *Encyclopædia Britannica* under the heading "Jazz." It also contains a definition of "blues."

To one not born in the environment and lacking a folklore memory, it is difficult to express in musical notation all that Negro music implies. Herein lies an enigma as deep as the secret of the blues. I hold that one must have been a part of the old life to bring out the old effects, Dvorak's *New World Symphony* and Stephen Foster's songs of Negro life notwithstanding. It is my contention that all real work in typical Negro music can come only from one to the manner born. It's his mother tongue. The art of writing blues or spirituals can be assumed but cannot be delegated outside of the blood.

Another active concern of mine has been the preservation of unusual arrangements of the spirituals. There has been evidence of an increased demand for this type of native American music. It was particularly noticeable during the first World War. A similar upswing in interest occurred during the years of the depression. I wasn't sure what to make of these cycles, but Noble Sissle suggested a reasonable explanation in 1934 on the eve of a pageant we were preparing for Soldier's Field in connection with Chicago's Century of Progress Fair.

All of our music is derived from suffering, as he explained it. During slavery the suffering was a result of the lash and the cruel separation of families and loved ones. Today we suffer as a consequence of the past, through man's inhumanity to man. Then as now our music was our consolation. The white man has always liked this music, but he has liked it as a thing apart. When he became involved in the World War, however, he became involved in similar suffering. The draft tore him away from his own loved ones, tossed him across the sea, showed him the horrors of bloody struggle and taught him in small measure some of the things that Negroes had been suffering constantly for generations. In this condition he found the spirituals an expression of the heart, where formerly he had looked upon them as a novelty of the mind. He welcomed the relief and release of jazz.

Then the depression came, and white people suffered the pinch along with their darker brothers. With us, of course, being broke and low-down is an old story. With us there has never been anything else but depression. We have known for years how to laugh under trying circumstances, how to go on living with nothing but song to sustain us. But it took a woeful depression to teach this trick to white America.

Now there seems to be a much greater appreciation for the little things of life, including music. Indeed, according to one university man, only steel and oil were larger industries than music during the worst of the depression. Proof again, if more were needed, that in times of suffering and uncertainty America must sing.

CHAPTER SEVENTEEN

No Fool No Fun

ALEX LOVEJOY gave me a laugh once when he said, "A fool at forty is a fool forever." I couldn't see the point. Then he told me how he and Joe Byrd had earned three hundred and fifty dollars each in a Philadelphia engagement. In the dressing room they had discussed what they were going to buy and the debts they were going to pay with this money when they got back to New York. As they walked out of their dressing room they saw several fellows down on their knees with the bones and one asked Alex to take a hand—two bits worth. Lovejoy faded him for twenty-five cents. Pretty soon they were ten dollars into his bankroll and Byrd got in the game to help him get back his ten. About five o'clock in the morning Joe said, "Alex, let me take a ten spot"—and this morning was his fortieth birthday. Lovejoy, in distress himself, looked at Byrd comically and said, "I ain't got nothing." Byrd said, "You broke too?" He looked at Lovejoy philosophically, got up and brushed his knees, and said, "A fool at forty is a fool forever."

C. Luckyeth Roberts, composer of *Junkman Rag, Heart Beats* and many production numbers, is called "Lucky" by his friends. He met with an automobile accident in which his ankles were broken and both hands crushed. All of his friends were wondering about his hands, whether he would be able to use them again since he is such a marvelous pianist.

His composer friends (members of the Crescendo Club) visited the hospital sorrowing, only to find him in a joking humor although he could not talk. His jawbone was broken and his teeth jammed into the roof of his mouth. He is "lucky" and no one would know today that he had even met with any kind of an accident. But Henry Troy handed us all a hearty laugh. He had made several trips to the hospital and on the last one he said to Lucky, "I am ashamed of myself that I haven't brought you anything before now. You know how it has been with me, but this time I managed to bring you something and I hope you can use it." He handed Lucky a beautifully wrapped package. Lucky was so pleased he couldn't wait for Troy to leave and began to open it. The present was wrapped in rolls of tissue paper that he began to unfold. Finally, he came to a small box. In this box was a toothpick.

I come from an eating family. People for miles around had heard about Uncle Buck Brewer's appetite. And my father never took a back seat for anybody when it came to boarding. That's why things panned out as they did, one Saturday when these two Methodist preachers were spending a weekend in the country with another of my uncles, Mose Brewer.

Uncle Mose had an old rooster who ruled the barnyard from his perch on the back fence, never leaving that throne except to knock off a younger rival or perhaps say howdy to a hen. The old bird was much too tough to eat, and he seemed to know it. Seniority exempted him from the Sunday stew or fricassee. But on the occasion of this particular weekend Uncle Mose was in a quandary. How was he going to supply three Sunday meals, plus Monday breakfast, to his two heavy-eating guests. Finally he reached a decision. The old rooster had to go. Uncle Mose found his hatchet and started toward the barnyard.

For the first time in years the old rooster could not be found in his accustomed place. The day passed, and no rooster showed up. Sunday came and passed. Monday dawned. Still no bird. About noon the guests packed their duds and departed. As soon as they were safely out of sight, however, the devilish old rooster strolled nonchalantly out of the nearby woods, returned to his customary place on the fence and crowed very distinctly, "Is H-a-n-d-y gone?"

Well, that is one I heard but this one is mine and no joke. One day in Memphis during the bitter cold winter of 1917, transportation had been tied up on railroads and street cars. Coal deliveries, however, went on as usual with the cheerful Negro drivers. Suddenly one of the mules balked and refused to take another step. I heard the driver say:

"G'wan mule. Don't you wanna work? Had no business bein' a mule. Oughta been a woman, I'd be workin' for *you*. G'wan, mule!"

On another occasion in Mississippi my musicians and I were out looking for adventure—and stimulation. We had played a Saturday matinee prom for university students. We couldn't get a Memphis train before next morning and during the long evening we felt the itch to go places. Accordingly, we were given written directions to the address of what promised to be a gay little festival. When we followed the directions, however, we came instead to a big house in an exclusive white neighborhood and immediately concluded that we had been given a bum steer. We had turned to leave when a flood of light suddenly streamed from the door of a cabin in a spacious backyard. This changed the complexion of things. We ventured in and found a group of dark merrymakers, rocking with joy and singing the blues to the accompaniment of a battered guitar. Well, we pitched in avidly, bent on pure havoc where the chitterlings and assorted vittles, the beer and corn liquor were concerned.

When the party reached its peak, our host had to raise a restraining hand. "Listen, folks, remember this here's a bone dry state." Things quieted down momentarily, but before long they were off again, making so much noise you couldn't hear your ears. Above the din our host shouted, "Have all the fun you want, but remember you're in the *sheriff's* back-yard, and this is *his* liquor I'm selling you."

I've seen some monstrous things myself, and I've swapped for a few others, like this one from Alex Rogers. Alex was a Nashville boy and had been a member of an early Fisk University Quartet. On one of the quartet's tours, he told me, they had been under the management of an absent-minded preacher, a man who turned out to be chain light-ning with the collection plate and at the box office but cold molasses at the pay-off.

Well, one night in Henderson, Kentucky, following a most successful performance by the quartet before a large audience, the manager stuffed his pastoral pockets with Ken-tucky's unblemished coin and hurried to his lodging house down on Water Street. The quartet members were annoyed, for as usual he was behind in their pay and they had looked forward to being taken care of at the conclusion of this pro-gram. They held a quick powwow. Then one of their num-ber decided on direct action. They guessed right, that he had gone to his bunk. There they found him asleep. The bass singer, arming himself with a long iron poker from a coal stove, approached the sleeping parson on tiptoes, raised the rod, and just as he was about to strike, the preacher jumped up out of his sleep, stood erect and said, "Let's bow our heads in prayer," and then prayed.

Alex Rogers put this in a comedy sketch for Bert Wil-liams. Bert used the piece and it never failed to lay the audi-ences in the aisles.

Theodore Metz, composer of *A Hot Time in the Old Town Tonight*, unwrapped one sixty years old when he and I had occasion to swap memories one day. In those days, it seemed, Metz had conducted an orchestra which boasted, among other things, a bass player who could not read music.

The musician, despite this serious handicap, was not a complete liability; he could play anything he heard—provided it was in the key of G. One night in Denver, Metz determined to do a set of quadrilles he had just received from London. Unfortunately they were written in the key of F. That meant that the bass had to be well-posted, so Metz made it clear to the man that he would have to get set for this departure and play in the key of F. When the music started, the man sawed away in G as usual. Metz immediately stopped, restrained the bull-fiddler and asked him, "Can't you hear we are playing in F?" Again the music started, and again as usual the bull-fiddler sawed away in G. Metz halted a second time, but before he could speak, the man leaned forward indignantly and said, "You go on and play your fiddle. I'm getting as much for playing in G as you are for playing in F."

During my sojourn in Henderson, Kentucky, I was a member of the Henderson Cornet Band. The last season with this band we decided to build up our treasury by taking out of each pay a certain amount of the money to be distributed pro rata at the end of the season. It was an organized band and we couldn't take an engagement until the proposition was voted on. I was financial secretary. At the close of the season our treasury held eight hundred and sixty-seven dollars. We voted on drawing this money out and dividing it. I was instructed to figure out each man's part and at the next meeting we met early and had to wait for the treasurer. At last he arrived on his bicycle. When the president ordered him to produce the money so we could pay off, he made this statement: "Gentlemen, I went to the bank and drew the money out, but on my way down here I fell off my bicycle and lost eight hundred and sixty-seven dollars."

In Memphis the Chickasaw band played for a barbecue and it rained all day. One of the shrewd members of the band figured that we would not get our pay and decided to take his in barbecue without letting us know. Some of the fellows asked him what he was doing with so much meat, but he didn't tell them until after we all got paid. Then he tried to sell his meat back to the barbecue man and he got mad at us because we wouldn't buy it.

Some of the richest humor of the past, I've noticed, has lost its laughter. Some stories that seemed wonderfully funny in one era are now pathetic. Professor Councill used to pull a corking good one about a command that was not in the manual. I put his anecdote which dealt with a military company in Reconstruction Days into verse and set it to music. Here it is for the first time in print:

RIGHT BLIVVY
(marching song)

Verse:
Captain Brown of Geechetown
Was an ebony-hued rapscallion
He made himself the Captain of
The twenty-third battalion.
He set aside a special day
To pass in grand review.
So blacks and whites to see the sights
Lined Thirteenth Avenue;
The bugles sounded notes that drowned
The discords of the band.
Above the thunder of the drums
Was Captain Brown's command
"Company attention! Forward march!
Keep step there Jonas Pollard."
Knowing nothing else to say,
"Right Blivvy," next he hollered.
"Right Blivvy" had 'em guessin'.
Never had that in their tactics;
So Captain Brown explained it
In the following didactics:

Chorus:
"Do somethin', brothers, for the
White folks is looking at us. . . .

Why I could get no further than this one line in the chorus is probably due to the passing of the inimitable Bert Williams who was the foremost purveyor of this type of comedy material. "Do somethin', brothers, for the white folks is looking at us" is characteristic and it is probably this sentiment that has spurred my people onward and upward.

I visited an orchestra rehearsal once in my early days and there was something lacking in the spirit of the players. They didn't have enough "umph." The leader stopped them in the rehearsal and said, "Yo'all ain't playing this music right. Put it where the white folks can 'git' it."

I told one of my stories to Mack, of the Two Black Crows of the Moran and Mack team. In return he told me this:

Some comedians were burying a pal and doing the best they could with an awkward job. In the absence of a minister someone suggested the Lord's Prayer. But it was discovered that none of them knew it entirely. Finally one fellow said he thought he could repeat some parts of it. To this a companion added, "Go ahead, buddy. Say what you can remember, and I'll ad lib the rest."

One night during the prohibition era I took a Jewish friend to an intimate little tea room in Harlem. The proprietor was a retired musician who had once featured songs of mine. My friend and I swapped yarns. When five o'clock in the morning came, we were still at it. By this time all the other guests had become our guests, and my friend's check had mounted to one hundred and seventy-two dollars. We had told stories till I was ready to suggest that we quit. It would now take a good one indeed to top some of those that had been told. But my Jewish friend was sure he had one. It was a Bible story—a serious one, he said.

A Jew died and went to heaven. When his name was announced, he was admitted and asked what he expected to do up there. He requested a hard job. He was given a pick and shovel and told to level all the mountains. After five

17

hundred years he returned and said that the job was completed. But it had not been hard enough to suit him. He craved something more difficult. Well, this time he was given a small dipper and directed to dip the ocean dry. This kept him busy for a thousand years, after which he returned, reported the job finished and complained that he wanted a really hard job. After a long pause the one in charge told him that there wasn't anything harder up there. If, however, he wanted to tackle a very hard job, he was told, "go down to New York City, to this proprietor's place in Harlem, and just sit there till J—— offers you a drink on the house." The proprietor tumbled.

Sitting in a place where drinks are bought reminds me of one day in Florida when our minstrel band suddenly missed Joe Ravizee, a tuba player. We did our parade without him, thinking that he would surely show up in time for the evening performance. Evening came, however, with no Joe. After the show, considerably disturbed by the loss of a member, we started toward our private car on its railroad siding. On the way we heard strains of *Dixie* played on a bass horn. Following the music, we came to a saloon and there discovered our missing member, his jaws puffed, sweat streaming from his head, eyes bright and big, tooting for all he was worth. Some townsmen, up to devilment, had compelled him to play *Dixie* as a tuba solo all day and until midnight.

Fabulous things always happened on Beale. Once I saw a "crippled" guitarist sitting on a curbstone, playing and singing the blues, with his right leg up behind his neck. He was a pitiful sight, and he had a mournful voice, so I gave him my last half dollar. Later that evening I passed Third and Beale again and saw this same "cripple" with his right leg in a normal position and his left leg behind his neck.

Another night my brother and I sat in a Beale Street barber shop till after midnight.

"When will you close up?" Charlie asked, yawning and stretching his arms.

"Humph?" the barber answered surprised. "I never close up till somebody gets killed."

That was my cue to write the *Beale Street Blues*.

My old friend Billy King, minstrel headliner of other days, dropped in one day and recalled a time in C——, Arkansas, when he brought legal action against a minstrel show that was carrying his name. Billy was a salaried actor with the outfit, not an owner or manager, and he hoped to be protected by the court in this contention. The judge agreed to look over Billy's contract before court opened. This would speed up action and enable the actor to catch a morning train. As the judge read the contract he turned a big wad of tobacco over and over in his mouth. When his eyes fell upon "two hundred and fifty dollars a week," they became fastened. He read no further but spat a stream of tobacco juice out of the corner of his mouth. Finally, he rubbed his chin and said:

"I'm goin-ta dissolve this here attachment. I'm goin-ta dissolve it on the following grounds: there ain't nothing any nigger can do anywhere that's worth more'n ten dollars a week."

CHAPTER EIGHTEEN

Down Memory Lane

ONCE a minstrel man, always a minstrel man. The call of the road still gets in my bones occasionally, and I get together a band or a group of entertainers and start in again where I left off years ago. Not infrequently the trail takes me back to Beale Street. I remember one time we played to such a crowd in the Lyric Theatre of Memphis that four hundred and fifty people gladly paid a dollar a head to sit on the stage.

Even in New York City the old weakness for a stage door has continued to tempt me. Benefit performances are always hard to resist. Occasionally I have even done a turn in vaudeville. It's too soon to become a has-been. Besides, I've enjoyed keeping in touch with the gray-haired favorites of the stage on the one hand and making the acquaintance of rising young stars on the other. I still consider myself a trouper.

I went out to Chicago for the *Tribune's* music festival which was held at Soldier Field, to hear Noble Cain's *a capella* arrangement of *St. Louis Blues* with a choir of three thousand voices and one hundred musicians. Al Jolson and John Charles Thomas sang. I was introduced and took a bow; the applause of one hundred and twenty-five thousand people was good for what ailed an old trouper. Since I was on the committee to help put on a giant pageant depicting the development of Negro music during the Century of Progress, I remained. This inspired memories of my first world's fair, the Columbian Exposition to which I brought a quartet, making most of the journey on box cars.

On the first night that sale of beer was again made legal in New York, J. Rosamond Johnson and I attended the gay doings at the Friar's Club as guests of Gene Buck. During the beer-fest, celebrities like Jack Benny and Jack Pearl and others acted as waiters. A host of stars of the old days were presented, and each responded with one of the songs or dances that had come to be associated with his name. The program came off so well that it was repeated at the New Amsterdam Theatre on 42nd Street.

Here Al Smith led the singing of *Sidewalks of New York;* Barney Fagan danced again, danced as he had done more than a half century ago; Harry Armstrong sang his own composition *Sweet Adeline,* and under his direction the audience joined in the chorus. Many other old troupers came before the footlights and did their bits.

A few days later I received a telephone call from Joe Laurie, Jr., the man who staged the old-timers' show. Would I come to Loew's Orpheum on 86th Street Thursday morning? And would I bring along an orchestration of *St. Louis Blues?* Of course I would. At the theatre I discovered that we were booked for three days. Well, the first thing for me was to send for my trumpet. This might lend more color, not to mention the fact that through it I could "sing" better.

We went on "cold turkey" that morning without a rehearsal. When the manager showed surprise, Joe laughed.

"Rehearse?" he said. "Why? These old-timers are going to do what they were doing before you and I were born."

Four times that day we did our stunts, did them just as we had at the Friar's show, and my pay was not docked for appearing in a business suit. After the first performance another of the old-timers stopped me at the foot of the stairs.

"Where's your dressing room, Bill?" he asked.

"Five flights up," I said.

"But you don't have to undress."

"No," I said turning. "I'm just going up to leave my horn."

"Wait a minute, young fellar," he grinned. "You can't be running upstairs like this jest to carry a horn. Give it to me. I'll carry it. Come on," he added. "Let me have it. I've got to make a change. Besides, you can't expect to keep up with us kids."

He must have been between seventy and eighty, but there was no holding him. He was having a barrel of fun.

After every performance someone relieved me of the climb. Old troupers from here and there, meeting in memory lane—that described us. One thing we had in common—all of us had spent much of our lives on the road. Our years before the footlights bound us together in a sort of free masonry. The fellowship in *Memory Lane* (as the show was called) warmed the heart. It was the crowning glory of my life on the stage.

During the rehearsal I got an unexpected laugh from the orchestra. When I handed Teddy King, the leader, an original orchestration of *St. Louis Blues*, I simply remarked that perhaps it would be the first time they had heard it played without a special arrangement. They laughed and the performers were amused.

"Good line," Joe Laurie observed promptly. "Keep it in."

Well, I used it thereafter in all performances as a part of my announcement. It always worked.

Memory Lane clicked. Without altering Joe Laurie's original routine for the show, we appeared the next week at Major Bowes' Capitol Theatre on Broadway. As a prelude to the Broadway opening our company rolled down the main stem in horse-drawn carriages. We were dressed in styles of the gay nineties. The procession continued to the Empire State Building. On top of the building we were met by Governor Al Smith who gave us his blessing as newsreel cameras clicked.

In New York *Memory Lane* went over like Balboa's fleet, if the comment of the *Literary Digest* can be taken as an index. *Variety* was equally picturesque in its report of the show. My number, it thought, had plenty "of what it takes to get next week." With the echoes of this sort of thing ringing in our ears *Memory Lane* took to the road.

Mayor J. Hampton Moore greeted us at the City Hall in Philadelphia and seemed as proud as any of us to have himself photographed with the company. The same thing happened in Buffalo with Mayor Roesch. While down in Charleston, West Virginia, Governor Kumpf was our host on the steps of the capitol.

In Washington the *Memory Lane* company crossed paths with the Memphis Letter Carriers' Band. The band was on its way home from Atlantic City and had stopped in Washington to serenade Mr. Crump, then congressman from Tennessee. They invited me to join them as their guest. Unfortunately, however, Mr. Crump was catching himself some European air at the moment and could not hear the serenade. But there were others in his office at the Capitol who remembered me in connection with the *Memphis Blues* and expressed appreciation for my visit and the band's serenade. We marched to the Senate Building and struck up the band for Senator McKellar of Tennessee. The Senator came out and shook hands and assured us that Tennesseans were proud of our accomplishments.

We had hoped that President Roosevelt would be able to see the *Memory Lane* show. We thought he would enjoy the dancing of Tommy Harris. Tommy was doing at eighty-nine the same dance he had done for Abe Lincoln back in the "days when." He could look back on appearances, appearances in Washington at the old Comique, in 1873, when Bud O'Neill had that theatre. He had played at Barton and Logan's Museum. With his wife he had been in stock at the old Bijou. His old-fashioned dance, the least bit creaky now perhaps, was to us a very real link connecting our country's present with its memorable past. But problems of government had the President weighted down at the time of our visit, and he was unable to see Tommy Harris or the rest of us do our stuff in the *Memory Lane* company.

Linking the past with the present, too, was Harry Brooks, last of the old-time banjoists. He had been the original Peck's Bad Boy when that show played the Bijou in 1882. Then there was Bill Swan who had played at the Globe Theatre in '89 when that famous old structure stood on the site of the present post office on Pennsylvania Avenue. During an engagement there Bill Swan had called on President Cleveland, and the President had remembered him from Buffalo days when the actor had been a messenger. Even earlier Bill Swan had attended school with Frances Folsom, the girl who became the President's wife.

Still another link with the past became apparent when I discovered that no colored person was allowed to see our show in Washington. For there in the heart of our nation Negroes are systematically barred from most theatres. In this the Capital of the United States has gone a step beyond the deep South to keep alive an ugly thing that should have died before now in a democratic climate.

Presently we moved on to Pittsburgh. While there I visited a friend at whose home I had once written a song called *Long Gone from Bowling Green*. She reminded me of something I had forgotten. On my first visit to her home I had been everlastingly at the piano, forever picking out notes and chords for *Long Gone* but never playing anything consistently. A victim of all this plunking had been her parrot.

There was no escape for him, no closing the door or slipping into the next room. The poor bird must have known what he was in for when he saw me come back the next day and take my seat at the piano. Otherwise he would not have muttered so disconsolately and with such obvious disgust, "Aw, hell!"

The newspapers turned hand-flips for us as we made our tour. One pointed out how wrong Bernard Shaw and Dr. Osler were in contending that old people are not much good. "Quality is always in style," it held, quoting Joe Laurie's curtain speech. Another pointed out that Gus Hill, making his first stage appearance in forty-five years, was the same chap who made his debut in Harry Hill's *Free and Easy* on Broome Street and the Bowery; the same Gus Hill who handled Montgomery and Stone, Bert Wheeler, Harry Richman, Weber and Fields, Sophie Tucker, John L. Sullivan, Sam Bernard, the Roger Brothers, Billy B. Van and Anna Held.

Others sang the praises of Annie Hart, a trouper for more than fifty-nine years. Since her first rôle, carrying a spear in *The Black Crook*, she had been a hit as Mrs. O'Dare in *Irene* and acted in every form of show business except the talking pictures—and she was sure that there was still plenty of time for that. Annie Hart had known Al Smith when he was just big enough to creep on the sidewalks of New York. She had been an associate of Weber and Fields before they rose to fame.

Billy Maxwell was with us too. Born the year the Civil War broke out, he had also been a member of the cast of *The Black Crook*. Then there was William Renard, who got his start with Primrose and West Minstrels. The year 1865 seemed like just yesterday to him. And Eddie Horan, just past eighty-one, was another. He used two canes for his dance, but not because he needed them—not by a jugful. Eddie Horan originated the cane dance back in Primrose and West's Minstrels. He used two instead of one in the *Memory Lane* show simply to prove that he was better than ever.

Lizzie Wilson, an old-timer, went back and dug up *Schnit-*

zelbank which always got laughs. Dave Genaro, credited with originating the cakewalk dance, and Emma Francis who did five cart wheels at the end of her own stunt, closed the show in a cakewalk just as Genaro had done forty-five years before in the team of Genaro and Bailey.

All this gave newspaper reporters and dramatic critics a busman's holiday. It made them happy to hear J. Rosamond Johnson play *Under the Bamboo Tree* again. Not a little of this generous praise came my way. Isaac Goldberg, critic for the *Boston Transcript*, was especially impressed with the influence of the blues. He saw in them sociological meaning as well as a marked imprint on all the popular music of our day, and he loudly cheered the "Father of the Blues." Ardis Smith made a similar point in the *Buffalo Times* and then added, "Why, if I had the author of *St. Louis Blues* in my theatre, I would scream the fact with a banner eight feet wide, hung from the highest cupola. I would have a band play about the St. Louis Woman all day in the lobby. . . . I would have Mr. Straud stop at the end of every piece of syncopation and confess that the very style of arrangement was directly attributable to Mr. Handy's boyhood composition. . . . I might make Mr. Handy a bore to the populace but, by cracky, I would point the finger of significance to him a dozen junctures in every program.

"It is hardly an exaggeration to say that every piece of polyphonic ragtime is traceable to *St. Louis Blues*. It has made musical stars, it has made orchestras, multiplied the clarinet and helped the sale of throat lozenges. It has even made literature. It has focussed the attention of the world on the high-brown gal and her gold-toothed dude's amorous and nostalgic ways. It has sent to the four winds the cacophonous tidings of such places as Beale Street and undoubtedly accounts for the notoriety of Harlem. It probably stimulated the vogue of Spirituals too."

In December of that year *Memory Lane* played the Ambassador Theatre in St. Louis. As usual the audience was warmly appreciative. They gave my playing of *St. Louis Blues* a fine hand. But here again I made an astonishing discovery. The only Negroes who heard the performance were the employees of the theatre. These employees did their best to make the most of their situation, however. They entertained J. Rosamond Johnson and me one night—at the manager's request.

Oh, well! I had slept on the cobblestones of the riverfront there in St. Louis just forty years earlier, hadn't I? So what? But looking back at those three seasons I spent with Joe Laurie, Jr.'s *Memory Lane*, I feel that they were three of the happiest years I have spent in all of show business, to be privileged and honored to work with those great old troupers. It was "*great*" strolling down Memory Lane.

From the day I donned my father's "jim-swinger" (Prince Albert coat) to be a walking gent in the home town minstrels, I felt I was closely identified with the theatrical profession. Almost from the time of my entrance, however, I was conscious of the social ostracism, and harsh words heaped upon its members. "Show folks ain't nothin'." I realized that organization alone could correct this false classification. It cannot be denied that in the field of entertainment the Negro has made a proud and enviable record. Despite this fact, there had never been an organization honestly and sincerely devoted to his best interests, morally, spiritually and financially, until the Negro Actors Guild of America, Inc., was founded.

To Noble Sissle must go credit for the inspiration as well as the six years of untiring effort he put forth to bring into being this medium of dignified representation for his people of the theatrical profession. It might still be but a dream had not sparks from his own persistent enthusiasm been caught by others, whose ability and influence, given without stint, helped to make the task less difficult.

Sissle, and other members of the profession working in cooperation with Alan Corelli, Executive Secretary of Theatre

Authority; Elmer A. Carter of the N. Y. Unemployment Insurance Appeal Board; Hubert T. Delany, City Tax Commissioner; Robert P. Braddicks, one time vice-president of the Dunbar National Bank; Dr. Louis T. Wright, noted brain specialist; and the Reverend A. C. Powell, Jr., of the Abyssinian Baptist Church, gave their invaluable services to this cause in which they believed. High hope was held that the charter of the Negro Actors Guild of America, Inc., for which application had long been made, would be granted. Finally, Simon S. Feinstein, Sissle's attorney, obtained the necessary approval and a charter, bearing the signatures of Leigh Whipper, Rex Ingram, Muriel Rahn, Hamtree Harrington, Noble Sissle, Ada Brown and W. C. Handy, was obtained. Dave Ferguson, executive secretary of the Jewish Theatrical Guild, and Dan Healy, president of the Catholic Actors Guild, gave the accumulated wisdom of their many years of experience toward perfecting the structure of the infant organization.

The appointment of Fredi Washington to the position of Executive Secretary was a happy selection, for she brought to the office that capable, dynamic quality which is always a guarantee of success. Membership to Theatre Authority was applied for and accepted shortly after the Guild was founded and it became a part of that impressive and important body, whose function is to control the benefit situation, as it relates to theatrical folk. The Authority exacts a percentage from all benefit performances and these monies are allocated to the member groups each year. That a Negro organization should be here represented is simple justice, for it is a historical fact that no benefit has been held in many decades, on whose program some great colored artist did not make a contribution of his time and talent. If the NAGA had accomplished nothing more, this alone would seem to justify its existence. However, in spite of the difficulties with which all new and struggling organizations are confronted, its aims have been magnificently achieved, and these include every phase of social and material welfare and betterment.

We realized that the Guild must necessarily have the backing of a solid treasury. It is to the credit of its Honorary President, Bill Robinson, that our first big finances came as the result of the benefit performance staged and managed by him at the 46th Street Theatre, which grossed nine thousand dollars. Add to this the proceeds of the annual boat rides and dances, the active and life membership dues, and you will have some idea of its sources of income. Annual donations come from eleven kindred organizations, namely: Theatre Authority, League of New York Theatres, Screen Actors Guild, Jewish Theatrical Guild, Catholic Actors Guild, Actors Equity, Chorus Equity, American Federation of Radio Artists, American Guild of Musical Artists, American Guild of Vaudeville Artists, and Authors League Fund. Thirty names constitute its Board of Directors, all of which are outstanding in the theatrical, business and social worlds.

For the time being, Acting Executive Secretary Edna A. Thomas, dramatic actress, has given up stage work in order to devote herself entirely to her duties, considering it a labor of love, though a financial sacrifice.

The annual budget is prepared by Lucas and Tucker, Certified Public Accountants, in collaboration with the Board of Directors. They have the financial guidance of Robert P. Braddicks, Assistant Treasurer, whose experience of years in official capacities with metropolitan banks assures that its golden eggs have a protected nest. Cab Calloway is chairman of the Board, but because of professional activities the Guild carries on under the able leadership of Elmer A. Carter, its vice-chairman. During its three years of existence I have had the honor of being its treasurer.

The accomplishments of the past lead to a justifiable belief in a future, rich in continued achievement.

CHAPTER NINETEEN

"'Way Down South Where the Blues Began"

IN HIS book *The Bright Side of Memphis,* published in 1908, the late G. P. Hamilton wrote, "As a rule, the bright side of the Colored Race is not given its due share of publicity to the world. Its mistakes, misfortunes, weaknesses, and crimes are minutely published, while its abilities and worthy achievements are too often overlooked and unmentioned. It is left to the colored people themselves to show to the world what they are doing and what they are capable of doing to promote the welfare of society. It is left to them to publish the deeds that do them honor."

On March 14, 1931, I received a letter from M. Thornton which told in effect that the colored people were taking Hamilton's advice in a big way. On the corner of Hernando and Beale Streets stood for years the historic Market House of Memphis. This had recently been torn down, making a new thoroughfare and leaving open an old plot belonging to the city. Someone had suggested that the site be converted into a city park or square and named in honor of some Memphian who had contributed to the welfare of the city.

The suggestion was timely and church organizations proposed ministers, schools suggested educators, in fact to my way of thinking there were any number of people in many walks of life who had done much to entitle them to this honor.

Therefore, you can picture my surprise when notified by a committee that the majority were uniting to have the square named after me, and requesting my presence at the dedication ceremony, to be held on March 29, 1931.

On the 27th I left New York City for Memphis, to find that the leading newspapers, the *Commercial Appeal* and the *Press Scimitar*, had been squarely behind the movement which I learned had been inaugurated and carried to its successful conclusion by Lieutenant George W. Lee, who three years later wrote a book entitled *Beale Street* with a glowing account of this memorable event. He had the whole-hearted support of Allen Fisher, John Ross, J. W. Hewitt, Congressman Crump, Bob Church and C. H. (Doc) Hottum.

That Sunday was one to be remembered, at least by me. On the speakers' stand, besides representative members of my race, were City, County, State and Federal officials. The parade was so long it took hours to reach the stand. I could witness only a part of it as I rode at its head in Lieutenant Lee's car, together with M. S. Stuart, General Manager of the Universal Life Insurance Company. Although we rode together I saw little of them for my mind was reviewing former large events in Memphis and contrasting them with the present one. Mounted police led the parade followed by an escort of motorcycle men and back in line were five thousand school children riding on floats, singing societies, marching clubs, fraternal organizations with bands and more bands: the longest parade of its kind in the history of Memphis, more than two miles long, it was reported.

I was rolling through familiar streets, smiling here, removing a tear now and then, tipping a silk topper to a happy multitude, while catching the sound of voices, some of old men and women saying, "That's him . . . Yes, here he comes . . . that's our Handy!" But as the auto sped along my mind was kaleidoscopic and my band was playing again for a cooking contest at Dixie Park. Cooks by the dozens were lined up, racing each other in killing, dressing and cooking a chicken in less time than it would take to tie a Jesse Owen's record. I heard the applause for the winner—or was I riding in an automobile and were all those cheers intended for me? Then I seemed to see the Ice Men's contest, where marching men with active tongs would catch and toss two-hundred-pound cakes of ice along the line as if they were tossing the medicine ball—or were they flashes of sunshine lighting up one white banner after another? And I paraded again and played once more for the Cotton Men's and the Trucking Men's contests, where cotton bales and barrels of flour were handled with incredible speed and astonishing skill. Yonder marched fraternal orders to which I had belonged, and through my memory marched Captain Brown's military organization of men who had seen service in the Spanish-American War; and beyond them older soldiers of the Civil War, the gray-haired heroes of the G. A. R. And here Church's Auditorium loomed, from whose rostrum had spoken Frederick Douglass, Booker Washington, Roscoe Simmons, B. K. Bruce, John M. Langston and even Theodore Roosevelt. And suddenly an embarrassing happening reoccurred: meeting for the first time the daughter of R. R. Church, Sr., Mrs. Mary Church Terrell, as she advanced toward the orchestra platform to greet me, and I, anxious to be introduced and proud of the honor, stepped down so rapidly from the stand that a sound of ripping trousers was heard and cold air, a draughty feeling, suggested that something was amiss, then with dignified mien I was backing and bowing—or was I riding forward, lifting my hat to a great lady and that sudden noise, was it a reminder of the present motor police and not the memory of a distant past?

But now we were approaching the speakers' stand where bands were blaring out the *Memphis Blues*, and again the *Beale Street Blues*. Then a great chorus was heard, led by Miss Lucy Campbell, in *Lift Every Voice and Sing*, the Negro National Anthem, and then my own *Aframerican Hymn*.

Following which, some of the most forceful speakers of both
races began a flood of oratory covering every phase of achievement in Memphis relative to our race. Many speakers were
veterans and others brilliant young men just out of their teens.
Some were humorous, others serious, but all contributed to
the greatest experience of my life.

The Reverend Benjamin J. Perkins introduced the Master
of Ceremonies, George W. Lee, who stood before the micro-
phone and eloquently told the enthusiastic crowd and the listening thousands whose radios were tuned in what it was all
about. Behind this scene could be felt the powerful hand of
Bob Church and the magical name of E. H. Crump, finding
expression through the eloquent, dynamic personality of the
Master of Ceremonies.

The program was scheduled for 2:30 P.M., yet even before
the vertical rays of the sun had rested on her bosom, Ole Beale
began to "strut her stuff" from Main Street to Turley, with
her maids and matrons all in fashionable array.

Mayor Overton, confined to his home, was ably represented
by the Honorable Clifford Davis, who was at his best in relating stories to drive home important points. In encouraging
Memphians to be boosters for their city and loyal to their own
people, he fabricated the following instance. While visiting
New York, a friend of his decided to call upon Professor
Handy and after having been passed through seven doors succeeded in reaching a girl who announced his presence and
then told him to return at two o'clock. At the appointed hour
he again had to mention his name at every door until he was
finally admitted into the eighth room, where he beheld Professor Handy seated behind a mahogany desk so highly polished that a fly could not alight on it; and according to the
tale, there he was in evening clothes and white gloves. "What
can I do for you?" Handy inquired, and the visitor barely had
time to mention the fact that he was from Memphis when
Handy said, "Why in heck didn't you say so in the first place?

18

My doors are always open to anybody from Memphis."

In his splendid speech that followed, Commissioner Davis mentioned that some objectors to the idea of naming the square in my honor had referred to the fact that parks and other public places were usually named after celebrities who had passed on and whose records, therefore, were entirely known—involving a subtle inference that being numbered among the living, W. C. Handy might, by some future act, prove to be unworthy of this honor. I listened intently to his comment in reply, and as near as I can remember Commissioner Davis stated:

"You have honored your educators, your leaders, your ministers but you have failed to give public recognition to your talented artists. We want this place to be an inspiration to our boys and girls who are artistically inclined, and we feel quite sure that the habits Professor Handy has cultivated and lived up to will justify our faith in him. We wanted him to come down here and let us show him what Memphis thinks of him while he is still living."

Never before had I heard so much Negro history as was related by the principal speaker of the day, Judge Harry B. Anderson. Among other things I remember, he stated that to his way of thinking, Alexandre Dumas was a greater writer than Shakespeare in that Dumas was the father of fifteen hundred works and five hundred children. In referring to the source of my compositions he paid me a compliment by again mentioning Dumas who, "when the color scheme of Paris was black and white, wore a red vest and didn't give a hang who liked it." The inference being that my color scheme was "blue" and I didn't give a hang who raised an eyebrow at it.

Next on the program was George J. Strong, editor of the *Mid-South Liberator*, himself a lad, but filling a man's boots as he presented the talented scholar and minister, Dr. W. Y. Bell, Dean of Gammon Theological Seminary, Atlanta, Georgia, and pastor of the local Mt. Olive C. M. E. Church, who received the park in behalf of the colored people of Memphis. Dr. Bell brought back a story from Europe and told it on the platform that day. He said that a waitress in Paris asked him if he were not an American, and from what part. On being told Memphis, she laughed smartly and said in broken French, "Oh, I know, that's the place in 'Beale Street.'"

Others on the program were Professor Frank Sweeney, President of Le Moyne College; Dr. L. A. West, head of Mercy Hospital and former President of the National Medical Association; Colonel Bacon, Sheriff of Shelby County; and mine host, John R. Love, dean of local musicians, who in his modest and effective manner presented me as guest of honor. The band broke into *Beale Street Blues*, and the jubilant crowd yelled and waved until made hoarse by their weakened voices, as I stepped forth to speak with swelling heart. My mind reached back into archives of the past and I spoke of the many pleasant memories experienced on Beale and attempted to cite their importance in the development of my career.

After I had finished speaking, only the masterful address of Judge Harry B. Anderson of the U.S. District Court, who was introduced by Professor G. P. Hamilton, was sufficient to rekindle the high enthusiasm of the vast multitude. This was a prepared address which made a direct appeal to the hearts of my people, extolling their rare gifts and virtues, and depicting the glory and grandeur of the future that awaits them.

The program ended with the presentation of trophies for the best float and the two best school units in the parade. The former was given by His Honor, Mr. Crump, whose name linked with that of Bob Church was many times mentioned by various speakers on the program. I was told then that I would be invited to be Memphis' guest every five years.

Five years elapsed and on the occasion of the Memphis Cotton Carnival, an affair similar to New Orleans Mardi Gras, my invitation came in the form of national press announcements giving wide publicity to my return. The *New York Evening Journal* offered on its editorial page, which was syndicated, an item headed "Beale Street Papa—Celebrating the Birth of the Blues."

My wife, daughter Elizabeth, and secretary Mrs. Pearl Carn and I motored to Memphis via Fisk University, where my youngest son Wyer joined us. The park had grown shade trees and street cars had been rerouted in order that passengers waiting for transfers might find rest and comfort. The city was decorated, and naturally Beale Street was all dressed up.

Watching the easy-going people sitting around in the park reminded me of a laugh that Bessie Smith (celebrated blues singer) had given me back in New York. Exclaimed Bessie, "Mr. Handy, you ain't seen that park since they fixed it up, have you?"

"No," I replied.

"They sit out there and sleep day and night," she said.

"Is that so?"

"Yes," she concluded. "One fellow was sitting on a bench asleep when a passing policeman tapped him under the feet and said, 'Wake up and go home.' The lounger brushed his eyes, looked at the officer and said, 'Y'all white folks ain't got nothin' to do with me sleepin' here. *This is Handy's Park.*'"

In the publicity preceding my arrival, Harry Martin of the *Commercial Appeal* had been sounding the sentiment of Southerners in regard to having me conduct Whiteman's orchestra in the rendering of the music I had written on Beale Street. One unfamiliar with the South might not understand this rather unusual gesture; nevertheless, the broadminded young Martin received letters of commendation from the surrounding territory. One of the most typical was received from Mrs. Frank Hayden, widow of the Memphis banker, who told Martin she would love to see the white people pay W. C. Handy this tribute which she thought he so justly deserved.

I was presented by Attorney Howard Netterville to a gay carnival crowd at the Floral Ball in the Municipal Auditorium that night amidst five thousand enthusiastic cheering people, as Paul Whiteman and his orchestra struck up *St. Louis Blues*. Due, however, to faulty vision which I feared would prevent proper reading of the score, I declined Whiteman's proffered baton as the press photographers snapped us there in front of his band. Since the NBC network was to broadcast thirty minutes of the Whiteman music from coast to coast that night, at Harry Martin's suggestion the broadcast also included the tribute to me in order, as Martin stated in his Footlights & Flickers column, "that the world can hear the white people of the South honor a Negro who deserves such recognition and who will accept it humbly, yet happily, in the spirit in which it is given." Among the stage and screen celebrities I met there were Mary Carlisle, Allan Jones and Irene Hervey.

In the parade of the Cotton Carnival where Cotton is King, Main Street celebrated with floats and bands characteristic of such pageants, wherein even neighboring states, also producers, were ably represented. To Beale Street came the actual producers, the cotton workers from these same neighboring states to celebrate with their own floats and bands.

The Beale Street parade took place after dark, starting at Mississippi Avenue between Booker Washington High School and the undertaking parlor of T. H. Hayes, whose son Thomas Jr. was master of ceremonies. The committee arranged for my wife and me to ride in the first car heading the parade and my son and daughter, Wyer and Elizabeth, followed in the next. It was largely a repetition of what had taken place five years previously at the time of the park dedication, only this time I sat on the reviewing stand and watched an entire spectacular pageant go mirthfully rolling by.

In Court Square, Main Street, in Memphis, there is a monument to Judge Walter Malone, with his poem *Opportunity* inscribed thereon: "They do me wrong who say I come no more," etc. Under the inspiration of the honor Memphis bestows on her sons, native and adopted, I set this beloved poem to music with a choral arrangement, which had its initial rendition in St. Louis by twelve hundred voices, accompanied by the St. Louis Symphony Orchestra. In due time I was presented with an achievement award by the St. Louis branch of the National Association of Negro Musicians.

Drawing upon the same source, another composition was born, 'Way Down South Where the Blues Began.

First chorus:

Down South in Nature's own garden
Where hearts never harden
Like the grinding stone on old Miller's wheel,
You'll find the world there like a grand pageant
And all a free agent, in peace alone where love is real.
Lawd sent down hardships yet all of our hardships
We understand, 'twas His command and His demand
That the world give in to life worth livin',
'Way down South where the blues began.

Second chorus:

Want to go down where the Father of Waters
And all of his daughters like the human stream
Flow leisurely 'long,
They wear the world there like a loose garment
And without adornment,
All day a dream, all night a song.
Lawd sent boll-wee-vil,
All kinds of upheaval; like Egypt land
He had His plan, He had this plan—
Made the world borrow gladness from sorrow,
'Way down South where the blues began.[10]

[10] From *'Way Down South Where the Blues Began,* copyright 1932 by Handy Bros. Music Co., Inc.

CHAPTER TWENTY

ASCAP

How often have you heard the price of some valuable article quoted with the expression, "You can get it for a song"? If you have ever been told to "sing for it," you have found that a song is considered of little value. But what can give us more comfort than a song or be more soul-stirring than a military band march? And yet a great composer can write his heart on a page of notes that will thrill the world, and that composer may starve to death.

This has happened before the inception of The American Society of Composers, Authors and Publishers, often referred to as ASCAP. Was this organization needed? This chapter will write the answer and you will be the judge and jury.

Gussie L. Davis, a Negro composer of more than six hundred songs, died in poverty. Did his work rate such a poor end? He was the author of *A Lighthouse by the Sea, In the Baggage Coach Ahead* (a song that swept the country at one time) and, again back in the days of the Columbian Exposition or Chicago World's Fair, his famous song *The Fatal Wedding* matched in popularity Charles K. Harris' *After the Ball*.

Why should such talent die in want? Simply because a great artist will pour out his heart and hard-hearted people will take it, unless that artist is protected. If you leave your door open, someone will walk in and help himself; it is as simple as that.

The composer of *Maple Leaf Rag*, Scott Joplin, wrote an entire ragtime opera, *Tremonishia*. He was driven insane by overwork and underpay.

Samuel Coleridge-Taylor, two years my junior, who died the year in which I published the first blues, is without a doubt the greatest name in the list of Negro composers. This celebrated Afro-English composer wrote the incidental music to successful plays by Stephen Phillips: *Herod, Ulysses, Nero, Faust*. The picturesque and melodious choral work, the trilogy of *Hiawatha*, is considered his best work. His first symphony was performed the year I joined the minstrels. J. Rosamond Johnson tells me that he attended an opera with Coleridge-Taylor and when the conductor spied him in the box he stopped the orchestra and they all rose and faced Taylor in an orchestral salute. I have heard that had it not been for England pensioning his family they would have been left in humble circumstances.

And, it is said that John Howard Payne, writer of *Home Sweet Home*, had no real home and his lonesome wanderings around the world inspired this deathless song.

It is hardly necessary at this time to speak of what most European masters had to undergo by way of privation of the necessities of life while creating works that still fill the coffers of others long after they have joined the Immortals.

The French, who set a premium on the arts, taking advantage of this situation, organized the French Society of Composers, Authors and Publishers to safeguard their interests. Thus, France collected a fee for each public rendition of a composer's work. My royalties from this source mounted higher as time passed.

It is said of Saint-Saëns, the great French composer, that his funeral was a state function comparable in this country with that of a great warrior or statesman. But in America it was inconceivable that a composer who wrote a song to gladden the hearts of millions, who inspired men to march to the defense of their country, who supplied the words with which a mother croons her baby to sleep, was destined to fill other than a pauper's grave.

Even justice seems to adjust the balances in favor of the man with the most money. Here may be hidden a reason why America has inadequate copyright laws and is not a party to the International Copyright Treaties at the Berne Convention. Prior to 1909, in this country a phonograph company could reproduce an American composer's works and sell them for profit, without his permission or without pay or royalty to his publisher.

The copyright law protects against similarity of melody, as presented to the eye by a written score. When' an unlabeled Sousa's march could not be identified by its author—grooves on a disc couldn't be read by the keenest eye—trickery entered and composer and publisher had no redress.

It is to the credit of the composer and publisher that a corrective copyright law was enacted, providing for a royalty of two cents per record on each composition reproduced mechanically for nationwide distribution.

Through the creative genius of young America, gigantic organizations flourished and, with millions flowing into their money chests, music lovers bought as many as two million copies of a single song. And that's what composers and publishers call a "hit."

Victor Herbert had written as many operettas as any European. John Philip Sousa had played his marches around the world. Nevin had given us *The Rosary, Narcissus* and *Mighty Lak A Rose*. Burleigh had transcribed the spiritual so the white man could sing *Deep River*. Cole and the Johnson brothers had electrified two continents with their songs, while the Witmarks, the Von Tilzers, Joseph W. Stern Company, Feist and Frankenthaler were supplying the hits which America whistled when not singing Howley, Haviland and Dresser's *On the Banks of the Wabash*. To include all the song writers who produced songs that made stars, who in turn made more songs, is not the purpose of this chapter. The point is that American composers all over the map became conscious of an American music that replaced the compositions from overseas, wherein fashions were set in song much as they were in clothes. It was popular to imitate patterns worn by Prince Albert, or the ladies copied designs of French origin.

New York composers, out of a desire for intimate acquaintance and more good fellowship, met at Luchow's on 14th Street and formed an organization without regard to race, creed or color. H. T. Burleigh, the Johnsons, Will Marion Cook, R. C. McPherson (Cecil Mack) and Will H. Tyers (all Negroes) were in on the ground floor. It was fortunate for this body that in their first meeting the eminent attorney, the late Nathan Burkan, took an active and brotherly interest by giving advice which transformed the group into more than a social organization. They hit upon the idea that a musical composition should not be performed for profit without some of these profits finding their way back to the composer's purse.

George W. Maxwell, of the G. Ricordi Company, owing to his knowledge of the inner workings of foreign organizations of composers, became the Society's first president. Since that time the Society has made reciprocal agreements with all such Performing Rights Societies throughout the world and acts as a clearing house for its 1285 American members and over 42,000 foreign authors and composers and their estates. These reciprocal agreements are respected by the countries of Europe not under the dominating influence of the Hitler régime. It was the vision of Victor Herbert and Gene Buck that made this Society a reality.

Without the inner workings of the Society, how could I know that a talkie was singing my song in the Fiji Islands, or that China was listening to Mae West singing the *Memphis Blues* in her motion picture, "The Belle of the Nineties"? How could I, one individual, demand recompense from seven hundred or more radio stations in the United States alone? How could I collect performing fees from the thousands of cabarets and restaurants?

When a man operates a restaurant and supplies a sandwich for a dime, with coffee for a nickel, then adds an orchestra and raises the price of the sandwich and coffee, presumably he adds this charge to pay for the music. We call such use of our music, performance for profit. The same holds true where ten-cent bottles of ginger ale reach the delightful high of one dollar in a night club. All clubs where music is used commercially pay a music license fee, and from this and all sources mentioned, I receive my share as a composer through ASCAP.

Only recently, ASCAP fought to defeat a new copyright bill which favors the users of music (such as radio, talking pictures, television, hotels, night clubs, theatres, etc.) without due regard for the makers of music (who are authors, composers and publishers).

As stated before, our copyright law in its present form has not fully protected us. As late as the year 1940 bills introduced would make it next to impossible for an individual composer or publisher to secure redress through the courts. Many states hostile to ASCAP have enacted laws which deprive me of rights guaranteed by Federal copyright. If there was an infringement, we'll say, of my music by some radio station on the Pacific coast, ASCAP could collect by law two hundred and fifty dollars minimum damages. Let's see how this would work under one proposed law. There would be a minimum damage of one dollar and the court could fix the damages for more if it saw fit. I should have to cross the continent to appear before a court that could postpone the hearing to a future date. Meanwhile, similar infringements might be going on in all parts of the country simultaneously, making court hearings necessary at one and the same time. If I could be one dozen individuals "we" would be worn out defending and proving.

You have doubtless seen song sheets containing one hundred late songs, words only, peddled on street corners near theatres for only five cents. Our various protective organizations have spent many years of hard work and a lot of money in an effort to stamp out this piracy. The buyer goes home, turns on his radio and learns the latest songs without buying a copy of the regular sheet music. This practice has cost the music industry millions of dollars through loss of sheet music sales, and yet there was an imperfection in our copyright law that left the industry practically helpless. Some provisions have been made for our protection and the evil has diminished perceptibly through the efforts of the Music Publishers' Protective Association.

At the semi-annual banquets given by ASCAP and held at the Ritz-Carlton or the Hotel Astor, or wherever they may be, it is refreshing to hear reports of the Society's growth and the restatements of its objectives.

The Society has had many honored guests at these dinners, one of whom was the aged daughter of Stephen Collins Foster, who never dreamed that one day an organization would be formed to see that no widow or orphan of one who writes the nation's songs shall know want or lack the necessities of life. Another guest was Mrs. Edward MacDowell. At other times we have had as our guests, lawyers and judges from all parts of the country who have helped in their districts to protect our work from infringement.

Two of these gentlemen from Memphis and Atlanta, when time permitted, sat at my table and spoke words of encouragement, since they considered me a representative product of the South. Senator A. O. Stanley was once our guest, the man who danced to my music thirty years before at a Kentucky barbecue. At another time our guest of honor was Congressman Sol Bloom, himself once a song writer and publisher. Benjamin Franklin's maxim, "Fools make feasts and wise men eat them," though true, is not applicable to ASCAP dinners. The Society's reserve fund has stood solidly behind its members and is always accessible in case of sickness or any other form of distress. It has gone further than this by giving such aid even to non-members who have contributed to creative art and through no fault of their own have become impoverished.

When banks were crashing and gigantic corporations were financially on the rocks, and even governments were becoming insolvent, thanks to the integrity and vision of our Board of Directors, we received our royalties promptly on the same date each quarter of the year.

Another observation highly commendable is the fact that during the depression no member of our Society applied for or received relief from the government.

During the latter part of 1940 there was difference of opinion between ASCAP and the major networks on the terms for renewal of license agreements terminating December 31st. A music publishing firm was set up with the idea of providing the networks with music to replace that controlled by ASCAP, so on midnight, December 31st, all of ASCAP's vast reservoir was replaced by publications, most of which are in the public domain.

The vast majority of the press was sympathetic to ASCAP and countless columnists expressed in no uncertain terms their disapproval of the stand taken by radio. One of the most outstanding articles, by Louis Sobol, nationally syndicated writer for the Hearst papers, appeared in the *New York Journal-American* of Friday, January 10, 1941.

In his column New York Cavalcade, and headed "Life Was No Song For These Composers," he tells in a few words what I am trying to tell in a whole chapter. By kind permission, I quote:

"About Composers—By this time the public is beginning to realize, I imagine, how truly boring radio can be when it tries to force music upon listeners who prefer to hear melodies they want to hear. But this department's real interest in ASCAP goes beyond that. He knows that but for ASCAP, many of our songwriters would have died penniless. He knows two cases at least where one-time well-known songwriters who had not joined the Society were nevertheless taken care of by the organization in their final days—also given a decent funeral. Not much, you might say, but more than these boys who write words and music could count upon before ASCAP.

"A composer's life was never too happy a one in other years. When Claude Debussy died on March 25, 1918, for instance, he left no estate except his author's rights, his manuscripts and his fame. To supplement his income, he had edited Chopin's works, revised Bach's violin sonatas and offered to write a method for teaching piano. Then take Robert Schumann, a gay, light-hearted fellow as ever you'd want to meet, but after he married Clara Weick and they had several children, he discovered he couldn't support his family on the musical pieces he was turning out. So he went insane.

"Franz Schubert died at the age of 31 leaving a 'few articles of clothing, a mattress, bed coverings and some old music.' During his lifetime, he had received approximately $6.00 in payment for his Trout-quintet, $4.40 for the beautiful Trio in E Flat and about 20 cents apiece for the Winterreise cycle of songs.

"Mozart died at 36 and was buried in a pauper's grave. His friends would not even defray the expenses of his funeral and when his wife appealed to them frantically, she received advice as to the cheapest way to bury him! At one time Hector Berlioz, famous French composer of *The Damnation of Faust*, lived on raisins, bread and salt in order to meet the debts incurred when he paid to have one of his own Masses performed. Boccherini (1743–1805), composer of the famous minuets, was constantly in want and was reduced to making guitar arrangements for wealthy dilettantes.

"Ludwig van Beethoven lived on handouts most of his life. From 1800 on, Prince Lichnowsky contributed to his support and in 1808 three Viennese noblemen guaranteed him 4,000 florins a year if he would stay in Vienna instead of going to Cassel. But sooner or later they dropped the payments and Beethoven was forced to sue them all in order to collect a small part of what he had been promised.

"Frédéric Chopin, ill and poverty stricken, made his last public appearance at a ball in the London Guildhall (which was destroyed by bombs last week) for the benefit of the Polish refugees. No one listened to him—no one seemed to care even that he was there, although some mourned when a few weeks later he was dead—of tuberculosis, aggravated by undernourishment. Johannes Brahms was never very affluent but in later years when he earned some money, he still lived alone in a furnished room and got up every morning at 5 o'clock to make his own coffee, so uncertain was he that this 'affluence' would last.

"George Friedrich Handel died in London on April 14, 1759. According to Samuel Butler in his note-books: 'People say the generous British public supported Handel. It did nothing of the kind. On the contrary for some 30 years it did its best to ruin him, twice drove him to bankruptcy, badgered him till in 1737 he had a paralytic seizure, which was as near as might be the death of him and if he died then we should have had no *Israel*, nor *Messiah*, nor *Samson* nor any of his greatest oratorios. What kept Handel was not the public but the court. It was the pension given him by George the First and George the Second that enabled him to carry on at all.'

"In this battle between radio and ASCAP, the air people are crowding the waves with Stephen Foster masterpieces because they are in the public domain. Foster, unfortunately, was not a member of ASCAP and so today his song, *Jeanie With the Light Brown Hair* is a No. 1 melody. But the announcers forget to introduce the song by revealing that Stephen Foster was forced to sell most of his beautiful tunes for petty cash—and that he died penniless."

The Federal government stepped into this controversy by commencing anti-trust proceedings against both ASCAP and radio's competing publishing house, and both organizations submitted to "consent decrees" eliminating such details of their systems as the Attorney-General criticized from the public standpoint. As there were no trials, it is impossible to know how the Court would have ruled on these questions after hearing the evidence, but what I wish to emphasize is that whatever criticisms our government had to offer still recognized the essential world-wide protective functions of ASCAP itself, which would be utterly beyond the powers of any individual.

In looking over a copy of the *Literary Digest* one day, I ran across a criticism of the Society reprinted from a Nashville paper to the effect that the Society was good at collecting money but wondering what was done with it after it was collected. Being a former Tennesseean, I undertook to explain by letter what I knew of the workings of the Society, stating as best I could how its revenues were divided—one-half to the publisher-members and one-half to its authors and composers. These sums are redistributed to the members according to the volume and quality of their music used. I made it clear how I had been voluntarily raised from a low rating up to almost the highest classification in the Society. My letter evidently carried the necessary information, for the Tennessee newspaper printed it.

ASCAP considers a song as intellectual property, and it believes that a composer's song is entitled to the same protection as an inventor's patent or a realtor's holdings.

You know by this time that in 1912 I sold *Memphis Blues* outright. At that time radio, motion pictures, television, etc. had not been anticipated. Yet since the formation of ASCAP, it and its affiliated foreign societies have collected fees for public performance of *Memphis Blues*, which go into the writers' share of the quarterly distributions and thus indirectly benefit me. Performing Rights Societies, in short, say to the publisher in effect, "Yes, you own the copyright but you didn't write the song, so the author and composer are justly entitled to some of its benefits even after parting with their ownership."

One of the great assets of our organization is its president, Gene Buck, who has held that office for many years now and who was well prepared by earlier activities for handling the problems of the creators of music. He has designed as many as three thousand title covers for sheet music. For almost twenty years he was associated with Florenz Ziegfeld, Jr., writing as many editions of the *Follies*, not to mention sixteen editions of the *Midnight Frolic*. There are more than three hundred song lyrics to his credit. Among the best known are *Tulip Time, Hello Frisco, Sally, Won't You Come Back?* and *No Foolin'*. He has collaborated with Victor Herbert, Dave Stamper, Lou A. Hirsch, Jerome Kern, Raymond Hubbell, Rudolf Friml and Mischa Elman.

There have been times in my life as a composer here in New York when to march onward seemed almost useless; then the memory of speeches made and plans laid by E. C. Mills, chairman of ASCAP's Administrative Committee, gave renewed strength and determination to carry on. There has not been one time when the way looked dark, and when I sought advice and guidance, that he failed to give the best in him. This is true of all ASCAP officials and the staff, but Mr. Mills somehow just seems to hold reality as in a closed fist. I had known him when his was the guiding hand of the Vaudeville Managers' Association in the days of Pat Casey; also as chairman of the Board of Directors of the Music Publishers' Protective Association, until succeeded in that capacity by John G. Paine, now general manager of ASCAP. Mr. Paine has brought to ASCAP the personality and understanding which enabled him to create great good will among the music industries of America. He was succeeded by Harry Fox who licenses the use of our music for phonograph recordings, electrical transcriptions and talking pictures. Walter G. Douglas, chairman of the Board of Directors, has brought to the Publishers' Association the valuable experience of a lifetime devoted to executive work as a music publisher.

Among the 1285 members of the American Society of Composers, Authors and Publishers there are approximately fifty members of my race who have contributed to the vast

19

reservoir of American music compositions ranging from symphony to swing. They also belong to another organization of which I am justly proud, the Song Writers' Protective Association, under the leadership of Irving Caesar, successor to Sigmund Romberg, who is securing for the song writer further benefits.

In Manhattan the original inhabitant could look across the Hudson, but his loudest cry could not penetrate beyond the Palisades. Today, seventy stories above the street from the RCA Building in Radio City, Father Knickerbocker can look across Long Island and see the Atlantic Ocean. He can chat with Singapore or London and broadcast his music around the world. Perhaps out where morning stars sing together, ether waves may have carried, "I hate to see de evenin' sun go down." Yes, along these waves my songs reach unbelievable lands and entertain numberless unknowns. On such a broad highway of life why should one not feel repaid for any hardship endured along the trail?

Just come with me off Fifth Avenue at 50th Street, to the greatest music center of the world and through the halls of Radio City with its gold, granite and marble walls which no palace can surpass in architectural splendor. Take the elevator up to the forty-fifth floor—that is the home of the American Society of Composers, Authors and Publishers.

It is a far cry from Handy's Hill to Harlem or from a rock quarry to Radio City, but we live in a new day and this is America.

CHAPTER TWENTY-ONE

Treasure Island

IN THE old Florence District School, during oratoricals, one of my favorite declamations was that from McGuffey's Fifth Reader, "No Excellence Without Great Labor," by William Wirt of Maryland, a former attorney-general of the United States. I recited this so often and with such great emphasis that it became a governing factor in all my subsequent undertakings. "There Is No Excellence Without Great Labor. It is the fiat of fate, from which no power of genius can absolve you," etc. I quote the last line: "This is the prowess, and these the hardy achievements which will enroll your name among the great men of the earth."

I had seen a Negro's name, B. K. Bruce, registrar of the U.S. Treasury, on Uncle Sam's currency. I had read *The Black Phalanx, The Rising Sun*, and other books which told of the achievements of our race. Young as I was, I knew we were limited and proscribed. But "what man has done, man can do." At the New York World's Fair, 1939–40, I saw, in small degree, a fulfillment of "No Excellence Without Great Labor." There on the American Common, tablets were erected containing the names of six hundred men and women selected from all races who had contributed in some degree to American culture, and among those names I saw mine.

Eduard C. Lindeman, Professor of Philosophy at the New

York School of Social Work, in dedicating this site (the gift of Sears-Roebuck Company to the American people) said in part: "We have gathered at this place, the American Common, for a unique and a sublime purpose. The event is unique because it is highly probable that it could not at this moment be duplicated in any other country in the world. The occasion is sublime because it is concerned with human personality, and with that most subtle of all human equations, the relation of the citizen to his nation."

On this same site a week was devoted to the achievements of the Negro with programs worthy of mention. However, it should suffice to say that the ceremonies were opened by an address of welcome delivered by the Honorable Fiorello H. La Guardia, Mayor of New York City. Other speakers were Harvey D. Gibson, Chairman of the Board, World's Fair 1940 in New York; Harvey W. Anderson, Director of the American Common; the Reverend John H. Johnson, Rector, St. Martin's Episcopal Church, Chaplain, Police Department, New York City. Throughout the week, music, drama and esthetic dancing studded each program with such outstanding artists as Todd Duncan and Anne Brown of *Porgy and Bess;* the Rose McClendon Players; the Karamu Dancers of Cleveland, Ohio; Eddie Matthews, celebrated baritone; the best choirs in and around New York; Negro authors and composers; celebrities of stage, screen and radio, assisted by the World's Fair band.

T. Arnold Hill was General Chairman; Geraldyn Dismond, Chairman, Program Committee; Lawrence D. Reddick, History Committee; and Channing H. Tobias, Religious Activities. The committee was wise in its selection of W. E. Burghardt DuBois, author and philosopher, who spoke of the achievements of the race, of its aspirations and its part in the "World of Tomorrow."

ASCAP celebrated its Silver Jubilee at Carnegie Hall in New York City, during the week of October 1, 1939. It was the greatest program of all-American music ever staged—and free to the public. Each night the program was of a different character.

It opened Sunday evening with excerpts from outstanding musical comedies. Monday evening had a program of Negro music from symphony to swing. Tuesday evening was devoted to various military bands; Wednesday—folk and heart songs; Thursday—symphonic works; Friday—American symphonic jazz, melody and swing, purveyed by Paul Whiteman, Glenn Miller, Benny Goodman, and Fred Waring with his orchestra and choir. The demand for seats was so great that in order to accommodate the overflow the bandsmen repeated their respective performances immediately following at the 71st Regiment Armory. The Saturday matinee performance was devoted to compositions of children's music, for an audience mainly made up young people. On Saturday evening, the second concert was devoted to symphonic works.

The entire festival was produced under the personal direction of Gene Buck, assisted by Deems Taylor, Frank Black, John J. O'Connor, W. C. Handy, George W. Meyer, Abram Chasins, Roy Harris, and Fred Ahlert, with R. H. Burnside as stage manager.

I should like to go into the details of the composers who took part and how the audience thrilled at hearing their works played and sung by the authors and composers themselves. These programs were repeated in San Francisco at the Golden Gate International Exposition on Treasure Island and at the New York World's Fair, "The World of Tomorrow," a month later. So to avoid repetition we pass along to the all-Negro program from symphony to swing that took place on the evening of October 2, 1939.

The committee thought it fitting and proper that this night be set apart to show the creative and interpretative gifts of the Negro. Another committee consisting of J. Rosamond Johnson, Harry T. Burleigh and myself was designated to arrange matters. The actual labor fell upon the capable shoulders of Charles L. Cooke, Joe Jordan and my secretary, Pearl Carn.

ASCAP empowered me to engage the most outstanding concert artists, and the Negro Symphony, whatever the cost. The program proved a real success due to the cooperation of the choirs of the Abyssinian Baptist Church, Wen Talbot, Donald Heywood and Juanita Hall, plus renditions by Jessie Zachary, Clyde Barrie, the Southernaires, Minto Cato and my daughter, Katherine Lewis. The program opened with the three hundred and fifty voices of the combined choirs, accompanied by the seventy-five piece orchestra under the baton of Joe Jordan, in *Lift Every Voice and Sing*. Then followed excerpts from three symphonies conducted in turn by their respective composers, James P. Johnson, *From Harlem*; Charles L. Cooke, *Sketches of the Deep South*; and William G. Still, *American Symphony*.

The second half of the program opened with a minstrel first part, consisting of members of the Crescendo Club, of which J. C. Johnson is president. Henry Troy acted as the interlocutor, with Tom Fletcher and Laurence Deas as end men. Plantation melodies ranging from the earliest minstrel days to songs from the various musical productions of Williams and Walker, Cole and Johnson, Sissle and Blake and others were rendered. Each member of the club, being a song writer, presented in turn his own famous compositions many of which had ushered in various dance crazes: *Pas-a-ma-la, Ballin' the Jack, Shimmie, Charleston*, etc. Maceo Pinkard and Clarence Williams were ably assisted in their respective songs, *Mammy o' Mine* and *Baby, Won't You Please Come Home?* by their vocalist wives, Edna Alexander and Eva Taylor.

The minstrel grand finale was Cramer and Layton's *'Way Down Yonder in New Orleans*, thrillingly sung by the entire company, followed by a wild orgy of blues, jazz, jitterbug and jive, now called swing, in which the following bands participated: Cab Calloway, Noble Sissle, Louis Armstrong and Claude Hopkins. Although they were unable to be there in person, Duke Ellington, Thomas "Fats" Waller, Andy Razaf, Benny Carter and Jimmie Lunceford were represented by the playing of some of their noted compositions. In this concert, as has been the case in all others in which I have had managerial interest, the Musicians' Union, Local 802, A. F. of M., gave wonderful cooperation through its secretary, William Feinberg.

Previously, ASCAP had released through the press of the country a biographical sketch, in cartoon form, of my life as they knew it, which inspired a seventeen-year-old colored girl, Mary Annie Bunting of Columbia, S. C., to write and produce a play, *Cavalcade of the Blues*. I was invited to witness its presentation and to be crowned. Youngsters sang and played themes of their own compositions as part of the play. At the time, I was appearing nightly at the Cotton Club but my contract permitted me to witness this one performance. I was compelled to board a plane, fly to Columbia, then back, to insure my being on time for my regular nightly performance where the Davis-Coots song-tribute, "Thanks To You, Mr. Handy, For Giving Us the St. Louis Blues," was my entrance cue. This was followed by a grandiose arrangement of *St. Louis Blues* played by the orchestra, the entire cast marching on stage; beautifully gowned and glamorous courtly ladies, trailed by tinseled chorus girls and dancing boys, the gay lights playing upon their brilliantly attractive costumes. From high up in a staged organ loft came the thrilling voices of a trained choir, chanting and contributing to the grand finale led by the one and only Cab Calloway.

The Cotton Club celebrated my birthday that year by inviting friends and acquaintances in the theatrical profession and music industry. One hundred special invitations were sent to outstanding members of my race to witness the unveiling of a bust by Augusta Savage. Among these special guests was none other than my old friend from Memphis,

Bob Church, together with his beautiful daughter. That night I had the extreme pleasure of relating to him how his father, the late R. R. Church, had been instrumental in training my mind to look at music from a business standpoint. I spoke of the time when I had appeared late for an appointment with the latter, and was reprimanded with, "Young man, I take care of my business and my business takes care of me. If you'd take care of your business, your business would take care of you." Coming from an ex-slave, who in an ordinary lifetime had amassed a fortune of two million dollars, this advice stung me so forcibly that its significance was indelibly impressed upon my being. As a boy I went to Memphis just to see the home of this man whose fame had gone abroad during the yellow fever epidemic that had stricken Memphis in the early seventies. The Beale of that day was not the street I praised in song, for there was a gay, glamorous social circle among the colored aristocrats which created within me that restlessness and urge to do worth while things and to be a somebody in this life.

My telephone rang one day seemingly louder than ever. I took up the receiver eagerly and a voice on the other end said,

"Hello, Bill, how would you like to go to San Francisco?"

I answered, "I'd like it fine. I haven't been out there in forty years."

"George M. Cohan, Irving Berlin, Harry Armstrong and Joseph E. Howard are going to fly out there. Do you want to take the plane with them?"

"No, I would rather take the train and get a good look at the towns, rivers, plains and mountains over the route we took in the old minstrel days."

"All right, meet us at the Grand Central Station, five-thirty Tuesday afternoon, and bring along your trumpet. About fifty members of ASCAP are going along to present a festival

of American music at the Golden Gate International Exposition on Treasure Island at San Francisco."

The voice on the telephone was that of Gene Buck. At
the appointed time I was at the station, where his invaluable
secretary, Miss Sylvia Rosenberg, provided tickets for me and
my assistant, Louise P. Logan, for the Twentieth Century
Limited.

Three days of travel on a streamlined train with every
modern convenience, covering the route I had so many times
traveled before, afforded much time for reflection. No riding
the rods, blind baggage, nor bumming my way to a World's
Fair this time! No telephones to answer, no mail to be both-
ered with, just sleeping, eating and reminiscing . . . Paul Wyer,
the tattered clarinetist when we met on the banks of the
Mississippi, and who played with our original blues band,
now a successful orchestra leader in Buenos Aires, after writing me from Asia, Africa and Europe. Thinking of how I'll
run down to Los Angeles to meet old friends and relatives,
then to Pasadena which I once thought America's most beautiful city. Thinking about the song I wrote, *Pasadena*, that
opened with these lines:

> Out where the Serri Indian treasures buried lie,
> Sierra Madre tiptoes to kiss the azure sky.
> Where golden sunsets woo silv'ry twilights in a sapphire sea
> My Pasadena is calling me. . . .

Occasionally I was aroused from my reveries by members
of our party, in particular Jean Schwartz and Dave Stamper,
who inquired whether or not I was comfortable and enjoying
the trip. Indeed I was, thanks to the constant and thoughtful
attention which I was receiving.

Time on my hands, in my comfortable compartment, I
thought about the time when a Negro porter managed the
affairs of a great railroad line between St. Louis and Memphis.

I had a very important engagement in Memphis and phoned the Union Station to make reservation, inquiring about the next train and the fare. I checked out at my hotel, went to the station and a redcap hustled my baggage to the ticket office. I called for a ticket to Memphis, at the same time passing the money through the window. The agent looked at me very thoughfully and then said, "You will have to see the conductor."

"See the conductor for what?" I inquired. While I was trying to straighten out the matter the redcap said, "I'll get the conductor for you."

He brought the conductor to me and I explained to him the importance of making the train. The conductor said, "See the porter."

"But why should I see the porter?" I asked.

Again the redcap spoke. "I'll take you to the porter."

Loaded down with my luggage he walked me past nine cars and found the porter. I told him of my experiences and that the conductor had sent me to him. He told me to give him the money for the ticket, showing me a little seat in a corner that would cost four dollars and fifty cents extra but I would have to get off the train at Metropolis, Illinois, and wait for the accommodation train. I didn't go to Memphis!

For the moment forgetting such injustices long endured, I picked up my trumpet and blew a few notes in an effort to get my lips toughened so that I would not make any flukey tones in our concert at the Fair.

The service on the diner and the chef were par excellence. Here I had no petty annoyances like one a month before when I was motoring from New York to Chicago. A little way out of Columbus, our party consisting of a white gentleman, my chauffeur, secretary and myself stopped at a roadside restaurant for luncheon. We all ordered "steak-ett" and coffee. I noticed preparations were slow for the secretary and me. My chauffeur, being rather light, must have been taken for a foreigner and was served promptly along with the white gentleman. Finally, the waiter brought my lunch in a brown paper bag and laid it on my plate. My secretary, knowing that my sight is impaired, told him to serve me properly. So we ate our steak-ett and drank our coffee and I asked for a glass of water. The waiter served water to all, but mine came in a paper cup which he placed in the glass. I drank out of the paper cup, laid down a ten-dollar bill to pay for our luncheon, and the waiter had to go to several places outside to make change. When he brought my change back I asked him if he had ever heard the *St. Louis Blues* and he began to tell me how he liked it. I told him that I happened to be the writer of that song and that I am an American. I reminded him of the great pains he took to humiliate me probably because he didn't like the color of my face. He looked sheepish and muttered something about the boss. I told him to tell the boss that America is appealing for unity now while one-half of the world is warring against the other half or making preparations to fight because of racial antagonism. As our party was entering the car another waiter who had seen the incident and overheard the discussion apologetically expressed his regrets for the happening and he stated that he personally had no antagonism, as he was working on a project in a local high school with colored school-mates. From his tone of voice he was sincere.

To remove the grief from what is to follow I repeat here the story I once heard and have used for illustration. During the World War, Negroes were migrating North in great masses. The story goes that all were leaving a town in the deep South and a little white child was crying as though her heart would break. A visitor asked her why she was crying and she sobbingly replied, "All the niggers are leaving."

The visitor remarked, "I thought you would be glad to see the colored people leaving."

The innocent child said, she didn't want to see *all* of them go "because if *all* of them go there won't be anybody left for us to be better than."

"Somebody to be better than," on trains, in restaurants, in theatres, yes, from the cradle to the grave.

Even in democratic Manhattan this monster prejudice had to show its head in a hospital where my wife in her last days was kept outside one hour in an ambulance after arrangements had already been made for her admittance. The head nurse told me, "There must be some mistake," and while waiting anxiously I asked the telephone girl what was wrong. She replied, "We don't take colored people in private rooms."

Well, no more reminiscing. Our train had come to its final stop, Berkeley, and I alighted with a song in my heart and ASCAP on my mind. We were met by the composer of *Smiles*, Lee S. Roberts, a native son of San Francisco. Here we took the boat and cameras clicked all the way to 'Frisco. Then to the Hotel St. Francis where we met other writer-members from Hollywood and Los Angeles. A huge banner of welcome greeted us and as if this were not enough to make us feel at home we were promptly notified that we would be recipients of California's hospitality on various occasions. There we met Marshall Dill, president of the Golden Gate International Exposition, who invited us to Mrs. Dill's cocktail party. Then there were invitations for luncheons from the Press Club, Club Bohemia and the Government Building on the Exposition grounds.

Give Mr. and Mrs. America something tingly to sing and perhaps the composer to play it, or a concert artist accompanied by the San Francisco Symphony Orchestra of one hundred and ten sterling musicians to voice it, and they'll never go home. This is just the way officials of the Golden Gate Exposition felt the day following the performance of the Music Festival presented by ASCAP on Treasure Island, September 24, 1940.

Twenty-five thousand persons attended the open air concert 'neath the glorious California skies that afternoon, and twenty-five thousand more attempted to squeeze their way in at the evening performance held at the Coliseum which could seat but twelve thousand. Another ten thousand heard the program "piped" into nearby Festival Hall. Although it sounds like something emanating from a Hollywood press agent, the counter at the front gate showed sixty-six thousand eight hundred and five persons attending that day.

Quite naturally, the afternoon symphony program held in Federal Plaza called forth the attention of lovers of such music, plus the music critics and editors. As a result, American music was heard and cheered by more auditors than had ever assembled in that part of the world for a strictly American musical program.

The mind of the audience was prepared at the start by Gene Buck, introduced by Marshall Dill, who gave a comprehensive idea of the purposes of the Festival, in his eloquent yet direct and simple manner.

The concert opened with Roy Harris' *Johnny Comes Marching Home*, and Dr. Howard Hanson, Director of the Eastman School of Music, Rochester, N. Y., conducted Harris' work and his own work, *Third Symphony*. This was followed by ballet music from Richard Hageman's opera, *Caponsacchi*, conducted by the composer. Then came Charles Wakefield Cadman's *Dark Dancers at the Mardi Gras*, the composer at the piano and the orchestra under the baton of Edwin McArthur. William Grant Still introduced his *La Guiablesse* and two movements from his *G Minor Symphony*. According to the critics, Still proved a composer who can qualify as one of the most graceful conductors ever seen on a podium.

As the concert began, I was seated together with Shelton Brooks, Irving Berlin and Harold Arlen in the first row where a local news photographer caught us enjoying the program. Had it been a sound movie camera, it would have saved for

posterity the unusually hearty laughter of Shelton as he guf-
fawed at the seven trombones' imitation of a herd of elephants
trumpeting during the playing of Deems Taylor's *Circus Day*.
Mr. Taylor had declined to conduct it, because he "wanted
it heard to the best possible advantage" and so invited Conductor Edwin McArthur to direct the performance while he
himself "could tell the audience how good it was." The
combined efforts of Mr. McArthur and the orchestra saved
him the task, for the audience showed their approval of some
of the most entertaining music ever introduced on a symphony program.

When my taxi arrived at the Exposition grounds that night
I was met by a young man and escorted to a box seat which
I shared with George M. Cohan, who on various occasions
had displayed a most kindly, friendly attitude toward me.
Shortly after, this same youngster invited me from that box
to a more advantageous spot. Here I gazed directly into the
beaming face of Dr. Hanson as he led the orchestra in memo-
rial tributes to John Philip Sousa and Victor Herbert. Touch-
ingly beautiful and thrilling, American music!

Gene Buck had begun this performance with a beautiful
tribute in memory of those departed members who had dedicated their lives to the building of this great reservoir of
music. One outstanding statement that I shall never forget
was, "There is nothing finer than a song to hang a memory
on." Were I able to recapture the remarks he made while
introducing the contributors to the evening's program and
place them herein, this would be indeed a marvelously written
chapter.

There's Lee S. Roberts, composer of *Smiles*, walking over
to the piano. My mind flashed back to the old days when
he headed the Q.R.S. Roll Co., and to J. Russel Robinson,
then a staff artist, billed "the white boy with the 'cullud'
fingers," first to record my blues on hand-played rolls. *Smiles*
put them in a singing mood and turned this vast audience

into one magnificent choir which accompanied Roberts and all of the composers who followed with their respective songs.

Two pleasant young men, writers of hundreds of famed Paramount Picture songs, Leo Robin and Ralph Rainger, sang and played their always beautiful *Love in Bloom*. The onetime Broadway "hit" writer and publisher, now retired, Albert Von Tilzer, started the opening strains of *Take Me Out to the Ball Game*. The audience caught the spirit of "buy me some peanuts and cracker-jack." Billy Hill offered his *The Last Round-Up* and little did the cheering audience realize his own "last round-up" would be in Boston during the coming Christmas holiday season. Ex-vaudeville headliner and show stopper Shelton Brooks walked over to the piano to deliver in his own inimitable manner *Some of These Days*. A gay young motion picture star, Judy Garland, acknowledged the welcome from the audience to her and friendly Harold Arlen as they proceeded to give out Arlen's popular *Over the Rainbow*. Dapper Ernie Burnett, witty and affable but withal the composer of the torchiest of all torch songs, *Melancholy Baby*, struck a few arpeggios and to his delight the vast crowd picked up the chorus. ASCAP's Los Angeles representative, L. Wolfe Gilbert, lifted the crowd with his zippy song of the levee, *Waitin' for the Robert E. Lee*. Still partners after a quarter of a century together, the Messrs. Bert Kalmar and Harry Ruby made merry, to the happiness of all, with one of their many compositions, *Three Little Words*. Walter Donaldson occupied the spotlight now. George Whiting wrote the lyric of his first offering, *My Blue Heaven*, which was a favorite of my late wife. He next rendered *My Buddy* with its touching lyric of lament by Gus Kahn. A distinct hush overcame the audience as Mr. Buck presented the beloved Mrs. Carrie Jacobs Bond, America's most successful woman music publisher and writer. As she played *The End of a Perfect Day* it took me back to the days of my dance orchestra when we always closed our sessions with this lovely melody. It was sung by Allan Linquist.

The ever changing mood of the program was never more noticeable than when young Miss Ann Ronell put a laugh in the hearts of all with her famous song of Disney's "Three Little Pigs," "*Who's Afraid of the Big, Bad Wolf?*" The petite composer proved as witty and cute in her rendition as the song itself. Arthur Freed, lyrist and producer with MGM, and his suave composer partner, Nacio Herb Brown, kept up the fast and furious pace of the program with their great novelty contribution, *Singing in the Rain*. The crowd sang out, "I didn't want to do it, I didn't want to do it," as James V. Monaco offered his famous old *You Made Me Love You*. Someone yelled for his then current hit-craze and he was forced to let them have it, *Six Lessons From Madam La Zonga*. High-stepping seventy-two-year-old Joseph E. Howard of the "Gay 90's" radio program was welcomed next and like the veteran performer he is bowled them over with *I Wonder Who's Kissing Her Now*, followed by his cake-walk specialty, *Goodbye, My Lady Love*.

The appearance of the king of the musical comedy field, Jerome Kern, was a most auspicious occasion, for it was but the second time in his life that he had ever performed in public. Tony Martin did justice to *All the Things You Are* and *Smoke Gets in Your Eyes*, with Kern's mastery of the piano asserting itself in the background. Harry Armstrong next addressed the audience with a brief discourse on *Sweet Adeline* in her youth and the romance surrounding her. After a solo chorus, he invited all the barber shop tenors, back room baritones and basso profundos to join in the answers to the lead of his sweet pseudo soprano as he demonstrated his handling of mass conducting.

My eyes followed the next performer, Sigmund Romberg, as he walked to the piano. Serious of mien, this foremost composer of light opera played his *Lover Come Back to Me* with the touch of genius in beautiful, simple, melodic style and the audience demonstrated its appreciation. Another very impressive tribute followed as Mr. McArthur led the orchestra in George Gershwin's *Summertime* and *I've Got Rhythm*. While the audience responded with thunderous applause, my mind reverted to that evening when I dined at the home of a friend in the company of Gershwin, Cadman and Whiteman, and of how we had discussed the great potentialities and possibilities of American music. It reminded me of the untimely passing of this youthful genius. I felt that he too was conscious of this tribute. When Harry Warren and Johnny Mercer stepped out and swung into their recent favorite novelty composition, *Jeepers Creepers*, I became aware that what I had thought was hodge podge was really a swell piece of work done in the American idiom, at which this team excels. *I Can't Give You Anything but Love*, with its composer James McHugh presiding at the piano, came in for a burst of applause and memories of a first nighter at Lew Leslie's *Blackbirds of 1928*. As though it were prearranged as part of the setting, Hoagy Carmichael and his *Stardust* were accompanied by a shower of skyrockets overhead which had somehow been touched off accidentally. It created a spectacular effect, however unintentional, and didn't put a damper on the audience's enthusiasm for the composer and his grand song. Peter DeRose, accompanied by his wife, May Singhi Breen, known to radio fans as "The Ukulele Lady," presented his recent hit, *Deep Purple*, the lyric of which was written by the author of *Stardust*, Mitchell Parrish. Then followed a medley of past hits which the audience knew and adored as sung by this clever man and wife, *When Your Hair Has Turned to Silver*, *Have You Ever Been Lonely?* and *Somebody Loves You*. Laughs and more laughs, that's what any audience gets when they rate the services of lyric writer Mack Gordon, round of girth and fond of fun. To watch him, accompanied on the piano by his partner, Harry Revel, as he spoofed the audience while singing their *Did You Ever See a Dream Walking?*, was

20

to receive more laughs than I ever thought possible in such a short space of time. *Chinatown, My Chinatown*—my favorite fast tune for three decades. The first time I ever heard it created a deep respect for the ability of its composer, though it was many years before I had the opportunity of meeting Jean Schwartz. The lyric was the product of his partner for many years, the lamented "song-boy," William Jerome.

Next I heard Gene Buck announcing my name and after giving my trumpet a few toots to see if my lip could make it, I walked with him to my place before the mike. The orchestra gave out an eight-bar grandiose introduction of *St. Louis Blues* and we all went to town. At Mr. Dill's request a photographer caught me in several action shots which have given me and my friends some laughs. John Charles Thomas followed me as guest soloist with Eugene Heyes conducting as the orchestra played David Guion's song of the Texas plains, *Home on the Range*, a truly great melody; Ethelbert Nevin's *Mighty Lak a Rose*, a song of tenderness which has done much to create sentiment favorable to my race; *Old Man River*, with Mr. Kern again at the piano; and then, *Sally Won't You Come Back*, with composer Dave Stamper at the piano. In this latter number, it was the first time to my knowledge that Gene Buck had ever exposed himself as a writer, for in everything I have ever heard him say in his championing the writer's cause he has never led one to suspect that he once authored the famous Ziegfeld Midnight Roof productions. If John Charles Thomas had sung the concluding number, *The Lord's Prayer*, with piano accompaniment alone, it would have been sublime; but with the orchestra in back of him, as I sat watching the exalted face of Albert Hay Malotte, its composer, conducting, the feeling that came over me was indescribable, especially at its climax as Thomas sang, *"For Thine is the Kingdom, and the Power, and the Glory Forever."* Its divinely spiritual melody brought the feeling of being lifted straight up to the Throne of God, so profound and reverent did it sound—the feeling that Sir Arthur Sullivan's *The Lost Chord* has always inspired in me.

When Gene Buck next appeared with George M. Cohan at his side and attempted to go into his introductory remarks, the applause was so enthusiastic he was forced to cease his attempts. Soon, however, the influence of his skill and technique in audience handling brought on the desired quiet and he reminded them of the "Yankee Doodle Boy's" great gifts and unparalleled contributions to America in both the theatrical and musical worlds. Cohan opened with *Yankee Doodle Boy* ("I'm a Yankee Doodle Dandy") and upon the conclusion of his second number, *Grand Old Flag*, the audience rose with an overwhelming surge of patriotic fervor.

The thirty-third and final performer of the evening was Irving Berlin. Years ago, in an article written for a music magazine, Berlin was quoted as saying that he would rather have been known as the composer of *The Rosary* or *St. Louis Blues* than of anything he had yet written. As he stood there this night of nights, singing along with the combined voices of that tremendous audience, I felt his old statement was jeering at him. At the time he was credited with making it, *God Bless America* had already been written by him for a Yip Yip Yaphank production while he was in the U. S. Army encampment there, and he had laid it away in mothballs, so to speak. It takes talent to write a song. None will deny that Berlin is talented, but it requires real genius to "time" a song —to resurrect it when the nation is in need of it. Irving Berlin is that genius, sane, sympathetic, sincere and unaffected; one of the kind of men who have made America great. He is the Francis Scott Key of our time—*God Bless America*.

Thus the curtain came down on a program that was never before nor can ever again be duplicated this side of Kingdom Come.

As the audience was filing out and we were leaving the

stage, the same youngster let me know that a rolling chair was awaiting me if I cared to accompany him. I did so, still wondering why he should be so interested in my welfare. Along the way to the taxi-stand a half mile distant, I was besieged by autograph seekers whom he did not permit to interfere with his plans. Finally we reached the taxi-stand and finding none there he ordered one by telephone. While waiting I handed him and his companion a substantial tip which both refused. Although I became inquisitive it availed me nothing other than this statement, "I have kept watch over you all the time you were on the grounds, but why, is a secret I cannot divulge."

CHAPTER TWENTY-TWO

Black and White

RETURNING to New York by way of Los Angeles, my cousin Llewellyn Brewer bade me farewell and invited me to come again. I said, "I will if the Lord is willing, if I live, an' don't die, an' nothin' happens." Llewellyn, now in his eighties, had fought with the U. S. Regular Army in their battle with Geronimo. He was at John Wilson's "Big House" when the robbers shot Grandpa Brewer and hit Grandma over the head with a gun. From him I learned that Matthew Wilson gave his ex-slaves who headed families one thousand dollars in cash and forty acres of land each. Llewellyn laughed heartily at "if I live, an' don't die, an' nothin' happens," for he knew it as a characteristic old-time Negro expression. I told a story about this expression to one who is interested in this book and he asked me to tell it to my readers in a chapter on "black and white," which I agreed to do.

A colored man who was "passing" for white in a Southern town got a job at which he worked Friday and Saturday and the boss was well pleased. As he was about to leave, the boss said, "Be here early Monday morning." The "passer" characteristically replied, "If I live, an' nothing happens." The boss spotted him for what he was from this remark, and he was fired immediately.

On the way back to New York, as my thoughts reverted

to "black and white," I recalled some words a Texas girl once submitted to me for a musical setting.

One verse told how the white folks spend their summers getting tanned on the beaches while the colored folks spend their time looking for face bleaches. Another verse had to do with colored folks getting their hair straightened and white folks having kinks and waves put in theirs. The chorus ran:

> So when we get our colors changed,
> Fixed over and made all right—
> White folks will all be colored
> And colored folks will be white.

In Harlem I've often gone to musicales at which ninety-five percent of the program consisted of foreign music. I attended one such program where a great concert artist rendered five old English songs, four French and four Italian songs. A young woman seated at my right jabbed me in the ribs and whispered, "She is making a serious mistake!"

I asked, "What is it?"

"She isn't singing in German," was her reply.

This brings to mind the fact that prominent white orchestra leaders, concert singers and others are making commercial use of Negro music in its various phases. That's why they introduced "swing" which is not a musical form.

Louis Armstrong was a guest artist on Bing Crosby's program. Mr. Crosby in this nationwide hookup was enlightening radio fans on the subject of "swing"—or was he? Anyway, he said, "We have as our guest, the master of swing and I'm going to get him to tell you what swing music is." He asked Louis to explain it. Said Louis:

"Ah, swing, well, we used to call it syncopation—then they called it ragtime, then blues—then jazz. Now, it's swing. Ha! Ha! White folks yo'all sho is a mess. Ha! Ha! Swing!"

I received a letter from an admirer of my music living in Brazil, in which he stated he was the proud possessor of one hundred and twelve different recordings of *St. Louis Blues*. A farmer in Java wrote me that he had a collection of sixty-six, and at the time I didn't have one record of the many I have made for Columbia, Okeh, Paramount and Plaza. Recently I needed a copy of the original edition of *Memphis Blues*. Not even a member of my own family had any kind of a copy. No colored friend could supply me but I obtained a dozen perfect copies, kept for twenty-eight years by various white people, through the courtesy of C. H. (Doc) Hottum of Memphis.

Eubie Blake, commenting on backwardness, told me of a time when he was rehearsing a show for which he hoped to find an "angel." The cast was losing interest, the chorus girls were losing their pep and Eubie himself was at his wits' end as to how to cope with the situation. On his way to rehearsal one day he stopped for a shoeshine. When the Italian bootblack had finished, Eubie got a sudden inspiration. "Please put on your coat and come with me," he said, handing the man a dollar bill. Together they hurried to the rehearsal hall where Eubie yelled out, "Chorus girls on stage! Run down number three." They started to dance and all the while Blake kept up an animated conversation with the Italian, firing questions at him that required an affirmative answer or a nod of the head. Eubie could see that his stunt was fallen for by the psychological change which immediately came over the performers as they figured that a prospective backer was being impressed, and shortly thereafter the show was financed and successfully produced.

With white people the situation is sometimes reversed and quite to the black man's advantage. Although there were plenty available white troops, President Wilson, during the first World War, chose colored soldiers for personal guard duty around the Capitol. There is no "fifth column" in the colored race.

Joe Jordan related how when a lad his mother at great

sacrifice hired a German to teach him violin and to give his sister piano instruction. It seems that Joe progressed to the sixth lesson and the teacher was highly pleased with his efforts until he reviewed the first lesson and found that Joe couldn't play the first note. He wore out his bow strafing young Jordan, then took him to his mother and explained, "He never will be anything but a cheat! He'll never learn anything!" Joe soon got odd jobs around St. Louis that gave him opportunity to practice and obtain further study. Later on, coming to New York where he played in shows and composed music, he was afforded a chance to make a European trip during which he worked professionally and studied as well. Returning to America, he traveled west to Chicago and there was given the management of Robert T. Motts' Pekin Theatre, the first one to be entirely staffed by Negroes. It was at this theatre that the celebrated English Negro composer, Samuel Coleridge-Taylor, made his first Midwest appearance. Jordan induced Motts to bring Eph Thompson and his elephants from Germany where he had seen the act and knew it was a sensation. It was at this theatre that Chas. S. Gilpin and Miller and Lyles got their first opportunity. Jordan composed many hits which were published by the Pekin Publishing Company of Chicago. He built the Jordan Building, still standing at 36th and State Streets and bearing his name till this day. At the height of his success he brought his mother to New York to hear him play and witness the performance of his chorus, the Memphis Students, featuring Abbie Mitchell and Tom Fletcher at Hammerstein's Victoria Theatre, Broadway at 42nd Street. She sat through the performance with apparent lack of interest and when Joe asked her later what she thought of his work she replied, "Aw, son, you're just foolin' the white folks." After she had seen enough of New York Joe took her to board the train for St. Louis, putting five hundred dollars in her hand as he kissed her goodby. She tucked the money away carefully, with the remark, "I'm not goin' to spend a penny of this money. I'm goin' to keep it all, for I know I'll need it some day to get you out of trouble. You ain't doin' a thing but foolin' the public." What the German music teacher had told her years before still remained the predominating thought in her mind as far as Joe and music were concerned.

In a serious approach as to why we behave ourselves as we do racially, the whole subject could be dismissed with one word, "economics." I prefer to confine myself to those existing differences that provide Amos 'n' Andy, Octavus Roy Cohen and others with material that a waiting public devours with glee. I have always known the happy-go-lucky, slipshod, shiftless contingent, but needed a classifying word until recently. By chance I heard it: they are *"dat'll do* folks."

A friend of mine in Chicago hired a colored man to fix her doorbell which was out of order. He could have gone to the first five-and-ten and purchased a new button for a few cents, but instead spent hours whittling corks into button shapes which somehow refused to stay in place when inserted. Finally, however, one of them remained in, so he told the lady the job was completed and said his bill for repairs was $3.50. She complained of the cork button so he started to show her how well it worked when, lo, the cork dropped on the floor. While she was still voicing her objections he reinserted it, rang the bell once more and said, "It rings, don't it? Well, *dat'll do!"*

Sometimes when a colored man does an heroic deed the white people make much of it. The same deed done by one of their own often gets but passing notice. This was the case when a Negro down in Memphis saved about a score of lives when he saw a sinking steamer. He made trip after trip in his canoe, saving the lives of these white people, and after he had rescued the last one he paddled on up the river as though it was all in a day's work. Someone's voice rang out, "What's your name?" "Tom Lee," came his reply. So far as he was concerned, that was the end of it. But not so with the white people of Memphis who gave him a home, a life pension, and as though this were insufficient reward, took him to Washington where he was presented to the President. When I lived in Memphis and the Mississippi had one of its worst floods, I remember too well how a white man took his steamboat to Arkansas and Mississippi to save the lives of many colored people, together with their chickens, hogs and cattle, bringing them to Memphis where he provided them with food and shelter, yet making no more fuss about it than did Tom Lee. Nor for that matter did he receive any special acclaim from the public, although later on the government appointed him to supervise such humanitarian work. I did not know him personally at the time but afterwards made it my business to make his acquaintance and offer him my thanks. Since that time we have been close friends. I speak of C. H. (Doc) Hottum. Recently he showed me a five hundred dollar gold watch and other expensive gifts given to him at that time by colored people.

An African was seated under a cocoanut tree resting when addressed by a passing Englishman: "My, my, what are you doing for yourself, just idly sitting there? Why don't you get busy and develop these fields, these mines and build cities?"

The African asked, "What for?"

To which the Englishman replied, "To establish commerce."

"Commerce, what for?" the puzzled native queried.

"So you can make lots of money."

"What good is money?"

"Money will bring you leisure."

"What'll I do with leisure?"

"Then you can rest."

To which the black man replied, "Why do all that when I rest now?"

Yes, man is trying to move Heaven and Earth with his airplanes, submarines, armored cars and battleships with big guns, murdering one another to establish a new world order which may provide enough security to enable him to sit down and rest a little while.

Once I saw a colored man and a white man fighting when suddenly half a dozen other whites jumped in without ascertaining what the trouble was and proceeded to cuff and kick the colored fellow. After subduing him, one more kindly than the rest said, "What's the trouble, can I do anything for you?" One of them took him either to his home or to a hospital in his buggy—similar to starting a war and keeping the Red Cross in readiness.

Henry Troy pulled this one out of his bag: At a bar up in Boston he saw a white man hit a Negro, felling him to the floor. The colored boy whimpered a bit, felt of his head, then picked himself up and went home. A while later he returned and, starting with the bartender, made the rounds of the various persons in the saloon, with what seemed to be an appeal for sympathy because of his getting the worst of the recent fracas. As he left each one in turn he would extend both of his hands to meet the proffered friendly clasp of the other while murmuring a tearful "goodnight." When he finally made his exit the barkeeper brought his fist down on the counter with a bang exclaiming, "It's a shame to treat that Negro like that!" As he drew back his arm he felt a razor cut on it. Several of the others came over to have a look and then discovered with dismay he had "cut" them all "goodnight."

The late Dr. Isaac Goldberg, who was visiting with me one day, heard James P. Johnson play his rhapsody, *Yamekraw*, in which the music simulates an ante-bellum Negro preacher. Expressing his impressions of that hearing in an article appearing much later on in a widely read daily paper, he wrote of the uncanny feeling he had experienced while listening to its strains. I quote: "With a few minor changes, this might be an old-fashioned Jewish cantor going through the melodic labyrinths of the racial cantillation. There is more than one communal habit that links Jew and Negro, whether it is the inevitable lateness at which social functions begin, or the psychology forced upon intellectuals to whom is denied adequate opportunity for expansion. The 'old time religion' was good enough for the Hebrew chillun, and it's good enough for me. So runs the spiritual; and the spirituals, of course, are the ideology of the Bible shot through with the richly melodious gifts of the downtrodden slave. It is hardly an accident, then, that in the United States the Negro and the Jew, without premeditation, should have done so much for the rude rhythms, the sad melodic line, the 'pep' and abandon of popular music."

Apropos of this trend, he continued: "The prejudice against jazz and against the blues, as words and music, is very much of it a moralistic rather than an esthetic canon. Not a small portion of the self-same prejudice is racial. It happens that modern jazz has been developed, whether as to artistic expression or commercial exploitation, by the Negro and the Jew—two races against which, even in the United States, there still remains a remnant of, shall we say, ill feeling. I have pointed out before, certain curious affinities existing between these races—affinities that may be sourced in a common ultimate Oriental origin, as well as in their historical status as oppressed peoples. Whatever the reasons, surely these affinities exist, and achieve a strange blend in such phenomena as the development of jazz."

CHAPTER TWENTY-THREE

World of Tomorrow—God Bless America

WHEN I arrived in New York I learned that ASCAP would repeat the festival at the New York World's Fair. Whatever else transpired was of minor importance to me. However, the offerings of the New York composers who did not take part at Treasure Island deserve mention here.

The afternoon Symphonic Concert devoted to compositions by members of the Society was presented at the Music Hall, New York World's Fair, Thursday, October 24, 1940, produced under the personal direction of Mr. Buck. With Dr. Howard Hanson conducting and William Grant Still as guest conductor, the Rochester (N. Y.) Philharmonic Symphony Orchestra assembled there on the stage was introduced by Gene Buck. Deems Taylor again officiated as Master of Ceremonies and opened the concert by presenting His Honor Mayor Fiorello H. La Guardia, who in a sincere, musicianly manner proceeded to conduct the orchestra in *The Star-Spangled Banner.*

Dr. Hanson took the proffered baton at the conclusion of our national anthem and successively led the orchestra in Henry Hadley's overture, *In Bohemia,* and his own *Symphony No. 2, Romantic.*

Following a brief intermission, guest conductor Still offered the same two works of his own that he had performed on Treasure Island, excerpts from the ballet *La Guiablesse*, and two movements from *Symphony No. 2 in G Minor*.

A star conductor with one of the three big networks, Morton Gould presented next his *American Symphonette No. 2*, and the concert closed as in San Francisco with Deems Taylor's *Circus Day*. R. H. Burnside, stage director for many years of the famed New York Hippodrome, staged the concert as well as the afternoon of symphony given in San Francisco. The weather was the ideal, not too cool autumn temperature, and the large audience was highly appreciative. The Music Hall was filled to capacity and standing room only was to be had at the start of the night's program which opened with the glorious strains of *The Star-Spangled Banner*, conducted by Johnny Green. As on Treasure Island, Sousa's *Stars and Stripes Forever* conducted by Dr. Hanson was in turn followed with a tribute to the immortal Victor Herbert in which Johnny Green conducted a typical medley of Herbertiana. Then came the campaign song that precipitated President Roosevelt originally into office, *Happy Days Are Here Again*, with lyrics by Jack Yellen, now a prominent picture producer, and melody composed by Milton Ager, who rendered it to the delight of the audience. Fred H. Ahlert, long active in the affairs of both ASCAP and SPA, scholarly musician that he is, brought back memories of the early days of Bing Crosby's career as he played his *When the Blue of the Night Meets the Gold of the Day*, whose lyrics were co-written by Bing and the late Roy Turk. *Santa Claus Is Coming to Town* was sung and played with a bright lilt by its composer, J. Fred Coots. The lyric is the product of Haven Gillespie. Irving Caesar, president of SPA, accompanied by his melody writer and team mate of radio, Gerald Marks, did a few of their famous *Songs of Safety*, one of which he rendered in the manner of a precocious child prodigy. He kidded himself and the audience, whose gales of laughter mingled with applause showed that Caesar is a

stage comic as well as a song-writing genius. Paul Whiteman's former pianist and arranger, Ferde Grofé, now famed
for his symphonic compositions and orchestral endeavors,
picked things up where Caesar left off by conducting his very
fine and popular *On the Trail* from *The Grand Canyon Suite*.

Spry and agile as his perennially youthful appearance implies, Harry Von Tilzer, one of the oldest, still active writer-
publisher members, caused many a tug at the heartstrings of
the older generation in attendance as he sang and played
Wait Till the Sun Shines, Nellie. One of the several news-
columnist song writers of the land, Nick Kenny of *New
York Daily Mirror* fame, together with his brother Charles
sang and played one of their joint past successes, *There's a
Gold Mine in the Sky*. "The old sailor," as Nick is affectionately called by his friends, did an admirable job for an audience that must have contained countless fans made by his
various radio activities through the years. Sammy Fain sang
and played his and lyrist Lew Brown's sentimental hit of a
few seasons ago, *That Old Feeling*, and the response of the
listeners proved to me again that "once a good song, always
a good song." Ray Henderson and Lew Brown played two of
the DeSylva, Brown and Henderson hits of yesteryear, *Just
a Memory* and *Lucky Day* which were featured in George
White's *Scandals*. Next in turn came one of the newer lady
members of ASCAP, Ruth Lowe, who delighted everyone
with her rendition of her current smash hit, *I'll Never Smile
Again*. Our nation's President was again brought to mind as
Harold J. Rome, author and composer of the rousing *Franklin D. Roosevelt Jones* from *Sing Out the News*, rendered it
in clever, versatile style at the piano. Jules Bledsoe of concert
stage and *Showboat* fame, as guest artist, rendered the song
which brought him into national prominence, *Ol' Man River*.
Burleigh's *Deep River* was his next offering and a tremendous
favorite of all. Composer Burleigh, although not appearing in
person, is still active at the age of seventy-four. He is music

editor for G. Ricordi, Inc., and still sings at St. George's Episcopal Church in New York as he has done for about half a century. Jacques Wolf's *Short'nin' Bread*, with words by Clement Wood, was Bledsoe's closing number which caught the fancy of all with its appealing lilt and swing. Arthur Schwartz, fine musical comedy purveyor, played his and lyrist Howard Dietz's *Dancing in the Dark*. Another newcomer to the ranks of ASCAP, Clara Edwards, accompanied her co-writer, Jack Lawrence, who sang their lovely and popular *With the Wind and the Rain in Your Hair*. Richard Rodgers and Lorenz Hart did two of their many production numbers, *My Heart Stood Still* from *The Connecticut Yankee*, and *The Girl Friend* from the show of that name. Their music can never grow old, so outstanding and fresh sounding. Johnny Green's *Body and Soul*, lyrics jointly authored by Robert Sour and Edward Heyman, was skilfully and beautifully played by the popular composer-conductor pianist. A tribute to the late George Gershwin was rendered at this point, followed immediately by Hollace Shaw's singing of *Smoke Gets in Your Eyes* and *All the Things You Are*, to composer Jerome Kern's piano accompaniment. Margaret Speaks, niece of Oley Speaks, sang four selections, *Only a Rose* (Friml-Hooker), *Softly As in a Morning Sunrise* (Romberg-Hammerstein II) and her uncle's *Sylvia* (lyric by C. Scollard) and *Morning*, the lyric of which is the work of Frank L. Stanton. The song-writing cowboy, Gene Autry of motion picture and radio fame, more than filled his difficult next-to-closing spot on the program, for despite the lateness of the hour (due to the lengthy program) the audience was with him solidly. Illness prevented George M. Cohan's appearance, although he was scheduled along with others including the Messrs. Jean Schwartz, Buck and Stamper, Romberg, Donaldson, Burnett, Kern, Armstrong, De Rose, Howard and myself to give performances similar to those

previously given at Treasure Island. The program ended with
Irving Berlin and his *God Bless America*, just as it did in San
Francisco. Thus passed into memory two truly great occasions in the history of American music. Certainly no organization in the world save ASCAP could have put on such
a program of its own controlled music as I have just described, and the radio programs will be poor indeed so long
as such material as this is kept off the air.

In my music library, recordings of the entire program are
preserved for posterity with due acknowledgments to N. V.
Carlson of Photo & Sound, Incorporated, and ASCAP, and
on the wall as a constant reminder hangs a picture of all who
took part in these unforgettable performances, thanks to the
thoughtfulness of the latter.

"Histories," Bacon claims, "make men wise, poets witty,
philosophers deep, logic and rhetoric able to contend," yet
what biographies do for man, Bacon does not say. But the
logical reason for this book will be found in its purpose to
take a few chapters from yesterday and frame them in words
of today; to preserve spirituals of our own South and chant
melodies from the Congo; to tell the story of the blues honestly and sincerely; to entertain or inform the reader and not
to parade a writer's ego.

And finally in these pages, if my serenade of song and story
should serve as a pillow for some composer's head, as yet
perhaps unborn, to dream and build on our folk melodies in
his tomorrows, I have not labored in vain.

If, as my teacher predicted, "music brought me to the
gutter," I confess it was there I got a glimpse of Heaven,
for music can lift one to that state.

If, as my father often said, "You are trotting down to Hell
on a fast horse in a porcupine saddle," I rode with a song
on my lips and its echo in my heart.

If, as Gene Buck has so well said, "There is nothing finer

21

on which to hang a memory than a song," I also hang a memory on these words from my mother's prayer which so aptly express my inmost feelings, "Lord, I thank Thee that we are living in a Christian land and a Bible country."

God Bless America.

Compositions, Arrangements and Books

By W. C. HANDY

"Instr." refers to instrumental compositions
Italicized titles are arrangements of spirituals ("spir.") and
folk songs ("f. s."). Names of books appear in block capitals.

1907 In the Cotton Fields of Dixie (words by Harry H. Pace)
1909 Mister Crump (unpublished in original form)
1912 The Memphis Blues, or, Mister Crump (instr.; republished
         1913 with words by George A. Norton)
1913 The Jogo Blues (instr.)
         The Girl You Never Have Met (words by Harry H. Pace)
1914 The St. Louis Blues
         The Yellow Dog Rag (title changed to Yellow Dog Blues)
1915 Joe Turner Blues *
         Hail to the Spirit of Freedom (march)
         The Hesitating Blues
         Shoeboot's Serenade
1916 Old Miss (instr., 1918; words with J. Russel Robinson)
         In the Land Where Cotton Is King (words by Harry H.
            Pace)
         Aframerican Hymn (also for military band, mixed chorus
            and male chorus)
1917 Beale Street (title changed to Beale Street Blues)
         Thinking of Thee (words by Harry H. Pace)
         The Hooking Cow Blues (words by Douglass Williams)
1918 Keep the Love Ties Binding (with J. P. Schofield)
         The Kaiser's Got the Blues (words by Dorner C. Browne)
         No Name Waltz (with Charles Hillman)

* Published by Robbins Music Corp.

1919   Though We're Miles Apart (words by J. Russel Robinson, music with Charles Hillman)

1920   Long Gone (from Bowling Green) (words by Chris Smith)
The Rough Rocky Road (spir.)

1921   Loveless Love
Aunt Hagar's Children Blues * (instr.; 1922; words by J. Tim Brymn)

1922   John Henry Blues
Ape Mister Eddie
Sounding Brass and Tinkling Cymbals
Southside

1923   Darktown Reveille * (words by Walter Hirsch, music with Chris Smith)
Harlem Blues
Sundown Blues

1924   Atlanta Blues (Make Me One Pallet on Your Floor) (words by Dave Elman)
The Basement Blues
I'm Drinking from a Fountain That Never Runs Dry (spir.)
The Chicago Gouge
The Gouge of Armour Avenue

1925   *Careless Love* (f. s.)
When the Black Man Has a Nation of His Own (words by J. M. Miller)
Bright Star of Hope (words by Lillian A. Thorsten, music with Martha E. Koenig)
Ever After On (f. s.)
Steal Away to Jesus (spir.; funeral march for military band and choir)

1926   Friendless Blues (words by Mercedes Gilbert)
Blue Gummed Blues (words by Dave Elman)
Goin' to See My Sarah (f. s.)
BLUES: AN ANTHOLOGY (book, with introduction and notes by Abbe Niles, pub. A. & C. Boni)

1927   Golden Brown Blues (words by Langston Hughes)
The Birth of Jazz (words by Henry Troy, music with Chris Smith)
Pasadena

* Published by Robbins Music Corp.

Give Me Jesus (spir.)

The White Man Said 'Twas So, So It Must Be So (words by Chris Smith)

Let Us Cheer the Weary Traveler (spir.)

1928   *I've Heard of a City Called Heaven* (spir.)

Who's That Man? (words by Agnes Castleton, music with Spencer Williams)

1929   Wall Street Blues (words by Margaret Gregory)

1930   *Somebody's Wrong About Dis Bible* (spir.; words by Arthur J. Neale)

Go Down, Moses (spir.), for pipe organ, military band and two pianos.

1931   *Stand on the Rock a Little Longer* (spir.)

Chantez Les Bas (Sing 'Em Low)

We'll Go On and Serve the Lord (spir.)

1932   Way Down South Where the Blues Began

Opportunity (words by Walter Malone)

1933   *In That Great Gettin' Up Morning* (spir.)

I'll Be There in the Morning (spir.)

1934   Mozambique (words by Arthur Porter)

Annie Love

1935   Negrita (with D'Arteaga)

NEGRO AUTHORS AND COMPOSERS OF THE UNITED STATES (book, pub. Handy Bros. Music Co.)

Vesuvius (There's a Red Glow in the Sky Above Vesuvius (words by Andy Razaf)

I'll Never Turn Back No More (spir.)

'Tis the Old Ship of Zion (spir.)

The Bridegroom Has Done Come (spir.)

1936   The Good Lord Sent Me You (words by Elsie and Stella Francis)

Nobody Knows the Trouble I See (spir.)

1937   East St. Louis

I'm Telling You in Front (words by Andy Razaf, music with Russell Wooding)

Stand on That Sea of Glass (spir.)

1938   W. C. HANDY'S COLLECTION OF NEGRO SPIRITUALS (book, pub. Handy Bros. Music Co.)

1938 Beale Street Serenade (with Gene Van Ormer and Porter Grainger)

I've Just Come from the Fountain (spir.)
My Lord's Writing All the Time (spir.)
Room Enough (spir.)
Been a-Listening All de Day Long (spir.)
You Better Mind (spir.)
Get Right, Church (spir.)
See the Sign of the Judgment (spir.)
Children, You Will Be Called On (spir.)
I Want to Be Ready (spir.)
Gospel Train (spir.)
The Rocks and the Mountains (spir.)
Sunday Morning Band (spir.)
Turn Back Pharaoh's Army (spir.)
Judgment Day Is Rolling Around (spir.)
Rise, Shine, For Thy Light Is a-Coming (spir.)
Swing Low, Sweet Chariot (spir.)
Keep Me from Sinking Down (spir.)
One Found Worthy (spir.)
Jesus Goin' a Make Up My Dying Bed (spir.)

1940 Black Patti (Sissieretta Jones) (with Chris Smith and Henry Troy)

Finis (a tribute to Richard B. Harrison; with Andy Razaf)

Remembered (impressions of Florence Mills; with Olive Lewis Handy and Joe Jordan)

The Temple of Music (a tribute to Robert T. [Bob] Motts; with Joe Jordan)

The Memphis Blues, or, Mister Crump (new arrangement with lyrics by J. Russel Robinson)

Index of Names

Abbott, John J., 192
Actors Equity, 251
Adams, Kenneth W., 224
Adams, Teddy, 98
Addams, Jane, 221
Ager, Milton, 300
Ahlert, Fred H., 275, 300
Alexander, Edna, 276
Alexander, Edward, 172
Alice Townsend Company, 38
American Federation of Radio Artists, 251
American Guild of Musical Artists, 251
American Guild of Vaudeville Artists, 251
American Society of Composers, Authors and Publishers, 113, 261
Amos 'n' Andy, 295
Anderson, Judge Harry B., 256, 257
Anderson, Harvey W., 274
Archer, Mrs. H. E., 61
Arlen, Harold, 283, 285
Armstrong, Harry, 243, 278, 286, 302
Armstrong, Louis, 276, 292
Ashford, Hammitt, 92
Authors League Fund, 251
Autry, Gene, 302
Avery and Hart, 42

Banks, Charles, 87
Banks, Mrs. Charles, 87
Barbour, J. Berni, 197
Barnhouse, C. L., 35
Barrie, Clyde, 276

Bates, Will, 16
Beethoven, Ludwig van, 268
Bell, Dr. W. Y., 256-257
Benny, Jack, 243
Berlin, Irving, 278, 283, 289, 303
Berlioz, Hector, 268
Bernard, Al, 196-197
Bernard, Sam, 247
Bernie, Ben, 219
Bevard, Sylvester V., 172
Black, Frank, 275
Blake, Eubie, 293
Bland, Leroy, 42
Blanks, Osceola and Berliana, 110, 126
Bledsoe, Jules, 301, 302
Bloom, Congressman Sol, 267
Blues—An Anthology, 231
Bond, Carrie Jacobs, 285
Boni, Inc., Albert and Charles, 210
Booth and Barrett, 92
Bowes, Major Edward F., 244
Bowhee Brothers, 39
Braddicks, Robert P., 250, 251
Bradford, Perry, 200, 201
Brady, William A., 39
Braham, Philip, 218
Brahms, Johannes, 269
Breen, May Singhi, 287
Brewer, Reverend B. H., 234
Brewer, Christopher, 3, 4, 5, 291
Brewer, Ex-Gov. Earl, 82
Brewer, James, 20
Brewer, Llewellyn, 291
Brewer, Mose, 234

309